STRATEGY IMPLEMENTATION

Strategy implementation – or strategy execution – is a hot topic today. Managers spend significant resources on consulting and training, in the hope of creating brilliant strategies but all too often brilliant strategies do not translate into brilliant performance.

This book presents new conceptual models and tools that can be used to implement different strategies. The author analyses how market leaders have benefitted from successful strategy implementation and provides the reader with a comprehensive and systematic framework to tackle strategy implementation challenges.

Have clear strategic choices been made? Are actions aligned with the strategy? What's the organizational context for the strategy? In answering these simple questions, the book provides students of strategic management, along with managers involved in designing and implementing strategies, with a valuable resource.

Kurt Verweire is Associate Professor of Strategic Management and Partner at Vlerick Business School, Belgium.

'For managers wondering what to do to take their competitive strategy to the next level, this book is right on the mark. By focusing on the big leadership challenges of strategy execution, Verweire takes us well beyond established strategy concepts with astute insights and practice-tested frameworks that emphasize organization-wide alignment and commitment as key levers of marketplace advantage. Very incisive, very timely.'

Fred Wiersema, *Customer Strategist, Chair of the B2B Leadership Board, Institute for the Study of Business Markets at Penn State, USA, and co-author of the bestselling* The Discipline of Market Leaders

'The biggest challenge to success in the ever more competitive environment companies face is strategy execution. Kurt Verweire's very readable and comprehensive book provides important insights into the factors that undermine strategy execution and offers ways to overcome them. A must read for senior executives.'

Michael Beer, *Professor Emeritus, Harvard Business School and Chairman, TruePoint*

'Taking a simple savings bank model and changing the way customers think about their money was like baking a soufflé at high altitudes. Having all the right ingredients didn't compensate for the atmospheric forces that needed to be overcome for success. Strategy implementation takes commitment to the vision, the chemistry of a team, the indulgence of time, and a heavy dose of pixie dust for the market to adapt. The Strategy–Alignment–Commitment model describes well what the necessary ingredients are to make this happen.'

Arkadi Kuhlmann, *Founder and former CEO of ING Direct Canada and USA and founder of Zenbanx*

'Strategy implementation is one of the most important challenges that a company faces today. Unfortunately, there are few comprehensive frameworks and books that explain what the strategy implementation challenge entails and how to deal with it. This book is an exception to the rule. It provides the reader with some new insights how to turn strategy into results and how to commit the entire organization on the implementation journey.'

Hans Bourlon, *Co-founder and co-CEO of Studio 100*

'Integrating and analysing the best and most practical business strategy literature, *Strategy Implementation* offers a clear framework that has been successfully used with the many management teams the author has worked with. The result is a book that is equally comprehensive as an accompaniment to a business strategy course, as it is practical for executives that want to diagnose their firms' alignment and commitment around their chosen strategy. This book puts the frameworks, tools and illustration in your hands.'

Philippe Haspeslagh, Dean, Vlerick Business School, Belgium

'Verweire describes clearly the challenges that managers must tackle to turn strategy into performance. He builds on the value disciplines – operational excellence, customer intimacy and product leadership – to add new insights and has integrated frameworks on strategy formulation, alignment and commitment. Anyone who is interested in deploying strategy effectively should read this book!'

Michael Treacy, Co-author, The Discipline of Market Leaders, *USA*

STRATEGY IMPLEMENTATION

Kurt Verweire

Routledge
Taylor & Francis Group

LONDON AND NEW YORK

First published 2014
by Routledge
2 Park Square, Milton Park, Abingdon, Oxon OX14 4RN

Simultaneously published in the USA and Canada
by Routledge
711 Third Avenue, New York, NY 10017

Routledge is an imprint of the Taylor & Francis Group, an informa business

British Library Cataloguing in Publication Data
A catalogue record for this book is available from the British Library

Library of Congress Cataloging in Publication Data
Verweire, Kurt.
Strategy implementation/Kurt Verweire.
  pages cm
  Includes bibliographical references and index.
  1. Strategic planning.
  2. Organizational effectiveness.
  3. Organizational change. I. Title.
  HD30.28.V475 2014
  658.4'012–dc23   2013036576

ISBN: 978-0-415-73198-0 (hbk)
ISBN: 978-0-415-73199-7 (pbk)
ISBN: 978-1-315-84944-7 (ebk)

Typeset in Bembo and Stone Sans
by Florence Production Ltd, Stoodleigh, Devon, UK

CONTENTS

FIGURES

TABLES

FOREWORD

Airports bookshops over the years have seen a plethora of business strategy books, but few, if any, have offered deep and comprehensive insight into the key elements of strategy implementation. *Strategy Implementation* is such a book. It is the outcome of many years of strategy teaching and workshop practice by the author, with multiple organizations in the context of Vlerick Business School's executive education and its research for business partnerships.

Integrating the best and most practical of the business strategy literature it offers a clear framework which has been operationalized with the many management teams the author has been working with. The result is a book that is equally comprehensive as accompaniment to a business strategy course, as practical for executives and teams that want to diagnose their firms' alignment and commitment around their chosen strategy.

Naturally the book starts from the basics of what makes for a winning strategy, but really comes into its own when addressing the challenges of implementation. The author does not pretend to invent a new generic strategy framework. Rather, he gives credit to Treacy and Wiersema's widely adopted distinction between product leadership, operational excellence and customer intimacy. The strength of the book is in the systematic way in which the author examines how each of these strategies requires not only alignment of various processes, but also commitment; in the rich cases by which he illustrates his concepts; and in the practical approach and tools he offers.

Being a strategy academic myself, I marvelled at the way the author gives credit to some of the most insightful findings of others and weaves them into a coherent picture, bringing clarity and depth to what it takes to successfully implement a winning strategy.

Strategy Implementation does a great job of operationalizing alignment by examining five sub-processes that have to work in concert. One of the main contributions of the book also is to bring the concept of commitment into the strategy literature, and operationalizing it by distinguishing different levels of management maturity.

Finally, a contribution that speaks in plain language is eminently clear in logic, well-illustrated by cases and examples throughout, and which takes the operational-ization of the concepts all the way through practical tools for diagnosis. With the author's toolbox management teams can hold themselves a mirror to reflect on the clarity of their strategic choices, and the quality of their implementation efforts.

Each of the three generic strategies benefits from a chapter clarifying their true meaning and debunking superficial views, another delving in the alignment and commitment issues required to execute, and a third bringing a detailed case illustration.

Management teams striving for product leadership will be able to assess through the 'performance pentagon' how their processes foster both product performance quality and product conformance quality. The author also clarifies that while product leadership needs be innovative, being innovative does not necessarily equate into product leadership.

Managers striving for operational excellence will expand their view of the objective being the ability to compete on the lowest price to one that focuses on access, and on reducing the transaction costs of the customer. The book illustrates how despite being typically characterized by structure, processes and measurement operational excellence companies can still succeed in creating true commitment in their employees. The ING Direct case is a wonderfull illustration of the power of operational excellence also serves to show that even the best strategy can go awry when the macro environment shifts radically, as was the case for mortgage-backed assets in 2008.

Management teams going for customer intimacy will appreciate the distinction between going for extra services or solutions, and going for deeper relationships and connectivity, which may or may not go hand in hand. They may find it helpful to think along the author's service connectivity continuum distinction. They would also do well to heed the observation that many firms think they go for customer relations but fail to take up the customers' perspective or to think beyond their own product solutions.

Years of applying the concepts and tools to various groups of managers result in a holistic framework, which to seasoned managers will feel pragmatic and spot on, while many strategy colleagues will recognize their contributions decanted, put in context and given credit to.

Kurt Verweire's frameworks, tools and benchmarked assessments provide the meat in many of Vlerick Business Schools customized programs. Each time management teams discover how Kurt pushes them in the trenches to confront to what extent they are paying lip service to strategy or have the maturity to follow through. This book puts the frameworks, tools and illustration in your hands.

Philippe Haspeslagh
Professor of Corporate Strategy
Dean Vlerick Business School

PREFACE

I have been working on the topic of strategy implementation for a number of years now. It all started more than 10 years ago, when I met four managers from Electrabel, one of the business units of GDF Suez, who introduced me to their Internal Control System. After numerous discussions, I understood that they were showing me a performance management framework that helped to explain why some of their business units performed better than others. We wrote a book that we called *Integrated Performance Management: A Guide to Strategy Implementation*, without really knowing what strategy implementation actually entailed. At that moment, I thought the book marked an end to an intensive research period. I now realize that that book was only the start of a much bigger research project, which I have finalized with this new book. Therefore, I would like to thank my sparring partners at GDF Suez – Bernard Hindryckx, Philippe De Cnudde, Mario Bauwens and Bernard Carrette – for the inspiration that they provided so many years ago. I've since renamed the Integrated Performance Management Framework the Strategy Implementation Framework, but the building blocks of the framework remain unchanged.

The strategy implementation research moved into a higher gear when I used the Strategy Implementation Framework to do a research update on the three value disciplines that were introduced 20 years ago by Michael Treacy and Fred Wiersema: product leadership, customer intimacy and operational excellence. I had the support of a wonderful team of great researchers: thank you Judith Escalier Revollo, Ghita Greef, Steven Carchon and Jonathan De Grande for all the hard work of going through numerous case studies, academic articles and management books, to develop the three alignment pentagons. Your efforts have helped me make strategy more operational!

Developing academic frameworks is nice, but it is equally important to find some good illustrations in practice. So, I was very happy when several managers allowed me to apply the tools and frameworks to their companies. Thank you to my Executive MBA students from 2009–11, who looked for inspiring case studies on strategy implementation. And thank you to the managers who allowed us to check their strategy implementation capabilities.

I would like to express my sincere gratitude to the managers of three wonderful companies – Studio 100, ING Direct USA, and Châteauform' – who allowed me to investigate their organizations in greater detail. I had great discussions with Hans Bourlon, one of the co-founders of Studio 100, and with Koen Peeters and Jo Daris on the challenges of a fast-growing and ever-expanding entertainment company. I have been following the ING Direct USA case for quite some time, and Arkadi Kuhlmann, the founder of ING Direct Canada and ING Direct USA, has always stood out as a visionary banker, a banker with a purpose. However, he showed me that ING Direct USA was a great case for strategy implementation too. Over the years, I have had extensive discussions on ING Direct USA's mission, strategy and strategy implementation initiatives with Arkadi, Hans Verkoren, Dick Harryvan, Brunon Bartkiewicz and Miguel Orti. Thank you for sharing your ideas and explaining what it means, and takes, to be a rebel in the banking industry. I'm also very grateful for the great and insightful discussions I've had with Jacques Horovitz, Gérald Coutaudier, Anne-Françoise and Pierre-Etienne Caire on how to run one of the world's most service-oriented chains of conference venues and seminar rooms. Jacques, you are fabulous at challenging people who wonder whether customer centricity is something relevant to them.

I would also like to thank my colleagues at Vlerick Business School, who co-authored the case studies on which the case chapters are based: Lutgart Van den Berghe and André Thibeault on the ING Direct USA case, Judith Escalier on the Studio 100 case, and Marion Debruyne and Ghita Greef on the Châteauform' case. A special thank you goes to Lien Vandenkerckhove, who processed all the alignment questionnaires for the three case studies (and for many other companies) and who makes the strategy implementation challenges visible to managers.

I am also grateful to Roger Hallowell, Geert Letens, Carel Boers and Phillipe Haspeslagh, with whom I had good discussions on some of the concepts of the book and who reviewed some of the chapters of the book. Your comments and suggestions on customer intimacy and operational excellence have definitely improved the book's quality. Thanks a lot!

I would also like to thank William Wright and the team at Routledge – Terry Clague, Alexander Krause and especially Sinead Waldron – who polished my manuscript into a book that is easy and pleasant to read.

Finally, a big thank you to my wife Lieve and my son Jens for all your patience and understanding when I was working on this project.

Kurt Verweire
September 2013

1

THE CHALLENGES OF STRATEGY AND IMPLEMENTATION

Some years ago, a friend of mine became a director and member of the executive committee of a European bank. Arthur Berthold was 33 and enthusiastic about his new assignment. After some management jobs in other financial institutions, he was now ready to lead a bank, together with two other directors. After some weeks, however, his enthusiasm had dropped significantly. Certainly, the bank had a nice mission statement and challenging goals, but already, in his first weeks, Arthur had noted that the directors and managers of the bank had totally different interpretations about how to reach those goals. The marketing and sales managers pursued market share without looking at profitability, whereas back office managers focused on efficiency but had lost sight of the customer. In addition, there were huge fights between the managers of the various departments of the bank. The culture was very competitive: every manager wanted to score, often at the expense of a colleague. Absenteeism and employee turnover were very high. On an average day, 9 per cent of the 335 employees did not show up. And the financial results were disastrous.

Despite all this, Arthur took the helm and was anxious to turn the company around. It was clear that the bank had to say goodbye to unprofitable customers and sell more products to existing customers. Furthermore, the bank needed to tap into new markets, either by selling new products or by addressing new customer segments. Over several months, Arthur engaged in strategy discussions with his managers. With the help of a performance management consultant, Hein Hilleman, he was able to confront them with the financial consequences of their *unclear choices*. It took time, but Arthur and Hein were able to generate discussions about whom the bank would serve (and not serve), what it would provide (and not provide), and where the bank would differentiate from the competition. Furthermore, they were working with the managers on specific approaches to analyse customer needs, sell and deliver, and develop further relationships with the bank's best customers.

The discussions that emerged were tough but necessary to create clarity, direction and cohesion within the organization. Furthermore, managers and employees were challenged to come up with solutions to address the many issues in the company. Whenever a problem was brought to Arthur's attention, he forced the employees to come up with solutions. He supported them when the solutions were in line with the strategic choices that they had agreed upon, but, often, Arthur refused their proposals and compelled the employees to rethink them.

Over time, the managers initiated new actions in the bank. For example, Gerhard Isenrich, a young manager who was responsible for about twenty bank branches, started a sales-and-service cultural change programme that helped grow sales spectacularly. This change programme forced employees to set targets and to debrief their results every week. In this way, a performance-oriented culture emerged, in which teams competed but shared best practices. Martin Schober, another manager, introduced a similar performance measurement initiative in the call centre. He also assigned new tasks to the call-centre employees by having them organize the sales meetings for the account managers. The account managers resisted this vigorously in the beginning, but Arthur and Martin were able to convince them that they could now spend more time with their customers, which further increased sales. Within 9 months, all of the managers had set up initiatives to help realize the bank's new strategy.

The new initiatives created numerous tensions within the organization and were greeted with a lot of scepticism. However, Arthur was committed to his project and refused to be distracted by the people who did not buy in. He personally explained the situation to all of the managers and employees. He required the managers of all departments to set goals and report on their performance on a monthly basis. The directors and managers discussed the results, which led to a more open and transparent culture. Furthermore, management's coaching in leadership style helped fuel a collaborative mindset throughout the organization. The results were impressive: after only 3 years, sales had grown spectacularly, and operating profits had doubled. Absenteeism and turnover decreased significantly as well.

When I invited Arthur to talk about his experiences in our school's programmes, I saw that managers struggle with many of the same issues that Arthur had dealt with. So, I decided to investigate strategy implementation in greater detail to figure out what effective implementation entails.

Strategy implementation: a hot topic

Strategy implementation – or strategy execution – is a hot topic today. Managers spend billions of dollars on consulting and training in the hope of creating brilliant strategies.[1] However, all too often, brilliant strategies do not translate into brilliant performance. Firms seem to experience significant problems with translating the strategy into concrete activities and results. This observation was also made by Lawrence Hrebiniak from the Wharton School: 'Formulating a consistent strategy

TABLE 1.1 CEO Challenges 2010: The 10 challenges (n = 444)

Relative ranking		Challenge	Cite challenge as being of 'greatest concern in the coming year', %	
Oct–Nov 2009	Oct–Nov 2008		Oct–Nov 2008	Oct–Nov 2009
1	1	Excellence in execution	42.3	55.4
2	2	Consistent execution of strategy by top management	39.9	47.0
3	5	Sustained and steady top-line growth	38.8	42.3
4	6	Customer loyalty/retention	33.5	40.1
5	3	Speed, flexibility, adaptability to change	29.0	46.6
6	15	Corporate reputation for quality products/services	24.1	20.2
7	16	Stimulating innovation/creativity/ enabling entrepreneurship	23.0	18.2
8	9	Profit growth	22.7	34.6
9	7	Improving productivity	19.9	36.9
10	26	Government regulation	18.9	12.6

Note: Respondents were allowed to rate multiple challenges as being 'greatest concern(s)' in the coming year. The global CEO Challenge rankings are weighted to correct for regional representation. Each CEO's responses are weighted by his or her respective region's representation in global GDP (Asia, 21.7 per cent; Europe, 36.4 per cent; the United States, 23.7 per cent; and other, 18.2 per cent), according to the GDP data from the International Monetary Fund World Economic Outlook Database (as of September 2009).

Source: The Conference Board (2010)[2]

is difficult for any management team, but making that strategy work – implementing it throughout the organization – is even more difficult.'[3]

Strangely enough, we have only recently come to realize that strategies are not implemented automatically. Nevertheless, for quite some time now, strategy execution has ranked high on top managers' agendas. For example, each year the Conference Board publishes the CEO Challenge Research Report. Strategy execution ranked as a top priority in the CEO Challenge 2007 and 2010 Reports (see Table 1.1 for the results of the 2010 Report).

At the same time, there is an increased awareness that developing strategy implementation capabilities is an important driver for competitive advantage. Nithin Nohria, William Joyce and Bruce Roberson have provided academic evidence for this observation. The three authors conducted a groundbreaking study on why some firms consistently outperform their competitors. They studied 160 companies – four companies from forty different industries. For every industry, they selected a winner, a loser, a climber and a tumbler. As Figure 1.1 shows, winners consistently outperformed their peers, whereas losers consistently underperformed. Climbers started off poorly but improved significantly, whereas tumblers started off well but then fell far behind.

Then Nohria et al. investigated which of the hundreds of well-known business tools and techniques help a company be great. The conclusion was surprising: companies that outperform their industry peers excel at only four primary management practices: strategy, execution, culture and structure. Winners supplemented their great skill in those areas with mastery of any two out of four secondary management practices: talent, innovation, leadership, and mergers and partnerships.

The message that I would like to emphasize here is that strategy formulation and implementation do matter – strategy (formulation) and execution are primary management practices – and that you need both a clearly stated and focused strategy and strategy implementation capabilities to be a winner in your market!

So strategy implementation is considered to be a prerequisite for high performance, but we all know that implementation is a source of frustration in many companies. Both academic and consulting studies report significant failure rates with strategy execution, ranging from 40 per cent to even 90 per cent. This made Larry Bossidy and Ram Charan conclude, in 2002, that execution is not only the biggest issue facing business today, it's something that nobody has ever explained satisfactorily.[5] Now, some 10 years later, nothing has really changed. True, there have been some good publications on the topic, but no generally accepted

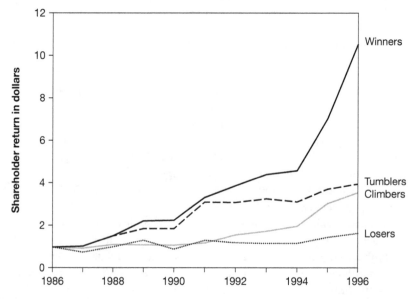

FIGURE 1.1 What really works

Source: Nohria et al. (2003)[4]

implementation framework has yet emerged. Unlike strategy formulation, strategy implementation is often seen as something of a craft, rather than a science, and our knowledge of the nature of strategy implementation and the reasons for its success or failure is still limited.[6]

Why is strategy implementation such a big challenge?

In my discussions with managers who struggle with strategy implementation, I have discovered that there are five root causes for an unsuccessful strategy implementation:

- there is too much focus on financials in strategy discussions;
- functional strategies are no substitute for a business strategy;
- strategy implementation is too fragmented;
- managers communicate about strategy but forget to translate strategy into action; and
- strategy implementation requires leadership capabilities.

Too much focus on financials in strategy discussions

Strategy implementation only succeeds if a company has a well-formulated strategy in the first place. In reality, however, few companies have a genuine strategy. Although everyone agrees that a superior strategy is critical to the success of an organization, after more than four decades of research, there is still no consensus among academics (or professionals, for that matter) with regard to the content of strategy and, in particular, what constitutes a great strategy. That is why, despite the thousands of books on the topic of strategy, good managers still set bad strategies. According to Michael Porter – one of the most influential writers in the field – managers often rely on a flawed definition of strategy.[7] For example, managers confuse strategy with aspiration. How many times have we heard or read: 'Our strategy is to be number 1 or number 2 in that particular industry', or 'Our strategy is to grow shareholder value by 30 per cent in the next three years'. Those statements are not strategies – they're goals or aspirations. These statements say what the company wants to be or achieve, not how it will get there. It's like an athlete declaring, 'My strategy is to win the 400 metres during the next Olympics by running faster than anyone else', which is wonderful, but the real question is how to achieve that.[8] Goals are important, but they are not a substitute for strategy. Great strategies provide guidance and coherence to the organization; financial goals, unfortunately, do not!

Functional strategies are no substitute for a business strategy

Many companies have problems with strategy implementation because they lack a good business strategy. They do, however, have a strategy for HR, for operations, for sales, for IT and for most other departments, but the more you break strategy up into various functional strategies, the less likely you will have a strategy at all. Strategy implementation is difficult – if not impossible – when a firm lacks a coherent business strategy.

Why do firms have functional strategies but not a business strategy? The answer lies in how many big corporations are structured today. About 10 or 15 years ago, most corporations had business units. Traditionally, a business unit is defined as any organizationally separate unit that has external customers. These units have profit responsibility, and there is functional integration within such business units, indicating that they are responsible for managing the entire value chain, including activities such as R&D, production, sales and marketing activities, and some supporting activities such as IT and HR.

Today, firms are organized differently. The corporation is unbundled, and the value chain is deconstructed by having separate sales and marketing units, production units and R&D units. According to John Hagel and Marc Singer, from McKinsey, firms should split up into separate units, because these three different sets of activities have divergent economic and cultural imperatives. For example, the focus of production management is on scale and efficiency, whereas R&D units focus on speed and creativity. For marketing and sales units, the high costs of customer acquisition will force companies to gain large shares of wallet (scope).[9] That's why many corporations now have big R&D units, production units and sales units. Managers call these units 'business units', but they're not: they are big functional units, not business units.

The problem with the deconstruction of the value chain is that managers and employees no longer see the big picture. Because different units pursue different goals, the coherence that strategy used to provide has disappeared. The enemy is no longer the competition; the enemy is within.

Strategy implementation is too fragmented

Although companies face significant problems formulating a compelling strategy, the issue of strategy implementation itself also poses some challenges. The first question that arises is: What is strategy implementation? Some management authors see strategy implementation as a performance measurement and management exercise, where you translate strategies into key performance indicators that you cascade further down the organization. Others see strategy implementation as creating an organizational culture that empowers people to act in line with the strategy. Still others see implementation as strategic project portfolio management.

As I will show later, strategy implementation is all of that, and even more. Too often, managers address only one item of the whole strategy implementation challenge, and they tackle execution in a way that is too fragmented. Strategy execution is a broad domain that touches many different management areas, from direction and goal-setting to HR, operations, culture, and so on. Strategy implementers need to be jugglers. Strategy implementation requires visionary capabilities, as well as process and people management capabilities. Although some managers often excel at one of these, they may not have the skills to perform the other tasks equally well.

Managers communicate about strategy, but forget to translate strategy into action

Although strategy implementation is about aligning different activities, it is also about creating commitment throughout the entire organization. Commitment is created when employees see where and how they can make a difference and are stimulated to take action within the boundaries set by the strategy. However, it takes time to create an organizational context that stimulates widespread action-taking. All too often, managers do not take the time to create that context. They communicate, but do not take the time to translate. Translating is tough: it means more work, more attention to detail and more attention to people.[10]

So, strategy implementation is about launching a whole set of activities, while, at the same time, stimulating the appropriate employee behaviour so that your strategy can be translated into activities and results. This requires the organization to be managed in a particular way. In high-performance organizations, employees do not just routinely perform tasks – they are allowed to take initiative, work collaboratively and supervise and regulate themselves. In other words, managers should pay significant attention to developing an engaging organizational climate and a collaborative structure and culture. Few managers really know how to do that.

Strategy implementation requires leadership capabilities

The four points outlined above indicate that the implementation job requires leaders, not just managers.[11] Strategy implementation is not about delegating the bits and pieces of a strategy to the functional managers, so that the marketing manager tackles the marketing issues, and the operations manager manages the operational issues. The chief implementation officer should be the business manager, or at least somebody from the business management team. Strategy implementation is difficult, because it forces people to change their behaviour. So, it's a job that should not be delegated to lower-level managers.

In summary, strategy implementation is difficult for at least five fundamental reasons. Some reasons have to do with the quality of the strategy itself; others deal with the quality of the strategy implementation efforts. And last, but not least, a final factor that drives effective strategy implementation is the quality of the leadership team that is in charge.

A new model for achieving competitive advantage

Over the last few years, I've conducted extensive research on how firms turn strategy into results. From my research findings, I've constructed a model to capture the essential elements of what constitutes effective strategy implementation. Although there is no step-by-step formula to translate strategies into great results, I have seen common patterns in how companies implement winning strategies and translate them into great performance.

As Figure 1.2 illustrates, there are three main levers for achieving a competitive advantage and a winning performance. The first lever relates to the *strategy* itself. It does not make sense to implement a low-quality strategy. Surprisingly, many firms struggle with defining a winning strategy. So, it is important to explain how and where a 'winning' strategy differs from a 'mediocre' strategy. In the next chapter, I will introduce a Strategy Formulation Framework that enables managers to assess the quality of their strategy.

The two other levers concentrate on how to translate a winning strategy into great results:

The first is called 'alignment' and defines which *activities* your company should set up to make the strategy concrete. Michael Porter has already stressed the importance of creating a tailored set of activities around a clear promise to your customers.[12] However, in this book, I want to take the concept further. What activities do winners choose to implement a particular strategy? Obviously, many

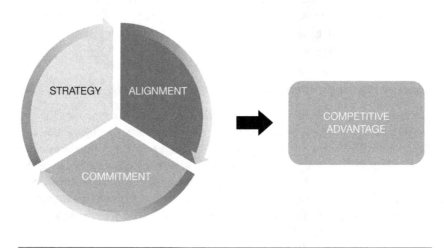

STRATEGY	Do we have a *winning strategy*? Have we made clear *choices* that provide guidance and direction to our people?
ALIGNMENT	Are all our *activities* aligned around a core competitive theme?
COMMITMENT	Have we created an *organizational context* that ensures that employees and managers are committed to make strategy work?

FIGURE 1.2 The levers of competitive advantage: strategy, alignment and commitment

activities that a company undertakes are driven by the firm's mission and, more particularly, by its core business. For example, airline companies have a different activity system from hotels. Apart from those industry-specific activities, however, firms also launch a set of activities that reinforce their chosen position in the market. In this way, the *operating model* of a low-cost airline company such as Ryanair or Southwest Airlines is strikingly similar to that of a low-cost hotel chain such as Formule 1. Alignment means that a firm has developed a whole set of activities around a core competitive theme such as 'low price' or 'great service' or 'great product'. The competitive advantage of winning firms stems from their ability to define an orchestrating theme and to set up a range of activities in line with one of the following three operating models: operational excellence, product leadership or customer intimacy.[13]

These operating models describe three common configurations that we recognize in high-performance organizations. Although we will discuss these three operating models extensively in the following chapters, let me explain very briefly what these configurations are. Operational excellence is an operating model that allows a firm to provide customers with reliable products or services at competitive prices, delivered with minimal difficulty or inconvenience. Product leadership is an operating model that allows firms to provide products that continually redefine the state of the art. Finally, customer intimacy is about selling the customer a total solution, not just a product or service.

The last lever of competitive advantage – 'commitment' – is an element that is often overlooked in the strategic management literature. Organizational and behavioural researchers, however, have investigated the topic in great detail for many years, and they've concluded that organizational commitment is a major determinant of organizational effectiveness.[14] Commitment deals with the organizational context in which a firm's activities occur. The key questions that I would like to address are: What is the *behaviour* that winning companies instill in their organization? How do these companies ensure that the managers and employees are committed to making the strategy work? We should not forget that strategy implementation takes place within an organizational environment that is shaped by the leaders of the organization. It is that organizational environment that produces the behaviour that you can observe in companies.[15] Winning companies have a highly committed workforce that is able to provide relevant input in the organization's strategic discussions, as well as to translate the strategy into the organization's day-to-day activities. The whole organization is strategy-focused, not just the executive team. The result is an organization that is performance-driven, yet thrives on a collaborative and participative culture.

Effective strategy implementation requires managers to work on all three levers – strategy, alignment and commitment – to create a sustainable competitive advantage. Strategy should lead to a set of coherent, reinforcing activities that lead to results only when these activities are supported by committed employees. Committed employees then provide further input that leads to further strategy refinements, and to new activities, which further augment the commitment within the organization. Winning companies are able to create a virtuous circle of strategy, alignment and commitment, and this is what ultimately drives performance. That is why I have depicted strategy implementation as a continuous process, rather than as a discrete process. Leaders from high-performance organizations do not develop strategies and then wait for the implementation to happen. They take an active role in the formulation of the strategy, the launching of the activities and the creation of a committed organization – and this is a continuous, iterative process.

Structure of the book

In order to provide the reader with a clear picture of the strategy implementation challenge, I have decided to divide the book into four major parts.

The first, more general, part is where I explain in greater detail the three levers of competitive advantage. Chapter 2 describes the characteristics of a winning strategy and helps you formulate one for your own company. In Chapter 3, I address the first of two strategy implementation concepts: strategic alignment. I will present a new Strategy Implementation Framework to explain what strategic alignment is all about. In Chapter 4, I will concentrate on the second lever that constitutes an effective strategy implementation, which is commitment. There I will show how effective strategy implementers commit the entire organization to think and act more strategically.

In the next three parts, I zoom in on the three operating models that I presented: product leadership, operational excellence and customer intimacy. I explain in much greater detail what strategy implementation for each of these three different configurations entails. The three operating models were introduced 20 years ago by Michael Treacy and Fred Wiersema, and are still used in strategy discussions in organizations today, but it is my experience that these concepts are often misunderstood and create confusion rather than clarity. That's a pity, because these three operating models can provide you with more concrete insights into how to build strategy implementation capabilities in your organization.

The second part, therefore, focuses on the challenges of *product leadership*. Chapters 5 and 6 present what it means and what it takes to be a product leader. It describes the capabilities necessary for building an organization centred around the competitive theme of 'continuous product innovation'. In Chapter 7, I describe the case of Studio 100, a creative media company founded in Belgium in 1996. Now, more than 15 years later, the company has more than 1,000 employees and dozens of popular characters, owns one of the largest independent catalogues of children's TV series in the world, and distributes TV series in more than 100 countries. From the beginning, the founders and managing directors have used the principles of product leadership to grow the company successfully. What started as an entrepreneurial initiative with seven employees has now become a fully fledged, innovative multinational corporation.

The third part focuses on executing a strategy built around *operational excellence*. Chapters 8 and 9 unfold what it means and what it takes to have an operational-excellence operating model. Whereas product leadership is the best understood, and customer intimacy is the least understood, operating model, operational excellence is probably the most *mis*understood operating model: I will explain why in Chapter 8, by going back to the roots of operational excellence. From there, I will investigate how the concept has evolved over time. New insights in management have given operational excellence a new meaning. Chapter 9 describes the implementation challenges of an operationally excellent firm, and, in Chapter 10, I present the ING Direct USA case to show what operational excellence means in practice. ING Direct USA is a very interesting financial services organization that is customer-centric and process-driven. This company has extremely high employee- and customer-satisfaction scores, which is atypical for a bank. The case study proves that, even in difficult industries, working on strategy formulation and implementation pays off.

The fourth part presents the challenges of implementing a strategy based on *customer intimacy*. Chapter 11 describes what it means to be customer intimate, and Chapter 12 clarifies what it takes to be customer intimate. In my strategy workshops, most firms aim to become more intimate with their key customers, but they do not have a clue how to set up and implement such a strategy. In Chapter 13, I use the Château*form'* case to illustrate how a firm can become more customer intimate. Château*form'* is a company of venues and sites dedicated to meetings and seminars, set up by Jacques Horovitz, a former services management professor at IMD. The hotel industry is a tough industry, with low growth rates and intense competition, but Château*form'* has reported double-digit growth per annum since its inception. The company has achieved those results by creating a unique environment for its guests, with all the elements necessary to turn a seminar into a memorable experience. The company has achieved this growth by applying the principles of customer intimacy.

Every chapter should provide you with clear frameworks that help you get a better view on your strategy formulation and implementation capabilities, and I hope that the numerous examples and case studies will provide you with lots of inspiration to start your implementation journey!

Notes

1 Pfeffer, J., and Sutton, R. I. (1999) *The Knowing-Doing Gap: How Smart Companies Turn Knowledge into Action*, Harvard Business School Press, Boston, MA, pp. 1–2, cited in Morgan, M., Levitt, R. E. and Malek, W. (2007) *Executing Your Strategy: How to Break It Down and Get It Done*, Harvard Business School Press, Boston, MA.
2 The Conference Board (2010) 'CEO Challenge 2010: Top 10 Challenges', *Research Report R-1461-10-RR*, The Conference Board, New York.
3 Hrebiniak, L. G. (2006) 'Obstacles to Effective Strategy Implementation', *Organizational Dynamics*, 35 (1), 12–31.
4 Bossidy, L., Charan, R., with Burck, C. (2002) *Execution: The Discipline of Getting Things Done*, Crown Business, New York, pp. 6–7.
5 Nohria, N., Joyce, W., and Roberson, B. (2003) 'What Really Works', *Harvard Business Review*, July, 1–11.

6 Noble, C. H. (1999) 'The Eclectic Roots of Strategy Implementation Research', *Journal of Business Research*, 45, 119–34.
7 Knowledge@Wharton (2006) 'Michael Porter Asks, and Answers: Why Good Managers Set Bad Strategies', 1 November, available at: http://knowledge.wharton.upenn.edu/article.cfm?articleid=1594
8 Vermeulen, F. (2012) 'So You Think You Have a Strategy', *London Business School Web Exclusive*, available at: http://bsr.london.edu/lbs-article/629/index.html (accessed 20 March 2012).
9 Hagel, J. III, and Singer, M. (1999) 'Unbundling the Corporation', *Harvard Business Review*, March–April, 133–41.
10 Scott, H. (2008) 'Lost in Translation', *Strategy Magazine*, 18 (December), 11.
11 De Flander, J. (2010) *Strategy Execution Heroes: Business Strategy Implementation and Strategic Management Demystified*, The Performance Factory, Brussels.
12 Porter, M. E. (1996) 'What Is Strategy?', *Harvard Business Review*, November–December, 61–78.
13 Treacy, M., and Wiersema, F. (1993) 'Customer Intimacy and Other Value Disciplines', *Harvard Business Review*, January–February, 84–93.
14 Liou, K.-T., and Nyhan, R. C. (1994) 'Dimensions of Organizational Commitment in the Public Sector: An Empirical Assessment', *Public Administration Quarterly*, Spring, 99–118.
15 Markides, C. C. (2004) 'What Is Strategy and How Do You Know If You Have One?', *Business Strategy Review*, 15 (2), 5–12; Markides, C. C. (2000) *All The Right Moves*, Harvard Business School Press, Boston, MA.

PART I

Achieving competitive advantage through strategy, alignment and commitment

2
FORMULATING A WINNING STRATEGY

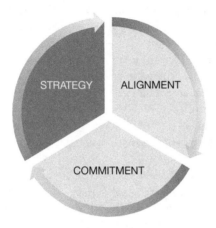

Robert Kaplan and David Norton started their highly influential book, *The Strategy-Focused Organization*, with the following statement: 'A study of 275 portfolio managers reported that the ability to execute strategy was more important than the quality of the strategy itself.'[1] One must, however, not forget that the quality of the strategy must be high for execution to be effective – and, in my experience, most companies struggle as much with formulating a winning strategy as with implementing that strategy. I very much agree with George Labovitz and Victor Rosansky, who stated that 'strategy is often like desert rain. Before the raindrops hit the desert floor, they evaporate, creating little or no effect below'.[2]

Therefore, I devote this chapter to outlining the characteristics of winning business strategies. I start by presenting the current state of the art of the field of competitive strategy. Today, strategy bewilders and confuses, and the quality of many strategies is not good. That's why I've decided to take one step back and define some essential strategic concepts. Then, I continue with outlining the elements of a winning business strategy. Strategy is a multidimensional concept, and so it is important to define the crucial dimensions of a winning strategy. I present a framework built around four key questions and discuss why only a few firms truly have a winning strategy. The chapter then elaborates on how providing focused and unique answers to all four questions is essential to developing winning business strategies.

Back to the basics

In the previous chapter, I stressed that a clear and compelling strategy is a pre-requisite for a successful implementation. However, it is also important to be aware that, of all management concepts, 'strategy is the one that attracts the most attention and generates the most controversy. Almost everyone agrees that it is important. Almost no one agrees what it is'.[3] It's no surprise, therefore, that managers get lost in the woods of strategic management. Although strategy consultants and academicians have developed a huge arsenal of interesting strategy frameworks, they have been less successful in providing an overall guiding and integrated framework for what constitutes a winning strategy. That's why managers often turn their attention to the hype of the moment – be it Total Quality Management, the Balanced Scorecard, Blue Oceans or ambidexterity – and, drawing on the jargon of the chosen methodology, infuse their strategies with sexy slogans. In this way, strategy can mean anything that an executive wants it to mean – which, needless to say, is not an ideal situation.

Why is there so much confusion about strategy? One major reason is that managers confuse strategy with mission, vision and goals. Let's pause a moment to clarify those concepts:

A *mission* defines who you are and why you are here – it should specify what your firm's core business is. For example, Disney's core business (as defined in the company's mission statement) is to develop the most creative, innovative and profitable entertainment experiences and related products in the world. The company operates in four business segments: media networks, parks and resorts, studio entertainment and consumer products. Defining your core business is difficult, but it has significant repercussions for what an organization does and does not do. A mission should also specify why you are here: it should clarify the firm's purpose. Several authors have stressed the importance of having a purpose that goes beyond just making money. For example, this is what purpose meant for Steve Jobs:

> My passion has been to build an enduring company where people were motivated to make great products. Everything else was secondary. Sure, it was great to make a profit, because that was what allowed you to make great products. But the products, not the profits, were the motivation. Sculley flipped these priorities to where the goal was to make money. It is a subtle difference, but it ends up meaning everything: the people you hire, who gets promoted, what you discuss in meetings.[4]

A *vision*, on the other hand, addresses the question: Where are we going? It describes a mental picture of what the firm wants to be in the future. Again, Apple is an illustrative case. Steve Jobs was really a visionary when he presented his vision for the Macintosh in what he called the 'digital hub'. He believed that Apple had a real advantage for people who were becoming entrenched in a digital lifestyle, using digital cameras, portable music players, digital camcorders and mobile phones. So Jobs transformed Apple from a computer company to a consumer electronics firm. Pursuing this vision led the company to develop the iPod and iTunes, the iPhone, the iPad and the App Store.

Finally, *goals* tell us what we would like to achieve in the longer term. Strategic goals are derived from the company's vision, but they are not a substitute for a vision! For example, 'Doubling our revenues in 3 years' might be a goal, but it's not a vision.'

A compelling business strategy

A *strategy*, then, specifies how to achieve the vision and the strategic goals. A strategy is an integrated set of decisions on where and how to compete. It is also very important to understand that strategy takes place at three different levels: the corporate, the business and the functional level.

Corporate strategy – or group strategy – defines *where* companies compete. For example, Stelios Haji-Ioannou, the founder of easyJet, a major European airline company, has also set up businesses in the car rental sector (easyCar), in the financial services industry (easyMoney), in the pizza business (easyPizza), in the cruise business (easyCruise), and in some other industries as well. However, should Stelios also set up easyBusiness School? Finding an answer to that question is what a corporate strategy should reveal. On top of that, a corporate strategy should also explain why the group is worth more than the sum of its individual businesses. What are the actions that a corporate parent performs that tie the different businesses together? And what is the logic of having different companies under the same corporate umbrella? Executives often refer to synergies, but be aware that synergies are often very difficult to realize.

Business strategy defines *how* companies compete. A business strategy – another term is competitive strategy – is about how companies position themselves in the market and how they make the difference relative to the competition. A business strategy should then be translated into *functional* strategies, such as a marketing strategy, an HR strategy, an IT strategy, an operations strategy, and so on.

As I have explained in Chapter 1, most organizations do have corporate and functional strategies, but they lack a clear and explicit *business* strategy, and yet, effective strategy implementation starts with formulating a winning strategy at the business level. That's where the competition takes place. In the end, companies earn profits when their business units – not the head office, and not the functional units – compete in the market successfully.

We are not saying that corporate and functional strategies are irrelevant, but, today, executives have forgotten to formulate compelling business strategies. Therefore, the focus of this chapter, and the remainder of the book, will be on *developing and implementing a winning business strategy*.

A 'winning' strategy vs a 'mediocre' strategy

So far, I have presented some generic strategy definitions, but these definitions will not help us construct a winning business strategy. What is needed is a simple and clear framework that helps us identify the elements and characteristics of such a winning strategy.

Elements of a winning business strategy

In my view, a business strategy should be a coherent, integrated set of decisions that addresses four fundamental questions (see Figure 2.1):

- Whom do we serve? What are the customer segments we want to target? And not target?
- What do we provide? What is our product offering? What do we not offer? And how does it relate to what competitors offer?
- What is our value proposition? Why do customers prefer us and not the competitors?
- What is our operating model? What are our resources and capabilities that underpin our value proposition towards our customers?

The answers to the first two questions specify where a company wants to play – they set the firm's *competitive arena*. As I have said, a corporate strategy defines the industries in which a company competes, but, once a firm has chosen a particular industry to compete in, it needs to delineate a particular competitive arena that it will concentrate on. For example, easyJet and Ryanair have carved out a very specific competitive arena in the European airline industry. Both companies have chosen to provide point-to-point flights on short-haul routes in Europe and the Mediterranean region. easyJet and Ryanair do not fly to the United States or to Asia, nor do they offer cargo or any other services. The motorcycle market provides another example: Ducati has focused on the sport bike market, in which its customers are 'racing aficionados' who seek extreme performance and top functionality.

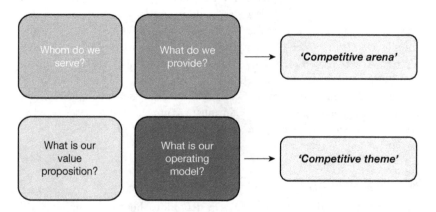

FIGURE 2.1 Elements of the Strategy Formulation Framework

Harley-Davidson (H-D), on the other hand, is strong in the cruiser and touring bike market, and its customers are the 'easy riders', who associate the motorcycle with a particular lifestyle.[5]

The questions 'What is our value proposition?' and 'What is our operating model?' force a company to specify how it can win in its chosen competitive arena. Answers to these questions describe the *competitive theme*, to both customers and employees. Customers are interested in a good value proposition, and employees need to understand what the company's operating model is.

It is important that the answers form a coherent whole. For example, IKEA's target market ('*whom do we serve?*') is young, primarily white-collar, not wealthy, and likely to have children. These customers can buy a wide range of well-designed, functional home furnishing products ('*what do we provide?*'). IKEA attracts customers by providing low-priced but stylish products. Its customers are treated to a fun experience as they wander through a visually exciting store. They can take the item home or have it delivered the same day, because IKEA carries an extensive inventory at each store ('*what is our value proposition?*'). IKEA is able to meet its customers' needs profitably because the company benefits from economies of scale and efficiencies of replication *('what is our operating model?*').[6] Although much of its low-cost position comes from having the customers assemble the furniture themselves, IKEA offers a number of extra services that competitors do not offer. In-store childcare and extended hours ('*what is our value proposition?*') are perfectly aligned with the needs of its target segment. In summary, coherence is essential to a sustained competitive advantage.

Characteristics of a winning business strategy

What makes a strategy a winning strategy? In the previous section, we defined a business strategy as a coherent and integrated set of decisions, addressing four questions. However, providing coherent answers to those four questions is not sufficient. If you want to develop a sustainable competitive advantage, your answers need to be 'more focused' and 'more distinctive' than the answers of your competitors.

What do I mean by that? First of all, strategy is about making choices. A strategy is a winning strategy only when *clear choices* are made: the essence of strategy is choosing what *not* to do.[7] A strategy can only work if it sets boundaries for what activities the organization does and does not perform. Attempting to be everything to everyone is a recipe for strategic mediocrity – that is why clear and explicit decisions must be made. If the strategy does not specify boundaries, the organization drifts in many different directions, probably provides inconsistent guidance to managers and employees, and deploys scarce organizational resources inefficiently. Too often, managers cannot resist the temptation to expand the boundaries, as they want to reach the growth targets that have been set, but, in the end, they are stuck with a number of unprofitable propositions.

Second, a winning business strategy is *different*. There is general agreement among strategists that successful companies choose a distinctive strategic position in their market. Strategy is about making a difference. You cannot outperform your competitors if you are just like them. This is a message that Arkadi Kuhlmann, the CEO of ING Direct USA, has understood well. In all that his bank does, it tries to create a feeling of 'unbank-ness', helping the company to differentiate itself from the rest. Differentiation is also key for companies such as Cirque du Soleil, Château*form'*, easyJet, and many others. It is the essence of their strategy and a prime source of their competitive advantage.

Let us explore what it means to be *more focused and unique* for each of the four questions of the Strategy Formulation Framework.

Whom do we serve?

Developing a winning strategy is about finding a unique strategic position in your industry. This is not easy, but I hope that the next sections provide you with food for thought about the position your company currently occupies in the market. Firms should define their competitive arena, either in terms of the customer segments they want to serve, or in terms of the choice of products or services they want to offer. In articulating arenas, it is important to be as specific as possible. Most firms struggle with this.

In a competitive market, managers should think carefully about whom to serve and whom not to serve. Some companies have become winners because they have a clear vision of what their target segment is and understand what it is that customers in this segment value. These companies continuously ask: Who are those customers? What do they need? And how are their needs evolving? They are also very explicit about which customer segments they do not serve.

Who is our customer?

This seems like an obvious question for managers, but the answer is sometimes surprisingly difficult. Who are the customers for an airport corporation? Are they the airline companies, or the passengers? And what about piping product companies? Should they focus on the retailer, or on the end customer? Or a temp agency? Whom should they serve? Is it the people who look for a job? Or the companies that provide the jobs?

So, a critical question is: Who is the company's focal customer? In order to answer that question precisely, firms should answer three questions: Who makes the purchasing decision? Who pays? And who consumes?[8]

A clear strategic segment

It is very important that firms make clear choices as to whom to serve and whom not to serve. Being sharper than your competitor in choosing your target market can be a source of competitive advantage. There are many ways to define your target market. For example, you can define a target segment by who the target customers are (e.g., in terms of particular demographics or other factors), when they buy (frequent users vs light users), what they buy (price buyers vs service buyers), or how they buy (perhaps through specific channels).

For example, ING Direct USA has defined its target segment in terms of what it buys. The company provides basic banking services to 'the average American', sensitive to price and convenience. This strategic segment is somewhat neglected by the traditional banks, whose focus is often on high net worth individuals, who have more money to spend on financial services (from the regular banking products to insurance and private banking). ING Direct USA serves the average American, as long as (s)he behaves in the way ING Direct wants. In 2004, the company 'fired' more than 3,500 customers who did not play by the bank's rules. Those customers relied too much on the call centres, or asked for too many exceptions from the standard operating procedures. Knowing who are good and bad customers is a starting point for a successful strategy.

Why does focus help? Companies that focus on one strategic segment have clear advantages over companies that address various marketing segments simultaneously.[9] Nirmalya Kumar, a marketing professor at London Business School, has provided some compelling arguments for why this is the case.[10] According to Kumar, marketers use *segmentation*, *targeting* and *positioning* (STP) to create a difference between their company's offering and that of its competitors. Such an approach helps the company to identify appropriate market segments to target, as well as to develop a *unique selling proposition* (USP) for the target segment, using the four Ps of the marketing mix – price, place, product and promotion. However, many firms are unable to create a perceptible differentiation among offerings. The tactical orientation has led marketers to rely too heavily on the marketing mix to make the difference.

On the other hand, some firms have used the entire value chain to make the difference in the market. For instance, Europe's Ryanair and easyJet target those customers who pay from their own pockets. The following example shows how Ryanair and easyJet have used their entire value chain to differentiate from the traditional flag carriers.

The more companies focus on one strategic segment, the more they can use the entire value chain to make the difference. Companies that address various market segments with the same business unit often have common purchasing and operations departments, which limits the differentiation possibilities. Targeting different customer segments with the same business unit also creates compromise costs.

For example, the traditional airline companies, such as KLM and British Airways, regard business travellers as their most valued customers. However, when British Airways wanted to attack the low-cost carriers easyJet and Ryanair, it set up a new company called GO, while retaining its traditional business traveller focus for the primary strategic business unit. When GO was part of British Airways, the temptation was to constantly seek synergies in the value chain, but the so-called synergies exploited in various parts of the value chain were optimized neither for the low costs necessary for GO, nor for the full service necessary for British Airways.

	Purchasing	Operations	Marketing	Distribution
Flag carriers	Integrated	• Multiple types of planes • Short- and long-haul routes • Prime airports (hubs) • Worldwide network • Assigned seating	• Semented customers • Varied meal services • Frequent flyer programme	• Travel agents • Worldwide reservation systems
easyJet/ Ryanair	Outsourced	• Single type aircraft • 149 versus 109 seats • Short-haul routes • Point-to-point lines • Rapid turnaround • No businessclass • No preseating • No in-flight meals	• No market research • No frequent flyer programs • Use of plane for advertising • Attention-grabbing campaigns • Variable pricing • One-way ticket only	• No travel agents • No tickets • No use of 'Sabre' • Direct sales (phone and internet) • Reservation agents on commission

FIGURE 2.2 Value chains of traditional flag carriers versus easyJet/Ryanair

Source: Kumar (2004)[11]

For them, addressing various strategic segments, even with two different business units, involved significant compromise costs, which can be high when focused competitors operate in the market. After 3 years, British Airways divested GO.

Unique customer segments

Having a differentiated approach to a target market can be a source of competitive advantage in its own right. Companies can even build a stronger competitive position by identifying potential new customers in markets that may have previously been considered to be uninterested non-customers. This occurs when firms 'create' uncontested market space in completely new industries, as Europe's Accor Formule 1 hotels did by focusing on the truck-driving segment. Formule 1 provided a good bed, easy check-in and checkout and enough parking space for large trucks, at the price of a one-star hotel. Formule 1 became a big success, and the customer segment extended to people other than truck drivers. In a similar way, Cirque du Soleil invented 'circus for adults' and has become a very successful market leader in that industry.

Checklist: 'whom do we serve?'

If you want to think strategically about 'whom do we serve?', the following checklist may be useful:

1   Does your organization focus on one strategic segment? How would you describe that strategic segment?
2   To what extent do your customers' needs differ from those of other customer segments?
3   Do you know what the customers in your strategic segment really want?
4   Do you know who your good and bad customers are? How many of the customers currently in your customer base are good customers?
5   Is there sufficient growth potential for your company if you simply focus on more customers in the strategic segment?

What do we provide?

Winning companies have a clear view on where they compete in their market. A strategy should not only specify which customers to target, but also the products and services the company is going to offer. One of the key decisions when defining your competitive arena is to identify the range of product lines you will offer – this is often referred to as the *product scope dimension*. A second important decision when you define your competitive arena concerns the *nature* of your products: should you trade up or trade down? Winners have made clear choices as to the product scope and the nature of their products. These choices are illustrated in Figure 2.3.

Product scope

The scope of a product mix – or the width and depth of the product line(s) – refers to how many different product lines the company carries (width) and how

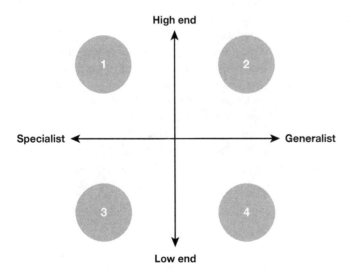

FIGURE 2.3 Making choices for your product portfolio

many variants of each product are offered in each line (depth). Companies that choose to develop a competitive advantage based on the 'what-do-we-provide' dimension of the Strategy Formulation Framework must decide whether they will consistently have the deepest selection of products in a particular product line, or the broadest assortment of product lines. It is very important to make clear decisions and to focus on one of the two extremes. Only then will it be possible to conquer a place of preference in the customer's mind.

For example, IKEA dominates its market by being a generalist in the furniture-retailing sector. Yet, at the same time, in many countries, other companies have specialized in offering beds or mattresses and can compete with IKEA through their expertise in these product lines. A similar example can be found in the insurance industry. DKV is a health insurance group with various European subsidiaries. All these subsidiaries profile themselves as specialists in health insurance. In contrast, Allianz is an insurance multinational that offers a broad range of life insurance, non-life insurance, asset management and even banking products in many of its western-European subsidiaries.

Focus on the scope dimension implies that a company must decide whether it is a specialist or a generalist in its chosen market.

Nature of your products

Winning companies have made a clear choice to target either the low end or the high end of their preferred markets. Do you want to offer the 'best' products, which are innovative and made to exact specifications? Or do you want to provide 'good enough' products? Bang & Olufsen (B&O) and Bose position themselves at the high end of the audio product market, and Porsche and Ferrari are examples of 'best product' providers in the car industry. Ryanair and Aldi are examples of companies focusing on the low end of the market. Focus means that you choose on which side of the spectrum you wish to compete.

Market research has yielded many interesting insights into the nuances of consumer market bifurcation. Consumers either *trade up* for products that meet their aspiration needs or *trade down* for products that they perceive to be commodities – like the customer who stays in a five-star hotel but travels with a budget air carrier. Boston Consulting Group has analysed why consumers seek value at the top and the bottom of markets – their conclusion is that, in general, the middle market is in terminal decline.[12] This reinforces the need for focus, which, in this context, essentially means choosing between high-quality, emotionally rich, high-margin goods and services, or basic, decent-quality, low-cost goods and services.

Making choices

All this means that there are four ideal positions that companies should seek to pursue. These four, ideal positions are situated at the four corners of each quadrant (indicated by the numbers 1–4). Examples of companies situated at position 1 (high-end specialists) are Ferrari, McKinsey, Bose and Apple. Lufthansa, Harrods and Allianz Germany occupy position 2 (high-end generalists). IKEA, Amazon and Walmart are low-end generalists, situated at position 3, and Aldi, McDonalds, ING Direct USA and Ryanair are great examples of 'type-4' companies (low-end specialists). It's essential to avoid the 'stuck-in-the-middle' position.

Managers do not always find it easy to position their company and their competitors on this framework. Nevertheless, by thinking about 'where you are' and 'where you ought to go', it's possible to stimulate interesting discussions that may help a company get a better view of the position it wants to occupy in the competitive arena. The more you are able to specify your competitive arena and the position you want to occupy, the better your chances in the market.

A unique position

Making choices is important, but it's not enough. Being a winner requires that you choose a product portfolio that you master best in your industry. This means that you need to have a distinctive set of capabilities and resources that help you be the reference in your market.

For example, Carglass® (like all the sister companies in the Belron® Group) specializes in automobile glass repair and replacement. The company has chosen to provide only a subset of the services that a typical competitor – a traditional car repair shop – offers. It has developed a set of specific competences in automobile glass repair, but it is also skilled in setting up partnerships with insurance companies and in marketing, all of which have made it the natural choice for most customers.

Châteauform' is another company that occupies a unique competitive arena by offering a different 'product offer'. Châteauform' is not a typical hotel chain in Europe: it is more a mix of hotel and seminar centre. The company calls itself 'The Home of Seminars' and focuses more on providing excellent conference centre facilities than on providing lodging. In this way, it is truly unique. It is one of the few 'hotels' that focus on corporate customers and their seminar participants, and Jacques Horovitz, the founder of the concept, has looked for many ways to offer this target audience a unique and differentiated experience. Since it opened its first site in 1996, Châteauform' has reported double-digit revenue growth every year, and this in a market that is considered to be mature and extremely competitive.

Checklist: 'what do we provide?'

If you want to think strategically about 'what do we provide?', the following questions need to be addressed:

1 For your product portfolio, have you made a clear and consistent choice as to where you want to be situated on the product scope axis? Are you a 'specialist' or a 'generalist'?

2   Have you made a clear and consistent choice with regard to the nature of your products? Are all your products or services focused on the 'high end' or on the 'low end'?

3   What are you doing to maintain the quality of your products and/or services?

4   How unique is your positioning in the market? Have you developed specific competences that allow you to be one of the best in that market?

5   Could you increase your product differentiation by specializing (like Carglass®) or by incorporating elements of related industries (like Châteauform')?

What is our value proposition?

Developing a winning strategy is about defining your competitive arena. In other words, you need to be clear about whom to serve (and not serve), and what to provide (and not provide). However, developing a winning strategy also requires that you develop a convincing competitive theme. Firms develop a competitive theme by formulating a focused and unique value proposition that is supported by a focused and unique operating model.

A value proposition can be defined as a particular bundle of benefits offered by the company and sought (and bought) by the customer. The value proposition communicates the reasons why a customer should buy your company's products and/or services in preference to those of your competitors.

In this section, I will focus on what it means to have a *winning* value proposition.

A focused value proposition

Winning companies have a compelling value proposition. A compelling value proposition is a focused value proposition. These companies have made up-front, deliberate choices regarding the benefits they are going to offer and those they are not going to offer. In contrast, many companies suffer from their desire to achieve across-the-board superiority, trying to outperform competitors on too broad an array of benefits – such as lower price, better service and more attractive products – all at once. This is the key message brought by Fred Crawford and Ryan Mathews in their inspiring book, *The Myth of Excellence: Why Great Companies Never Try to Be the Best at Everything.*[13] Crawford and Mathews provide managers with a very interesting framework that forces them to verify whether or not their organization has a focused value proposition.

Their basic assumption is that every business transaction can be broken down into five major value attributes:

•   Product: the set of core benefits a customer buys.
•   Price: the cost of the goods or services.
•   Access: how easily consumers can obtain and use the company's goods or services.

- Service: what a company does in addition before, during and after the sale. For example, a company that gives a lot of advice offers something extra before the sale. Offering flexibility in your product offering is a service during the sale. And offering performance guarantees clearly is an after-sales service.
- Connectivity: the feeling that customers have when they approach the company. Companies that are able to connect give their customers the feeling that they are more than a number.

Winning companies score well on all of these value attributes. They achieve a threshold level at which the customer says: 'I *accept* your offer – I trust you enough to buy your products and services, and I will consider coming back again.' You create a basic level of acceptance if your pricing is honest, your products are credible, you provide an accommodating service, you create easy access and you show your customers the respect they believe they deserve.

However, being 'good' is not enough to be a winner. Winning firms are 'better' than their competitors. Then, the customer says: 'I *prefer* your store, products and services, and – all things being equal – I will probably make my purchases here.' This happens when the company makes access to its facilities (or website) convenient, shows respect on a personal level, clearly presents consistently low prices, offers reliable, high-quality products, and is able to educate the consumer about how a product or service works.

Ultimately, the most successful companies do not stop at just differentiating themselves. They find ways to dominate, to further separate themselves from the pack, allowing them to become the one choice that springs automatically into the consumer's mind at the moment of need. Now, the customer is saying to the company: 'I trust you so completely that I will *seek* you out among all the other options.' This is the ideal position, in which the consumer not only prefers one company to another, but will actively seek out their company of choice. For example, some consumers will gladly wait 9 months for delivery of the new-model Ferrari, or will refuse to drink coffee if it does not come from Starbucks.

Companies with a winning strategy – Crawford and Mathews call these companies 'consumer-relevant companies' – never try to be the best at everything. They overcome the constant temptation to strive for universal excellence and, instead, decide to be the best ('dominate') in one primary attribute. In addition, they often select a secondary attribute that is strongly complementary to the first and helps to further 'differentiate' them from their competitors. Companies with a winning value proposition also realize that they cannot fall below the industry par for the other three value attributes; they must avoid slipping into the consumer underworld.

Again, the key message is simple: only through a proper focus will it be possible for consumer-relevant companies to create a meaningful image in the customer's mind. This is illustrated in Figure 2.4. Yet, even though the message is simple, few companies have a clear idea of where and how they can dominate

TABLE 2.1 Crawford and Mathews's Consumer Relevancy Framework

Level	Access	Connectivity	Price	Product	Service
'Best': Consumer *seeks* the company (dominate)	Turn my hassle into a positive experience	Establish intimacy with me by doing something no one else can	Be my price agent, let me trust you to make my purchases	Inspire me with an assortment of excellent products I didn't know about	Provide me with a solution, take away my problems
'Better': Consumer *prefers* the company (differentiate)	Make the entire interaction reliable and convenient for me	Care about my needs and about me as a person	Be fair and consistent in your low pricing (this does not necessarily mean the lowest price)	Offer high-quality products continuously	Educate me when I encounter a product or situation I do not understand
'Good': Consumer *accepts* the company (at par)	Make it easy for me to find what I need	Respect me, treat me like a human being	Keep the prices honest, do not jack them up or announce big savings when there are none	Be credible in your product and service offering	Accommodate me, bend over backwards sometimes to show me you care
'Failing, unacceptable': (consumer underworld)	Block my way, hassle me, keep me waiting, make it hard for me to get in and out	Dehumanize me, disrespect me, ignore my needs	Be inconsistent, unclear or misleading in your pricing	Offer me poor-quality merchandise and services that I cannot use	Give me an experience I'd just as soon forget, give me a reason to tell my friends and relatives to stay away

Source: Adapted from Crawford and Mathews (2001)[14]

and differentiate. Examples of consumer-relevant companies are Zara (dominating on price, differentiating on product, and at par for the other attributes), American retailer Dollar General (dominating on price and differentiating on access) and the Danish Jyske Bank (dominating on experience, differentiating on service, and at par for the other attributes).

A unique value proposition

Truly excellent companies not only have the right focus, they also look for unique value dimensions in their value proposition. A value dimension can be defined as a benefit that customers find in a company's product or service offering. Companies win because they offer the consumer something new. The value curve concept illustrates the value dimensions that can be useful to help a company differentiate itself from competitors (see Figure 2.5).[15] High-growth companies tend to look for totally new value dimensions and correspondingly under-invest in, or reduce, value dimensions that consumers do not value.

A critical aspect of value innovation is a managerial focus on creating value dimensions that an industry has never previously offered. For instance, Cirque du Soleil has combined value dimensions from the circus industry and the theatre industry to develop a totally new form of entertainment, and it has been very successful for many years with this 'blue ocean strategy'.

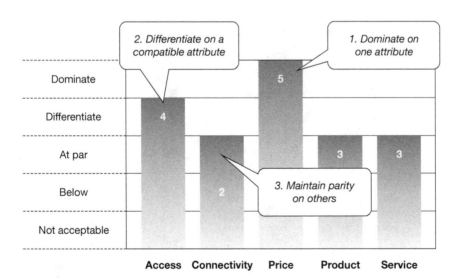

FIGURE 2.4 A focused value proposition

Source: Crawford and Mathews (2001)[16]

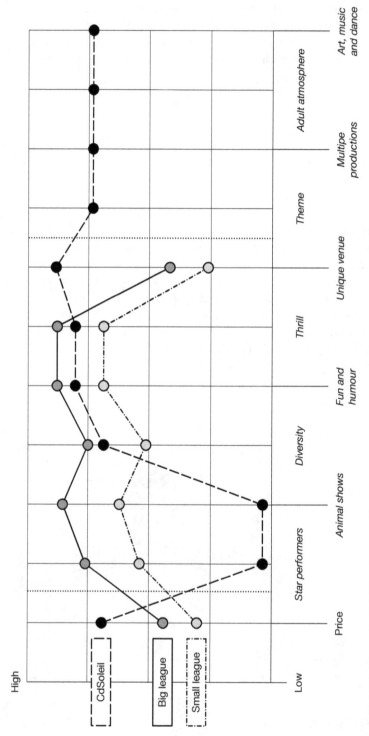

FIGURE 2.5 Cirque du Soleil's value curve[17]

Source: Kim and Mauborgne (2005)

Checklist: 'what is our value proposition?'

If you want to think about your value proposition, please consider the following questions:

1   Is your value proposition for your customers *clear* to you? Is this the same or similar for all your customers? Or do different customers have different reasons for coming to you?
2   When you compare your product and service offering with the competitors, is there a value attribute that you clearly dominate in and one that you clearly differentiate in?
3   Have you translated the Consumer Relevancy Framework into clear, specific, concrete benefits for your customers?
4   Do all people in your organization know where you dominate and differentiate? And does everybody in the organization know where you make the difference?
5   Is your value proposition really unique?

What is our operating model?

The value proposition is what a company offers to its customers. The operating model tells you how to make the value proposition come true:

- It consists of all of an organization's resources and capabilities that enable it to create and deliver the customer value proposition within a particular competitive arena.
- It reveals the underlying logic that explains *how* to deliver value to the customer at an appropriate cost.
- It includes what the company owns and what the company does, both in operational and managerial terms.

An operating model is industry-specific. For example, a hotel has a totally different operating model to that of a software company; the core resources and capabilities to succeed in those two different industries are indeed very different. However, companies such as Zara and Toyota have a number of striking similarities: they are both very process-oriented, they have a culture of continuous improvement, and they are fast in creating and delivering their products to their customers. Similarly, there are also striking commonalities between Apple's operating model and that of former top restaurant elBulli. Both companies are very innovative and cultivate entrepreneurship and creativity. They offer high-quality products and services, and they know how to market their products. Furthermore, to attract customers, they like to create mystery, either around a new product launch (Apple) or around the entire concept (elBulli).

This raises the following question: Are there some 'archetypal configurations' or 'generic operating models' that you find in successful firms?

A focused operating model

More than 15 years ago, Michael Treacy and Fred Wiersema wrote an influential book that provides an answer to that question. Their observation was that, 'companies that have taken leadership positions in their industries . . . have focused on delivering superior customer value in line with one of three value disciplines – operational excellence, customer intimacy, or product leadership'.[18] This means that the operating models of market leaders pursuing the same value proposition in different industries are remarkably similar. What are those three operating models – or, in the words of Treacy and Wiersema, value disciplines?

Operational excellence is an operating model that allows a firm to manage processes in a flawless and efficient way. Companies pursuing operational excellence are continuously managing their costs, and they optimize business processes across functional and organizational boundaries. ING Direct USA, Zara, McDonalds and Aldi are examples of operational excellence companies.

A *customer-intimacy* operating model allows organizations to segment and target markets precisely and then to continually tailor products and services to match the demands of those niches. This might be more expensive, but customer-intimate companies are willing to make investments in order to build customer loyalty in the long term. These companies look at the customer's lifetime value to the company, rather than at the value of any single transaction. Examples include Châteauform', Singapore Airlines (SIA) and Svenska Handelsbanken.

Finally, *product leadership* is an operating model that allows companies to win customers with state-of-the-art products and services. Great attention is paid to developing new products and solutions. A product leader looks for every possible opportunity to fuel creativity within the organization. In addition to their innovation capabilities, product leaders also have great marketing capabilities – they convince the entire market of the superiority of their products and services. Product leadership is the operating model of elBulli, Pixar, H-D and Apple.

So, in every industry, a firm can win by adhering to the principles of one of these three operating models. The key message again is that winning requires making a clear choice of one particular operating model. Each of these three operating models provides a clear competitive theme that aligns all employees throughout the company. And, as it also directs future investment in new projects, it helps the company stay ahead of the competition.

Strategic decision-making is essentially a never-ending series of trade-offs. Less-focused organizations find it more difficult to make such trade-offs, because they have failed to clearly identify which competences they need to win in the marketplace. As a result, resources are wasted on secondary objectives that do not always support the company's primary strategic goals.

Again, it is important to stress that an operating model is a business unit concept. I have seen many companies who strive to be operationally excellent in the production department, and customer intimate in the sales department, but that does not work! Operational excellence companies are operationally excellent in

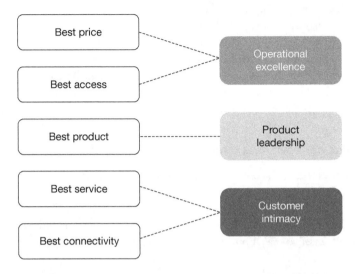

FIGURE 2.6 A compelling competitive theme

every department of the organization. The same applies to product leaders and customer-intimacy firms.

Furthermore, it's important to notice the link between a winning value proposition and a winning operating model. In the previous section, I identified five value attributes: product, price, access, service and connectivity. These can be linked to the three operating models, as illustrated in Figure 2.6. For example, a company that dominates through access, such as McDonalds, will only be successful if it has adopted an operational-excellence operating model. Firms that strive to have the best product are best served by a product-leadership model. And a customer-intimacy operating model is best suited to help companies dominate through service or connectivity.

A different operating model

Companies with a winning strategy not only focus, they also choose to be different. They consciously choose a different set of activities to deliver a unique mix of value. Indeed, the essence of strategy is in the activities: choosing to perform activities differently, or choosing to perform different activities, to your rivals.[19] For example, Amazon has been very successful because it masters a set of activities that others have not been able to copy yet: retail interface design, back-end supply chain, merchandising and customer relationship management (CRM).[20] Behind these capabilities is a set of activities that are unique, or uniquely combined.

Developing a radically new business concept compels a company to create resource bundles that are valuable, rare and costly to imitate, and that have few substitutes. This means that a company can only outperform its rivals if it can establish a difference that it can preserve. Such differentiation is not always easy to achieve, and it's still harder to maintain. Successful business ideas are quickly copied. If the original differentiators cannot rely on a continued first-mover advantage, the new profit pool will soon be shared with an increasing number of competitors, thereby reducing the basis for sustainable competitive advantage. Nevertheless, managers should constantly seek to achieve differentiation in their operating model, because that helps the company achieve a distinctive position in the market.

Checklist: 'what is our operating model?'

If you want to think strategically about 'what is our operating model', the following questions will be helpful:

1   Have you made a clear choice for one of the three operating models identified by Treacy and Wiersema: operational excellence, customer intimacy or product leadership?
2   Are all of your organization's departments focusing on the same operating model?
3   Are your core resources ('what you own') and capabilities ('what you know') aligned with the chosen operating model?
4   Is your operating model different from your competitors' operating models?
5   Do your employees know which core activities enable you to make the difference relative to the competition?

Key learning points

Effective strategy implementation starts with formulating a compelling, winning business strategy. Although there are numerous interesting strategy frameworks, it is surprising that few firms actually have a compelling and winning business strategy.

A winning business strategy provides a clear and coherent answer to four questions:

1   Whom do we serve?
2   What do we provide?
3   What is our value proposition?
4   What is our operating model?

Winning companies do not merely answer these questions – they answer them in a more focused and unique way than their competitors do. Making choices and being different are what set winners apart from other companies. In this chapter, I have provided you with some arguments as to why focus and uniqueness matter. If you feel that your strategy is not focused and unique, then I recommend that you first rethink your business strategy. Strategy implementation is effective only when the business strategy is clear. In the next chapter, I will describe what *effective strategy implementation* is all about.

Notes

1 Kaplan, R. S., and Norton, D. P. (2001) *The Strategy-Focused Organization: How Balanced Scorecard Companies Thrive in the New Business Environment*, Harvard Business School Press, Boston, MA, p. 1.
2 Labovitz, G., and Rosansky, V. (1997) *The Power of Alignment: How Great Companies Stay Centered and Accomplish Extraordinary Things*, John Wiley & Sons, New York, p. 92.
3 Margretta, J., with Stone, N. (2002) *What Management Is: How It Works and Why It's Everyone's Business*, Free Press, New York, p. 71.
4 Isaacson, W. (2011) *Steve Jobs*, Simon & Schuster, New York, p. 567.
5 Gavetti, G. (2002) 'Ducati', *Harvard Business School Case Study*, 9–701–132.
6 Hambrick, D. C., and Fredrickson, J. W. (2001) 'Are You Sure You Have a Strategy?', *The Academy of Management Executive*, 15 (4), 48–59.
7 Porter, M. E. (1996) 'What Is Strategy?', *Harvard Business Review*, November–December, 70.
8 Moenaert, R., Robben, H., and Gouw, P. (2011) *Marketing Strategy & Organization*, Lannoo Campus, Leuven.
9 We clearly refer here to business units. Obviously, corporations can have different business units that each focus on a different customer segment.
10 Kumar, N. (2004) *Marketing as Strategy: Understanding the CEO's Agenda for Driving Growth and Innovation*, Harvard Business School Press, Boston, MA.
11 Ibid., p. 39.
12 Silverstein, M. J. (2006) *Treasure Hunt: Inside the Mind of the New Customer*, Penguin, New York.
13 Crawford, F., and Mathews, R. (2001) *The Myth of Excellence: Why Great Companies Never Try to Be the Best at Everything*, Crown Business, New York.
14 Ibid., p. 27.
15 Kim, C., and Mauborgne, R. (2002) 'Charting Your Company's Future', *Harvard Business Review*, June, 76–83.
16 Ibid.
17 Kim, C., and Mauborgne, R. (2005) *Blue Ocean Strategy: How to Create Uncontested Market Space and Make Competition Irrelevant*, Harvard Business School Press, Boston, MA.
18 Treacy, M., and Wiersema, F. (1993) 'Customer Intimacy and Other Value Disciplines', *Harvard Business Review*, January–February, p. 84; Treacy, M., and Wiersema, F. (1995) *The Discipline of Market Leaders*, Perseus, New York.
19 Porter, M. E. (1996) 'What Is Strategy?', *Harvard Business Review*, November–December, 61–78.
20 Leinwand, P., and Mainardi, C. (2011) *The Essential Advantage: How to Win with a Capabilities-Driven Strategy*, Harvard Business Review Press, Boston, MA.

3

IMPLEMENTING A WINNING STRATEGY THROUGH STRATEGIC ALIGNMENT

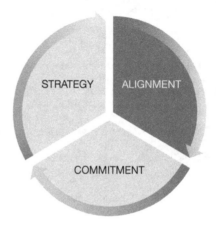

Strategy implementation is a stepchild in strategic management. Despite the significance of the topic, relatively little research attention has been given to it. However, Hamish Scott, a strategy professor from Ashridge Business School, rightly remarked that, 'it is essential to remember that an organization moves forward only when something is done – until that point everything is just words'.[1]

In this chapter, I will provide you with a new Strategy Implementation Framework and present some new ideas on effective strategy execution. Effective strategy execution is about aligning your organization's activities around a common core theme, but it is also about creating the right organizational context, so that employees and managers are committed to making the strategy work. So, in essence, strategy implementation is about creating alignment and commitment. In this chapter, I will explain the concept of strategic alignment in detail. Before that, let's take a closer look at what strategy implementation is.

What is strategy implementation?

Intuitively, strategy implementation is a simple concept: it is about taking action in support of a strategy. It's about translating the strategic choices into concrete actions to realize the organization's strategic objectives. Academics define implementation as a process of several steps that involves committing resources, setting up organizational structures and control systems, and managing people to transform strategy into a concrete reality.[2] However, that definition does not provide us with very concrete insights into how to tackle the strategy implementation challenge.

In order to define what constitutes effective strategy implementation, I have looked at strategy implementation from a process perspective. An organization can be seen as interconnected sets of processes – and processes are a collection of tasks and activities that together transform inputs into outputs. Within organizations, inputs and outputs can be materials, information and people.[3] I have identified five major sets of processes that managers must master to make strategy work. These are the five substantive levers you must pull to make strategy happen, and they constitute our Strategy Implementation Framework (see Figure 3.1).

Direction- and goal-setting processes

The first set of processes comprises direction- and goal-setting processes. In most organizations, developing a strategy largely occurs in an executive team – and those executives spend a lot of time and money with consultants to formulate a great strategy. However, the executives then often forget to take the time to translate the strategy down into the organization.

High-performing organizations, on the other hand, spend a significant amount of time involving their managers and employees in the strategy formation process. They ask their employees to provide input into the strategy analysis process, and they ask for input concerning important strategic decisions. Once a strategy is defined, it is then translated into departmental goals and action plans. Ask yourself how much time you spend each month translating strategy down into your organization? Is it hours, minutes . . . or seconds?

| Direction and goal setting processes | Operational processes | Support processes | Evaluation and control processes | Organizational behaviour processes |

FIGURE 3.1 The Strategy Implementation Framework

Operational processes

An effective strategy should also affect an organization's operational processes – the processes that create, produce and deliver the products and services that the company provides; they generate the revenues for the organization. Operational processes are more than just production activities – they also include product development, logistics, marketing and sales, and service activities.

Your strategic choices should have an impact on your operational processes. For example, the sales and service activities of a company that delivers exceptional service to a particular customer segment with a customer-intimacy operating model should be different from those of its competitors. If that is not the case – if the organization has more or less the same operational activities as its competitors – then its strategy is nothing more than a marketing slogan.

So, your strategy should drive your operational processes, but your operational improvement activities should also be driven by your strategy. Many companies today have quality programmes or re-engineering activities aimed at improving the operational processes of parts of the organization, but many of these activities are carried out across the organization, with no sense of priority or impact. Process improvement activities will only yield tangible results when they are in line with the strategy execution priorities that managers have set.[4]

Support processes

Support processes help improve the effectiveness and efficiency of the operational processes. They do not produce output for external customers, but are necessary for running the business. Support activities include workforce planning and resource allocation, information technology (IT) support and the definition of rules and methods in order to facilitate internal communication. Support processes are often neglected in strategy execution, but they often play a crucial (although sometimes less visible) role in making strategy work.

For example, successful implementation demands that managers collect and process particular kinds of information. Some companies consider information and knowledge as a strategic asset that helps build their competitive advantage. Some effective examples of companies that have adopted analytics are soccer team AC Milan (injury prevention), Tesco (customized offers) and Google (page ranks and advertising).

Evaluation and control processes

Once operations are underway, managers engage in evaluation and control processes to ensure that their organization is performing as planned. These processes detect perturbations, initiate corrective action and restore the organization to its previous equilibrium. Audit, risk management and management control are examples of evaluation and control processes.

Although, for some time now, academic researchers have stressed the importance of having the right performance measures, Robert Kaplan and David Norton convinced managers to translate a strategy into a comprehensive set of performance measures. The Balanced Scorecard emerged as the performance measurement and management toolkit that allows a firm to check whether it is on track. However, according to Kaplan and Norton, the Balanced Scorecard is not merely a control tool: they recommend using it also as a communication and motivation tool to create a high-performance climate in which individuals and teams take responsibility for the continuous improvement of business activities and results.

Organizational behaviour processes

This is the last set of processes that are crucial to implementing a strategy effectively. Organizational behaviour processes profoundly affect the form, substance and character of operational processes by shaping how they are carried out. These processes direct motives, influence and attitudes.[5] What do I mean by that?

Organizational behaviour processes direct *motives*: strategies are implemented effectively when people enthusiastically direct their efforts towards a common purpose. Human resources (HR) management practices, such as recruitment, training, promotion and rewarding, help to achieve this. An effective implementation requires that people have the right skills and attitudes to do the job. If managers do not provide HR support for their employees, their strategy execution initiatives will likely fail. In addition, the impact of incentives and rewards is often overlooked in strategy implementation. Nevertheless, rewarding can be an important tool for redirecting an individual's efforts towards the right behaviour.[6]

Organizational behaviour processes also include the processes that direct *influence*. By grouping specific tasks, specifying the hierarchical structure and establishing collaboration initiatives between departments, high-performance organizations use the organizational structure to implement the strategy more effectively.

Finally, organizational behaviour processes also direct *attitudes*. Attitudes, shared beliefs and values are elements of an organization's culture. Because the culture creates, and is created by, the quality of the organizational environment, it drives the extent to which teams cooperate and interact and how much everybody goes the extra mile.[7] Creating the right organizational context is an underestimated element in implementing an organization's strategy.

What is effective strategy implementation?

Effective strategy implementation requires organizations to use all five sets of processes to implement their strategy. Managers should translate strategy into concrete departmental goals, link strategy to operational activities, ensure that the right support tools are in place, measure and control, and create an energizing environment in which the employees can do their job and learn and improve as well.

In this way, implementing a strategy is like driving a car. Direction- and goal-setting processes provide an organization with the 'roadmap'. Not having goals or objectives is like driving a car without a destination. The operational processes can be compared to the actual driving: changing gears, accelerating, braking, steering, and so on. The support processes provide you with the fuel that you need to drive. Evaluation and control processes are the dashboard of your car: they tell you whether you are driving too fast or too slow, and they indicate how much fuel you have in the tank. The organizational behaviour processes represent the motor of your organization: they tell you how soon you will be able to reach your destination. Driving a car and reaching your destination on time require you to manage all five implementation levers.

It's not that one set of processes is more important than another – it's their interrelationship that makes firms distinctive and gives them a competitive edge. Effective strategy implementation is about combining activities. In the next sections, I show how these different sets of processes need to be configured in order to build a high-performance organization.

The main point that I would like to make here is that *successful implementation is about creating both alignment and commitment*. I will use the Strategy Implementation Framework to illustrate what alignment and commitment are all about. In the next section, I define strategic alignment; in Chapter 4, I will elaborate on how commitment helps create a winning company.

Defining strategic alignment

Alignment is a prerequisite for success. Some management authors see alignment as the essence of management.[8] In his outstanding book *High Commitment High Performance*, Michael Beer has argued that strategic alignment is one of the three pillars needed for building a resilient organization capable of providing a sustained advantage.[9] The view that strategic alignment is a driver of success is not a new theme in management. For example, more than 10 years ago, Danny Miller and John Whitney contended that,

> the heart of distinctive competitive advantage may lie not in the possession of specific organizational resources or skills, which can often be imitated or purchased by others, but in the power of an orchestrating theme and the degree of complementarity it engenders among the (implementation) elements. . . . In fact, companies may be seen as systems of interdependency among these elements, all of which must be harmonized to compete effectively.[10] Or, stated another way: 'High performance cannot be achieved unless all aspects of the organization's design are aligned or fit together and, in turn, are aligned with or fit the strategic task of the organization.'[11]

The clarity of a common orchestrating theme enables employees to work together towards common objectives. This should result in smoother collaboration, as everybody sees the big picture and understands what the main aim of the organization is. In turn, the smoother collaboration leads to more solid commitments. People do not have to guess about the motives and priorities of their colleagues from other departments. A commitment to do the right things together reinforces trust and openness, which makes teams operate more effectively. Moreover, the internal consistency that is created across a business unit makes it very difficult for a competitor to copy a firm's formula for success. Firms can copy some of the policies of SIA or IKEA, but they cannot copy the commitment and the energizing climate of those firms.

So, strategic alignment is important, but how do you know how well your organization is aligned? To answer this question, we need to define what an orchestrating theme is, and what crucial implementation levers need to be aligned with this theme.

What is your orchestrating theme?

Having a clear orchestrating theme is crucial to effective strategy implementation. You define a compelling orchestrating theme when you develop a winning strategy. In Chapter 2, I explained that a winning strategy consists of a clear, focused and distinctive competitive arena and competitive theme. High-performance organizations use that competitive theme as the orchestrating theme for their organization. An orchestrating theme has an external component – your value proposition – and an internal component – a clear operating model. A winning value proposition is built around one of the following themes: best price, best access, best product, best service or best connectivity. The value attribute that a company chooses to dominate in also determines its operating model. I reproduce a figure from the previous chapter to illustrate this point – see Figure 3.2.

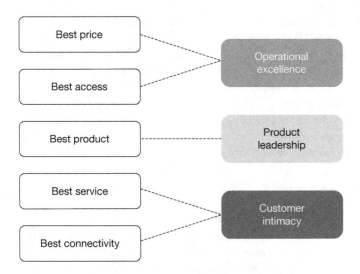

FIGURE 3.2 A compelling competitive theme

Aligning the levers of strategy implementation with your competitive theme

Choosing a competitive theme means choosing a winning value proposition and a clear operating model. The choice of a value proposition and the underlying operating model defines the very nature of a company. That is the essence of alignment. Alignment means that the orchestrating theme of an organization is reflected in each of the five process areas of the Strategy Implementation Framework. Let us explore what alignment means in practice by zooming in on the three operating models (see Table 3.1).[12]

Strategic alignment for an operational excellence organization

Operational excellence firms are companies that make the difference in their industry by being more process-oriented than their competitors. These process capabilities allow them to be the most efficient in the market, which they translate into the best price or the best accessibility (i.e. fastest delivery with minimal difficulty or inconvenience). McDonald's is known for offering, not best food, but fast food! Similarly, Dell made its name by offering computers, not only more cheaply, but also faster than any competitor.

Efficiency is the keyword in operational excellence organizations – and they achieve this by pursuing a process orientation throughout the entire company. Such a process orientation is positively associated with customer satisfaction, product quality, and speed of delivery and time-to-market.

Process-oriented companies typically view themselves as a collection of processes that must be understood, managed and improved, rather than as a collection of departments. In most companies today, few people are aware of the importance of processes, but this is not the case with operational excellence firms. These firms have process maps that present a picture of how work flows through the company, which serves as the company's organization chart. In all of its thinking, an operational excellence firm emphasizes process, as opposed to hierarchy, in order to offer maximum customer satisfaction.

No matter what formula it uses to combine price, reliability and hassle-free service, its operating model is based on a set of design principles handed down from Henry Ford. At Ford, there was only one way to do everything: the efficient way.[13] The main techniques and practices that are used to achieve maximum process speed and quality come under the umbrella of 'lean manufacturing and lean management'. At the same time, operational excellence companies constantly focus on achieving high quality. To deliver on the promise of consistently high and reliable quality in their value proposition, operational excellence companies strive for zero defects in their processes. Although total quality management (TQM) is sometimes regarded as management hype that was extremely popular when Japanese manufacturers were outperforming the rest of the world in terms of quality, a lot of these principles are very applicable to the quality approach that is found at operational excellence firms today.

TABLE 3.1 Strategic alignment for the three operating models

	Operational excellence	Product leadership	Customer intimacy
Orchestrating theme:	• 'Best price' *and/or* • 'Best access' ('fast, easy, painless')	• 'Best product'	• 'Best service' *and/or* • Best connectivity' '('relationship orientation')
Direction- and goal-setting processes:	• Efficiency through process thinking • Zero-defect service	• Best product through continuous product innovation • Clear innovation strategy: where to place the bets?	• Understanding the broader problem • Having expertise in the customer's business • Customers carefully selected
Operational processes:	• The operations department drives the company • Attention is paid to process speed and quality	• R&D is key: idea management • Marketing is also key: educate people with a missionary zeal • Get engineers, designers and marketers together systematically	• Demonstrate expertise and experience • Strengthen the relationship • Build loyalty: focus on customer retention
Support processes:	• Highly automated processes • Information systems increase control and coordination and streamline tasks • World-class supply chain management	• Clear innovation governance process • Systematic process for allocating resources to innovation programmes • Knowledge sharing and networks	• Systematic collection of customer and market information (through CRM) • Structured sales process
Evaluation and control processes:	• Strong, centralized control • Detailed measures on various aspects of the process	• Innovation performance measures • Control, learning, and experimentation	• Detailed measures about account penetration and loyalty • Lifetime value of the customer

continued . . .

TABLE 3.1 *Continued*

	Operational excellence	*Product leadership*	*Customer intimacy*
	• Setting higher thresholds		
Organizational behaviour processes:	• Centralized structure • Organization structured around core processes • Culture of continuous improvement	• Fluid organization structure • Stimulate diversity, tolerate mavericks • Low levels of formalization • Entrepreneurial culture	• Decentralized organization • Employee retention • Focus on quality, defined from the customer's point of view
Examples:	• Ryanair/easyJet • McDonalds • IKEA	• Cirque du Soleil • Apple • McKinsey	• SIA • Château*form'* • Jyske Bank

Operationally excellent organizations typically employ systems that increase coordination and control over the organization's complete business processes. Information (technology) plays a crucial role here. Information systems ensure the quality and availability of data and information needed for the organization's workforce, suppliers, partners, collaborators and customers, thereby expediting and streamlining all tasks. Furthermore, the organization provides tools and resources that support quality-driven efforts throughout the supply chain. Unlike product leaders and customer-intimacy firms, operationally excellent firms look beyond their own supply chain and involve their customers and/or suppliers in their quality and process management initiatives in order to achieve world-class supply chain excellence.

The evaluation and control processes of operational excellence firms are very peculiar. The ability to offer customers consistent quality, ease and/or speed of purchase at low prices requires strict discipline throughout the organization with regard to time, cost and quality. This is essential to sustain process speed and process quality – the critical elements of operations within operationally excellent organizations. Processes are highly regimented, and virtually all work is highly specified as to content, sequence, timing and outcome, in order to eliminate wasted time and resources. Technology facilitates the timely provision of detailed, accurate measurements concerning the products and services and processes. This provides the foundation for further data analysis and root cause analysis that stimulate ongoing improvements in cost, quality and process time. For each step in the organization's end-to-end processes, specific objectives are used to track progress and manage performance. In those organizations, there is a culture of continuous improvement, made famous by Toyota.

Firms achieve top-class operational excellence only with organizational discipline and a centralized structure. Some people refer to Charlie Chaplin's movie *Modern Times* to describe an operational excellence organization, but we should not forget that firms such as ING Direct, Carglass and IKEA have received 'best employer' awards with this operating model. Operationally excellent organizations are designed to enable the high levels of employee involvement that are required to support the efforts to continuously improve cost, quality and timeliness. The organizational design mobilizes employees to contribute to such continuous improvements, while simultaneously providing the necessary hierarchical structures and formalized procedures to avoid chaos and ensure efficiency. The organizational design typically found within operationally excellent companies can be classified as an 'enabling bureaucracy'. Such a bureaucracy serves to support the work of the doers, so that employees experience the organizational structure as a tool with which they can better perform their tasks. They are also involved in the design of the organizational procedures, so that best practices are identified. In this way, with extensive collaboration between the different levels, the hierarchy functions as an arrangement of expertise, rather than as a ladder of positional power.[14]

Strategic alignment for a product leader

Product leaders, such as Cirque du Soleil, McKinsey and Apple, dominate their markets with the best products or services. When consumers prefer a company for its products (or services), they believe they receive more benefits from those products than from any other competitor's products. The most important product attributes that are used to communicate product benefits are quality, features, style and design, and innovativeness. Some product leaders are able to create emotions with their customers through their products or services.

How do product leaders stay ahead of the competition? Product leaders continue to dominate their markets by continuously developing new versions of their best products or services and, from time to time, by coming up with radically new products. That's why product leaders embed innovation in their culture. Yet innovation must amount to more than catchy phrases at management rallies. Top managers must 'live' the innovation culture; otherwise, that culture becomes tricky to create and virtually impossible to sustain. In addition to creating an innovation culture, product leaders develop innovation vision and strategy. Senior management must give a sense of purpose, direction and focus, so that corporate objectives can be linked back into innovation initiatives. Again, this should be more than a marketing exercise. Product leaders regard innovation as essential to gaining competitive advantage, and its full value can only be realized when everyone is free to innovate. Although it is important to recognize the role those 'at the coalface' play in innovating, this does not mean a free-for-all for mavericks. Senior management must publicize the broad remit within which staff can be creative, through information gleaned from face-to-face meetings in the field, via staff intranet forums, at external networking events and through general awareness of relevant economic and business factors.

Product leaders realize that innovation is a core company-wide function. Systems to encourage ideas need not be rocket science. The humblest suggestion box may contain the germ of a product or service innovation that will delight the most demanding customer. The key is visibility – people need reassurance that their ideas will be considered, not stockpiled. This means publicizing ideas that are explored and followed up. Those being considered more seriously should involve top management across the company. Before going into full swing, management must also consider key commercialization factors, such as economic viability, target customers, market-leading features, brand 'fit', resources required and cost to customers. Product-leading companies often involve their customers – test-bedding ideas or organizing focus groups – so that their innovative activity remains relevant and does not become an outlet for over-ambitious or outlandish ideas that have little ultimate value.

The support processes that product leaders use transparently back up the innovation process. As a process, innovation ought to be auditable, just like purchasing, accounting or marketing processes are auditable. Consistency, ownership and resource availability are aspects of innovation that should be traceable, as time, effort and money are made available. It's critical to scrutinize finances and personnel. For instance, the rationale for selecting projects for development should be transparent, with senior management accountable for their decisions. More broadly, alongside their core responsibilities, employees should have an amount of time built into their job descriptions for investing in innovation. Formalizing the process of sharing ideas and discoveries outside the organization may also reap benefits. However free the company is with new insights, a degree of post-project introspection, formal or otherwise, is advisable, so that, going forward, employees will continue their innovative efforts armed with all available information.

Performance management is a major focus of every strategy-focused organization, but measuring the effectiveness of innovation is not as straightforward as, say, measuring sales or productivity. Product leaders see beyond these confines and link innovation success to their strategy by defining relevant innovation metrics. Thorough measurement entails a breakdown of the innovation process for tracking purposes – for instance, separating input measures (resources, such as spend, people and projects), process measures (such as cost performance and schedule performance indicators) and output measures (such as proportion of revenue or profit due to new products and services). However, restraint is called for: by its very nature, innovation may yield returns only in the long run, and senior management must bear in mind that failure and uncertainty are part and parcel of the innovation process, and that reflection and experimentation are necessary 'evils'. Terminating projects that do not promise immediate bottom-line results should not be an automatic response to disappointing measurements. Similarly, innovators need to be rewarded for their efforts, even if profitable outcomes remain on the distant horizon.

Finally, the organizational behaviour processes play a significant role with product leaders. Targeted talent management – covering attraction, selection, development and retention – is essential. Product leaders look for employees who demonstrate creativity, lateral thinking and alertness to customer needs. Diverse recruitment policies provide organizations with the widest possible creative input. Once the right people are on board, employers must continue to develop them, enhancing existing abilities and broadening skill sets, engendering motivation and loyalty. Employee well-being should be a priority, and it need not be costly. Improving the working environment and encouraging social and sports activities are small touches that result in happier, healthier people, who are more likely to come up with product-leading ideas.

Product leaders spend a lot of energy creating an innovative organizational culture that encourages curiosity, creativity and entrepreneurship among the employees and rewards 'can-do' types who try out new ideas. Such a culture features open communication, which might include a degree of challenging norms, constructive criticism and occasional disagreement. Taking risks is stimulated; learning from efforts is rewarded. Strict hierarchies and centralization stifle innovation. Companies with informal structures – where employees are empowered to make decisions, and where project teams, composed of employees from different departments, work together without interference from heads or functions – are more likely to benefit from their people's creative input.

Strategic alignment for a customer-intimate organization

Customer-intimate organizations build a competitive advantage by offering a great service and/or by creating and maintaining relationships with their most valuable customers. It is all about building lasting relationships – zooming in on customers who are already loyal and might be profitable, while not losing sight of those where cross-selling or up-selling opportunities exist. This means identifying where there are mutual benefits and where there's a strong level of trust, often as a result of perceived extra value or simply a positive customer experience. Most customer-intimate organizations are not intimate with all their customers. They serve customers differently, with the best customers getting the best treatment.

Customer intimacy demands personalized interaction in order to strengthen loyalty – but that interaction must demonstrate expertise and experience with specific customers on an individual basis, not simply in a sector-wide context. No matter how many key account directors or managers are drafted in, information must be disseminated effectively, so that all those on the ground understand the extent to which they have to inhabit the customer's world. Any customer relationship depends on personalized interactivity and in-depth knowledge to be sustained over the long term. In customer-intimate companies, certain customers are given single points of contact: individuals who champion their needs and feed essential information out to the relevant staff in branches or head-office functions.

When used with an accurate, well-segmented and scrupulously maintained database, CRM techniques provide a powerful marketing tool to support customer-intimacy objectives. Recording and understanding data on each individual customer's needs is critical for the lasting intimacy sought after by so many organizations. Effective CRM activities take both quantitative and qualitative information and evidence into account, but, ultimately, CRM still depends on human input. If databases are installed with greater attention paid to the system itself, rather than to the people who will be populating or querying it, your success will be limited. On the other hand, when customer-intimate companies use CRM well, and in conjunction with general market intelligence, they can drive cross-selling opportunities to loyal customers via continual personalization and anticipatory marketing action.

Do intimacy firms measure? Of course they do. These firms typically focus on account penetration, retention and lifetime value performance indicators, as part of a watching brief on customer loyalty. Tracking spending patterns and levels of satisfaction might influence marketing campaigns tailored towards specific constituencies or decisions around individual existing customers. Measures such as customer satisfaction and the Net Promoter Score (NPS) are studied intently by those charged with achieving greater, more meaningful customer intimacy. However, no analytic tool offers a cast-iron guarantee that certain activities will drive up revenues or win new business. A healthy dose of common sense, honest introspection and well-developed intuition must also be applied. Similarly, companies need to look long term to avoid investing disproportionately in accounts likely to have a limited shelf life – although this often amounts to a much tougher call, especially if periodic lapses in buying are not connected to any dissatisfaction on the part of the customers.

In the end, people buy people. That's why employee satisfaction – although appearing to be of greater concern to HR directors – may well have some bearing on customer intimacy and cannot be ignored. Unhappy workforces may be unlikely to invest time and energy in developing customer relationships, especially in highly competitive service industries, where client-facing people may move around frequently. Employee satisfaction is affected by the company's motivation and reward systems. In regimes where performance-related pay is based primarily on revenue, what incentive is there for people to behave in a way that promotes customer intimacy over short-term financial gain?

However, the groundwork is often laid much earlier: it's critical to recruit and train the right people in the first place. For customer-intimacy firms, soft skills are as valuable as, say, product knowledge or technical prowess at a particular task. Retention strategies must be put in place too – good people may leave if they feel undervalued or if they feel they do not get the support to do a good job.

Ultimately, a feeling of intimacy is created through one-to-one communication – asking the right questions of customers, responding well in uncomfortable scenarios and delving into the psyche of satisfied and unsatisfied contacts. The most customer-intimate companies are those in which the concept of customer intimacy is a given in the boardroom, embedded in best practice and accepted as the norm (rather than as the exception) by staff at all levels.

None of the three, or all three?

The three operating models I have described here represent ideal configurations that I have found in winning companies. Even companies that have reinvented their industry – such as Cirque du Soleil, which reinvented the circus industry; ING Direct, which revolutionized the banking industry; or Château*form'*, which created a new hotel and seminar concept – have grown further by aligning their organization with one of the three operating models. For example, Cirque du Soleil has become a product leader, ING Direct is a great example of operational excellence, and Château*form'* illustrates well what customer intimacy is all about.

Some people apply the three models to entire industries. In their view, the private banking industry is 'customer intimate', and the car industry is 'operationally excellent', whereas the pharmaceutical industry is about product leadership. However, that's not how you should use these models. The three operating models (with an associated value proposition) help you to think about where an individual firm can make the difference relative to its competitors. Of course, all pharmaceutical companies have to manage their R&D pipeline well – you need to have innovative products in this industry to remain competitive. But that is not necessarily how you win the game. I conducted a workshop with a division of a pharmaceutical company that had decided to differentiate from its competitors through a service and relationship orientation. This does not mean, of course, that

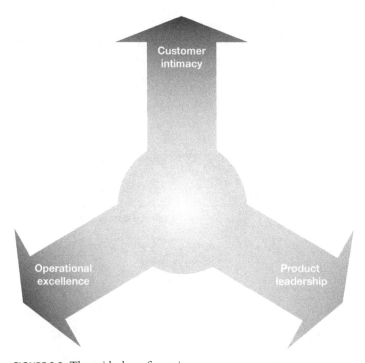

FIGURE 3.3 Three ideal configurations

that company will stop its R&D investments, but the division that came to the workshop realized that it needed to invest in more than R&D processes to make a true difference with the competitors.

Finally, some managers tell me that they find all three models within their organization. I did some work for a large European insurance company, whose three business units approached one country with three different operating models. Each business unit used a different distribution approach, had a different product portfolio and offered a different value proposition to its customers. Although that company was one legal entity, it ran the organization as three separate companies. This worked very well. Two of the three companies were among the top-performing insurance companies in that country. The managers of the business units attributed this success to the fact that headquarters gave them the freedom to develop and implement their own strategies, rather than forcing them to engage in costly and time-consuming synergy initiatives.

I am more cautious, however, when managers tell me that their sales department pursues customer intimacy, while the operations department goes for an operational excellence model, and the product development unit adopts the product-leadership model. If a company integrates all three operating models throughout the various functional departments, then I'm afraid that the company is 'stuck in the middle' of Figure 3.3. The problem in such organizations is not strategy implementation, but strategy *formulation* – and, more particularly, appropriate definitions of their business units. In the first chapter, I argued that many larger companies have problems with strategy implementation because they substitute functional strategies for business strategies. Many of today's corporations have big R&D units, production units and sales units, which they call 'business units' . . . but they're not. They're functional units! In such organizations, managers and employees struggle to see the big picture because they cannot see beyond the boundaries of their own department. This is a significant barrier to successful strategy implementation.

Everybody in the organization should be aware of the company's main competitive theme, no matter what department you work in – product development, operations, marketing, sales, IT or HR. Only then will you get the necessary

A misaligned organization

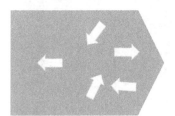

A aligned organization

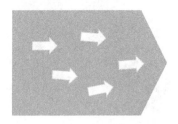

FIGURE 3.4 Examples of misaligned and aligned organizations

alignment in your organization. Unfortunately, in many organizations, different departments compete against each other – and this, obviously, has a devastating effect on a firm's performance. This is illustrated in Figure 3.4. The white arrows represent different departments of a business unit.

Checklist: 'strategic alignment'

The following questions are useful for checking how well your actions are aligned with your operating model:

1 How far down in the organization is your strategy transmitted? Do all of the departments in your organization know what the strategy is? Are each department's goals aligned with this strategy?
2 To what extent has your strategy led to the development of specific operational activities? Do you find some of the operational processes listed in Table 3.1 in your organization?
3 Do you have support processes that help you realize your strategy?
4 Do you have performance measures beyond financial figures? To what extent are these performance measures cascaded down through the organization?
5 To what extent do your organizational culture and structure reflect your organization's strategic choices?

Key learning points

In this chapter, I have stressed that strategic alignment is an important driver of success, but most firms struggle with it. The Strategy Implementation Framework gives you a better understanding of the strategic alignment challenge. Effective strategy implementation means aligning your actions with your value proposition and your operating model.

I have also presented three ideal strategy configurations – operational excellence, customer intimacy and product leadership – and I have shown what strategic alignment means for each of these configurations.

Unfortunately, creating strategic alignment is not enough – firms also need to create the necessary *commitment* to execute their strategy successfully. This is the topic of Chapter 4.

Notes

1 Scott, H. (2008) 'Lost in Translation', *Strategy Magazine*, 18 (December), 9.
2 Li, Y., Guohui, S., and Eppler, M. J. (2010) 'Making Strategy Work: A Literature Review on the Factors Influencing Strategy Implementation' in Mazolla, P., and Kellermanns, F. W. (eds) *Handbook of Research on Strategy Process*, Edward Elgar, Cheltenham, UK, pp. 165–83.
3 Garvin, D. A. (1998) 'The Processes of Organization and Management', *Sloan Management Review*, Summer, 33–50.

4 Kaplan, R. S., and Norton, D. P. (2008) *The Execution Premium: Linking Strategy to Operations for Competitive Advantage*, Harvard Business School Press, Boston, MA.

5 Miller, D., and Whitney, J. O. (1999) 'Beyond Strategy: Configuration as a Pillar of Competitive Advantage', *Business Horizons*, May–June, 5–17.

6 Hambrick, D. C., and Cannella, A. A. Jr (1989) 'Strategy Implementation as Substance and Selling', *The Academy of Management Executive*, 3 (4), 278–85.

7 Raps, A. (2004) 'Implementing Strategy: Tap into the Power of Four Key Factors to Deliver Success', *Strategic Finance*, June, 49–53.

8 Labovitz, G., and Rosansky, V. (1997) *The Power of Alignment: How Great Companies Stay Centered and Accomplish Extraordinary Things*, John Wiley, New York.

9 Beer, M. (2009) *High Commitment High Performance: How to Build a Resilient Organization for Sustained Advantage*, Jossey-Bass, San Francisco, CA. Beer uses the term performance alignment instead of strategic alignment, but he's referring to alignment between a winning strategy and organizational design, business processes, goals and measures, and capabilities. Beer also defines psychological alignment, which I will refer to in the next chapter when I introduce the concept of commitment.

10 Miller, D., and Whitney, J. O. (1999) 'Beyond Strategy: Configuration as a Pillar of Competitive Advantage', *Business Horizons*, May–June, p. 13.

11 Beer, *High Commitment High Performance*, p. 25.

12 In their book *The Discipline of Market Leaders*, Michael Treacy and Fred Wiersema describe the operating models of operational excellence firms, product leaders and customer-intimacy organizations. They also describe how a firm's core processes, organization, culture, management systems and IT are shaped by the choice of value discipline. This part of my book has been inspired by Treacy and Wiersema's work, although we have another definition of what constitutes an operating model. Furthermore, the management literature has evolved significantly since the two authors published their book in 1995.

13 Treacy, M., and Wiersema, F. (1995) *The Discipline of Market Leaders*, Perseus, New York, p. 51.

14 Adler, P. S. (1999) 'Building Better Bureaucracies', *Academy of Management Executive*, 13 (4), p. 36.

4
IMPLEMENTING A WINNING STRATEGY THROUGH COMMITMENT

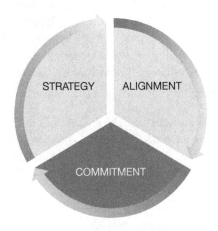

Whereas the concept of strategic alignment is quite well known in the strategic management literature, the concept of commitment is a rather neglected aspect of strategy implementation. Nevertheless, if managers want to implement a strategy successfully, they must also create an appropriate organizational environment that facilitates the implementation of that strategy. Obtaining employee commitment and involvement is necessary for successful strategy implementation. Winning companies are able to connect their employees to their strategy and get their employees committed to implementing that strategy. But what does commitment mean? And how, exactly, do winning companies use commitment to turn strategy into results?

I start this chapter by defining commitment and show that it is a crucial element for successful strategy implementation. A key message of this chapter is that commitment is affected by how firms are managed. I introduce a new concept – which I call 'management maturity' – to describe four configurations that are characterized by different levels of organizational commitment. Viewing organizations through this maturity perspective opens up a totally new view on the strategy implementation challenge. I conclude this chapter by linking commitment to alignment, the topic of the previous chapter, so that you have a clear and comprehensive idea as to how winning companies implement their strategy effectively.

Defining commitment

In Chapter 3, I referred to the book *High Commitment High Performance* (HCHP) by Harvard Professor Michael Beer, in which he examines why some legendary firms – such as Southwest Airlines, SAS Institute, McKinsey, Marriott and Nucor – have achieved sustained high performance for decades. One of the key messages of that book is that long-term success is driven by high levels of strategic alignment and by having a committed workforce that translates the strategy into actions and results. Those HCHP organizations are able to integrate a demanding performance culture, which is needed to win in the marketplace, with a collaborative and participative culture, which is needed to win in the workplace. According to Beer, high commitment goes hand in hand with high performance. All too often, managers formulate strategic decisions and then impose them on the rest of the organization, overlooking the importance of securing consensus with, and commitment to, the organizational strategy. Michael Beer argues for creating *psychological alignment* within the organization:

> Employees who are psychologically aligned with the mission and values of the organization are internally motivated. With psychological alignment, firms become communities of purpose. Relationships and teamwork become central drivers of behaviour. People become willing to sacrifice their immediate self-interest for the demanding goals required for high performance. . . . Firms seeking psychological alignment consciously develop a distinctive 'psychological contract' – a high investment, high return exchange between the firm and its employees (managers and workers). In a high-commitment culture, the psychological contract is the set of high mutual expectations and obligations that create high value for both parties. The unwritten contract is based on positive assumptions about people, what they aspire to and what they are capable of.[1]

Commitment: an HR perspective

Michael Beer is not the only one who has observed the importance of a committed workforce. For example, the HR community is aware that creating an organizational climate that triggers individuals and teams to give the best of themselves helps drive performance. Winning companies have employees who are engaged in their work and committed to the organization. Employees are engaged when they fully occupy themselves in their work and committed when they are willing to persist in a course of action and reluctant to change plans. Engagement and commitment lead to a distinct behaviour, as employees devote time and energy to fulfilling their job and eventually going the extra mile. However, engaged and committed employees also ask for something back from the company. This can be a good salary, a stimulating career path or some attention and recognition.[2] All these constitute the psychological contract that Michael Beer referred to.

Organizations need employees who are willing to go beyond the call of duty and engage in extra role behaviours: that makes the difference between a good product and a great product, or good service and great service. Some high-performing organizations – such as Southwest Airlines, IKEA and Apple – explicitly include commitment as one of their main values. Jack Welch, the former CEO of General Electric, argued that the best measures of organizational health are – in order of importance – employee engagement and commitment, customer satisfaction and free cash flow.[3]

Commitment: a strategic perspective

It is somewhat surprising that few strategy researchers have paid explicit attention to employee engagement and commitment as crucial drivers of effective strategy implementation. Some academics have pointed to the importance of gaining group commitment through shared understanding and extensive communication of the strategy and securing total organizational involvement through a strong corporate culture, but there are no generally accepted strategy models that incorporate the level of commitment and engagement of managers and employees within an organization. Nevertheless, in all the successful organizations that I have come across, the engagement and commitment of the managers and employees have always stood out. That made me conclude that strategy implementation is not only about taking well-aligned actions; organizations should also be concerned about the commitment with which their middle managers and employees bring the strategy to life. Do the employees just do what is expected of them? Or are they willing and committed to expend effort and resources in the pursuit of the strategy? This is illustrated in Figure 4.1.

Creating organizational commitment through management maturity

About 10 years ago, I met four managers of GDF Suez, one of the world's leading energy providers. These managers presented me their control and audit model,

Alignment – Low commitment

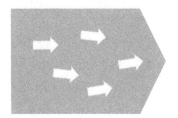

Alignment – High commitment

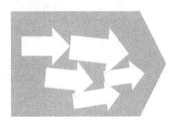

FIGURE 4.1 A committed organization

and I was immediately impressed by both the breadth and the depth of it. This was much more than a financial and operational audit model, it was a description of a series of management models that firms could adopt to implement a given strategy. In 2004, we wrote a book that provided the academic basics to that management model, with contributions from both Vlerick Business School faculty and GDF Suez managers. This was also the start of my research journey on the topic of strategy implementation.[4]

One of the key lessons of that book was that firms could be classified, not only according to their competitive theme and their operating model – operational excellence, customer intimacy, product leadership, or none of these three – but also by their *management maturity* level. In that book, we defined management maturity as the extent to which operational and management processes are set up and managed so that managers and employees are committed to making strategy work. In other words, your management maturity level tells you to what extent your workforce is committed to your strategy. The concept of 'maturity' was borrowed from the various capability and maturity models (CMMs) that are applied to management processes, such as software development, HR, process management, strategic management and innovation.

In that book, we identified the following *four management maturity levels*:

- Level 1: the entrepreneurial organization.
- Level 2: the structured organization.
- Level 3: the connected organization.
- Level 4: the committed organization.

Just as in creating alignment, we found that creating commitment requires managers to take actions in all five areas of the Strategy Implementation Framework: it's about direction and goal setting, setting up operational and support processes, evaluating and controlling, and developing and managing organizational behaviour processes.

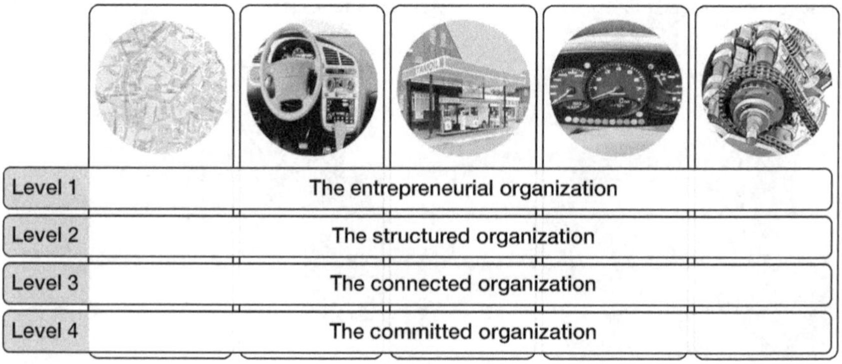

Level 1	The entrepreneurial organization
Level 2	The structured organization
Level 3	The connected organization
Level 4	The committed organization

FIGURE 4.2 Four different management maturity levels

The four maturity levels present four different stages of organizational development. Organizations always start as entrepreneurial organizations, but they can advance over time to the next level and become structured organizations. Some organizations move on to Level 3 and become connected. A minority even make it to the last level – the level of the committed organization.

Every new level constitutes a qualitative advance involving a new mode of managing. This new management approach allows the organization to tackle some of the problems inherent in the prior level of development. Already in 1972, Larry Greiner observed that management practices that work well in one phase may bring on a crisis in another. That's why firms go through periods of evolution and revolution. In those revolution periods, companies change their management model, so that they are better able to tackle the next growth challenge. As the term 'revolution' indicates, these changes are often resisted heavily, and it takes courage to take an organization to the next level.

For example, bringing structure and professionalism helps to control the chaos that entrepreneurial firms experience when they grow too fast. This does not mean that organizations that operate with an entrepreneurial management model are, by definition, unsuccessful. There are many successful, entrepreneurially managed organizations, but, when these firms continue to grow, they face problems that put a serious strain on their performance. At that moment, a structured management approach helps them grow further. In a similar way, a connected organization overcomes some of the problems of a structured organization. As they grow, some structured organizations tend to become over-structured and rigid. In this case, a connected organization helps build bridges between the various functional departments within the organization, and it can then move forward again.

The committed organization is the most advanced of the four organizational configurations, as it allows companies to be very adaptive and effective. The more difficult and complex an organization's external and internal environments are, the more managers need to raise their management maturity level. For example, if an organization is facing a tough competitive environment or a complex internal environment (e.g., because the company has grown very fast), it will not be able to sustain growth in revenues and profits with an entrepreneurial or structured management maturity model. Firms are only able to reconcile a performance-oriented, yet collaborative, culture by adopting management maturity Level 3 (connected) or Level 4 (committed). Only the connected and the committed organizational levels allow a company to execute a strategy effectively. However, before organizations can reach Level 3 or Level 4, they must first pass Levels 1 and 2.

Let us look at the four different management maturity levels, which are presented in Figure 4.2 in greater detail.[5]

Level 1: the entrepreneurial organization

When an entrepreneur decides to set up a new business activity or to explore new territories, he creates a new company. This new company can be part of a larger group, or it can be an independent unit. In this phase, the emphasis is on creating both a product and a market. The company is successful if it can find enough customers and if it can deliver the products or services well enough to meet customer demand and cover costs. The management system that is often found in these types of organization is one that supports an attitude of exploration and trial and error. The entrepreneurial spirit pushes employees to look for the next customer or to finalize the next new project. Attention is paid to operational issues, and managers and employees restrain from taking the time to think more strategically. Some organizations maintain this entrepreneurial management approach long after the company is established.

Do not bother managers of entrepreneurial organizations with advanced planning and control systems. In a typical entrepreneurial organization, formal planning is minimal or even nonexistent. There is no explicit vision, and goals are short-term oriented. There is no clear strategy, and the action plans focus on delivering immediate outcomes: solve what needs to be solved.

Certain *operational processes* are set up to provide immediate answers to the operational challenges the organization is facing. Make sure that you can deliver what you promised to your customer. Nothing more, nothing less! Products and services are produced and generated by trial and error. The organization continues what works and abandons what does not work. However, it's difficult to guarantee a certain quality level for the products or services and to produce repeatable results. Reactions to accidents are highly pragmatic. There is clearly no process-oriented approach, and there is frequent overlap between different activities.

Regarding the *support processes*: contributions and responsibilities are informally engaged and are based on interpersonal relationships, habit and individual good-will. Interfaces are fuzzy, and there is no clear distinction between operational roles and supporting roles. Material resources, methods, communication and documentation are provided according to need and by simple request, without strict accountability.

An entrepreneurial organization's main concern is to get some initial results – to see if the product or service works or is in accordance with expectations. There is no systematic data gathering; only ad hoc *performance measures* are collected. The control system itself is very informal.

Overall performance is driven by the enthusiasm of the employees to succeed, and they enjoy a high degree of freedom and creativity because the organization lacks clear procedures. A key person within the organization takes the lead and directs towards immediate implementation. The organizational chart is simple, and there is a certain degree of clannishness in the entrepreneurial organization. Belonging to 'the family' is important, and successes are celebrated. There are, however, no formal reward systems and no clear career paths for the employees. Individuals develop themselves by working hard and gaining experience. The leadership style is autocratic, meaning that managers make decisions unilaterally and without much regard for subordinates.

The strength of an entrepreneurial organization lies in its agility and flexibility. Entrepreneurial organizations are often close to their customers, and so they soon see what works and what doesn't work. This allows them to react quickly in the market – and this makes customers happy. An entrepreneurial organization is a *collection of individuals*, and the quality of the organization is in the quality of its people. However, if an entrepreneurial organization is too successful and grows too fast, the entrepreneurial spirit might no longer be adequate for managing the organization successfully. Then, it's time to adopt a new management approach. Sometimes this goes rather smoothly; but, in many cases, it takes a lot of time and effort to replace the entrepreneurial management approach with a more structured one.

Level 2: the structured organization

When firms have grown because they have defined a particular competitive arena, they will pay more attention to managing the company more professionally. In this stage, the company has grown large enough to require functional managers. The organization is no longer a collection of individuals but a *collection of departments*.

When an organization has become more structured, it is time to set up the first strategic *planning* efforts. This, however, is the responsibility of a small team, and that team also defines the vision, the mission, the values and the strategy. However, the strategy is often defined financially or operationally. In other words, this initial strategic planning is actually financial planning. The company has not made clear choices on where and how to compete; it is merely reflecting on how to reach the financial goals that have been set.

The company has adopted a functional organizational structure to separate various activities, such as operations, sales, product or service development, HR, IT and finance. Job assignments become increasingly specialized. The activities within the departments are planned, and there are well-defined expectations for each task. A few key processes are documented, and local improvement initiatives are organized in the various departments. The organization is internally oriented; only in exceptional cases is attention paid to external experiences and preventive measures.

Structure is gradually built up in the *supporting* activities. Budgets, IT tools and other elements of infrastructure are made available, if you can convince your management of the added value of your projects. Communication becomes more formal and impersonal as a hierarchy of positions grows. Communication primarily serves to coordinate activities within the different departments. Regulatory requirements and key technical issues are documented. Training and exchange of information occur on the job.

The operational budget is the main *control and evaluation* tool. Financial performance data are collected on a regular basis. Controls are primarily diagnostic, and quality checks are installed to see whether there are any unacceptable incidents or deficiencies.

The organization is structured functionally. Leaders still tell and sell, but gather feedback sporadically. As the organization has become a collection of departments, there is a feeling of togetherness within the departments and a lot of cooperation among team members. However, that feeling of togetherness does not always extend to the interdepartmental or company level. The organization establishes formal HR procedures and processes. The remuneration and career opportunities of the employees are mainly determined by their technical abilities and qualifications.

The strength of the structured organization is that the organization is managed professionally. The structure allows the company to grow further. However, this organization is very different from the original entrepreneurial firm, and one of the key problems that can emerge is the disappearance of entrepreneurship and the emergence of a silo mentality. This is the typical bureaucratic firm, where different departments pursue different goals – which can lead to the situation in which the departments do not work together but rather against each other. In that case, the enemy is not the competitor; the enemy is within. Firms can tackle this challenge by moving to the next management maturity level.

Level 3: the connected organization

In a connected organization, a company starts to think and act strategically. Business managers are increasingly aware that success is achieved, not only when departments perform well, but when they perform well *together*. The organization is no longer a collection of departments: the managers connect the departments around an orchestrating theme. In the previous chapter, I argued that an orchestrating theme has an external component – your value proposition – and an internal component – your operating model.

An organization that is connected has an unambiguous, well-disseminated *vision* and has defined, clear goals taking into account the expectations of its most important and relevant stakeholders. The company increasingly looks outward; it realizes that its success depends on how well it competes in the market. The company is aware that customers are very important stakeholders and it devises strategies with a clear definition of the competitive arena and a competitive theme. The company has set up action plans that tell how to reach its strategic goals. Departmental goals are derived from the overall business strategy.

Operationally, the process flow has been defined and implemented, the activities are well coordinated, and, in addition to product control, there is process control. Key processes are defined and documented, and process improvements are clearly linked to strategic goals. Undesired incidents are recorded and analysed in order to reduce their frequency and minimize their impact. Where necessary, re-engineering projects are initiated, and process activities are upgraded. The need for problem-solving is reduced owing to preventive actions.

Support processes are formal and powerful. Management accounting, documentation, IT tools and other infrastructure elements are well developed. Communication, both internal and external, is extensive and well structured. Special attention is paid to streamlining the interfaces between the various organizational functions. Knowledge management becomes a central theme on the agenda. Significant amounts are spent on competence development and training, which are both technical and value oriented. Widespread use is made of basic procedures, general rules and quality standards.

Performance measurement is an important activity in connected firms: key performance indicators, derived from the organization's strategy, are identified and measured. The performance measurement system also provides the input for the targets and objectives of the next period. There is room for flexibility: action plans can be re-oriented. System audits are common, and the organization seeks out good practice and obtains professional advice from outside experts.

Teamwork across departments has become key for connected organizations. Each employee is expected to work as part of a team and to observe standards that have been drawn up in common. The organization takes cross-functional process flows into account. Many initiatives and incentives are set up to promote a high degree of involvement and commitment, and organizational members are stimulated to participate in projects and to develop multidisciplinary skills. Performance assessment and remuneration increasingly relate explicitly to the objectives at the unit level (in addition to the team and individual levels). The remuneration consists of fixed and variable parts.

In connected organizations, the executive management and the middle management team discuss the organization's strategy. This creates a positive organizational climate, in which managers from different levels take action and are committed to delivering results. The output is what counts. (In bureaucratic organizations, it is the input that counts.)

Level 4: the committed organization

The committed organization is the most advanced organization in terms of management maturity. The organization is no longer a connection of departments, but a *connection of individuals*. This is a truly exceptional organization.

The mission, vision and values of the company are developed collaboratively and are fully integrated in the organization's culture. The vision and the mission really live. The company has a sense of purpose that is reflected in its culture. Company values have been internalized by all members – top management simply has to stress a few 'non-negotiable' rules. The vision and the goals are ambitious and foster a spirit of continuous innovation in the organization. All employees are invited to participate in strategic projects. The company has strategic plans that are developed and revised by cross-functional teams. On top of that, the action plans are initiated by the employees and help realize strategic goals. When personal objectives are set, care is taken to obtain a good fit between the company and individual objectives.

The *operational processes* are tracked and improved continuously. Process re-engineering is carried out quickly and efficiently, because the employees adapt easily to a changing work environment. Efficiency is increased through frequent consultation among team members in the course of the day-to-day activities. Wasted effort and variability in results are minimized.

Supporting activities are integrated within the operational process to a very great extent, thanks to the multidisciplinary skills of the employees. Team communication – which requires an open mind and a participative culture – is an ongoing activity. Routine work is facilitated by the extensive use of IT systems and other automation tools, so that employees can spend a lot of time on system improvements. This calls for an HR approach in which competence management is central. Domain experts are available internally to provide advice and assistance in exceptional cases.

Performance is extensively *monitored* and managed through performance indicators at all levels (company–department–individual). Measurement procedures are applied consistently and efficiently, using appropriate IT tools. Trends are carefully analysed, and targets are closely monitored. Action plans are reviewed dynamically. In the case of abnormal results, a detailed diagnosis is performed to determine the underlying causes of this variation. Measurement is part of the organizational culture, and decisions are evidence-based. The organization measures not only to control but also to identify best practices, which are then disseminated throughout the entire organization.

In a committed organization, responsibilities and authorities are assigned to the lowest hierarchical levels. All employees are closely involved in monitoring the results and are encouraged to provide suggestions for improving performance. The employees work closely together in teams, and 'delegating' is an important leadership attribute. Leaders and employees are engaged in a continuous dialogue founded on a team-based culture. In practice, it is sufficient to refer to a few non-negotiable rules and principles. A no-blame atmosphere prevails. Change and flexibility have become intrinsic to the organization. The organization is lean and mean. People are highly empowered and are highly committed to addressing the organization's strategic challenges. The mentality is very much performance driven: striving for excellence is a prerequisite. The remuneration system is based on the values of the organization, the results achieved and the attitude of the team and the individual.

Table 4.1 presents a brief summary of the characteristics of entrepreneurial, structured, connected and committed organizations.

Although I do not have any solid statistics, my experience in teaching executives tells me that the large majority of firms are entrepreneurial or structured. Only about 15 per cent are connected, and a really small minority – I guess not more than 1 per cent of all organizations – has reached the committed phase. Firms that have achieved the committed phase are the typical case studies that are taught at business schools, such as Southwest Airlines, Pixar, the former Dell and ING Direct USA. However, less-well-known companies – such as Carglass® Belgium, Château*form'* and French insurance broker Sofaxis – also qualify as committed organizations.

TABLE 4.1 Strategy implementation at four different organizations

	Direction- and goal-setting processes	Operational processes	Support processes	Evaluation and control processes	Organizational behaviour processes	
Level 1: the entrepreneurial organization	Planning is nonexistent. No clear vision, no strategy	Processes are isolated tasks providing an immediate answer to a request or problem	No clear support processes (such as HR or IT) created	No systematic data-gathering. Ad hoc performance measures collected	Autocratic leadership, no formal HR systems yet	±40%
Level 2: the structured organization	Planning is financial or operational. No clear strategic choices made	Few key processes are documented. Local improvement initiatives	Support structure built up gradually	Control through an operational budget. Diagnostic control	Functionally structured organization with formal HR systems and processes	±45%
Level 3: the connected organization	Strategic choices are made on the competitive arena and theme	The process flow is defined and implemented. There is process control	Support processes are formal and powerful. Focus on streamlining interfaces between departments	Key performance indicators are identified and measured	Teamwork across departments. Middle management involved in strategy discussions	±15%
Level 4: the committed organization	Vision and mission live within the organization. Values are internalized by all employees	Processes are tracked and improved continuously	Supporting activities are integrated within operational processes	Performance is extensively monitored, even at individual level. Control is used to learn	Responsibilities and authorities assigned to the lowest hierarchical level. The organization consists of self-directing teams	<1%

Raising your maturity level

As I have already indicated, the four stages correspond to different levels of organizational development. Table 4.2 presents the main differences between the various stages. The transition from an entrepreneurial towards a structured organization happens as the organization brings more structure to its operational and management practices. The company uses a functional organization to have more structured, task-based management. Structure allows for more professionalism and repeatability, and it is a first step in learning. However, the learning mainly occurs within functional departments.

The next transition – from a structured towards a connected organization – occurs when firms create structure, not within departments, but across departments. At this stage, firms adopt a more process-based management approach, where the focus is no longer on isolated tasks performed in various departments, but on a stream of tasks that involves various functional departments.[6] Strategy is the glue that brings the departments together. This management model requires substantially higher levels of collaboration and coordination throughout the organization. Process management, more structured forms of evaluation and control, and systematic strategic dialogues are becoming common practice in such organizations.

The last step – from a connected towards a committed organization – is achieved when everybody internalizes the values and the strategy of the organization. Everybody is invited to participate in the strategy dialogue. Empowerment is a keyword, and people work in self-directing teams, supported by a true learning organization.

Management maturity and effective strategy implementation

Successful strategy implementation requires firms to have achieved at least Level 3 of our management maturity model – i.e. they are connected or committed. These are the strategy-focused organizations with a well-defined competitive arena and a clear and compelling competitive theme that is the glue that holds the various departments together. Performance is measured continuously, and best practices are identified across the entire organization. A culture of openness and transparency stimulates others to adopt those best practices and further improve their

TABLE 4.2 Evolving in maturity

	Structured way of working	Process-based management	Values-based management
Level 1: entrepreneurial organization			
Level 2: structured organization	✓		
Level 3: connected organization	✓	✓	
Level 4: committed organization	✓	✓	✓

performance. This is an organization that combines a performance-driven culture with a collaborative and supportive mindset. Needless to say, this is difficult to achieve.

In 2006, I conducted a research project to test empirically whether management maturity and performance are correlated. In that research project, I examined the financial results of a large sample of Belgian insurance companies and investigated what drove the performance of Belgian insurance companies. The study showed that management maturity was positively correlated to the profitability of the insurance companies.[7]

Management maturity and strategy implementation challenges

The maturity framework helps to explain why many companies struggle with strategy implementation. Strategy implementation is not only a matter of defining a competitive theme and launching actions to make your value proposition come true – it is also about creating an organizational environment where middle managers and employees are stimulated to think and act strategically. This is done by creating a common perception and a shared understanding of the strategic priorities. Continuous communication and active involvement in the strategy formation process are activities that help create that strategic consensus. On the other hand, managers must ensure that their goals and those of their employees are aligned with the goals of the organization. Providing appropriate support tools and training and creating a supportive leadership style are crucial.

Strategy execution is a broad domain that touches many different management areas. Effective strategy implementation requires that managers use *all* five levers of my Strategy Implementation Framework simultaneously to work towards the desired maturity level of an organization. In many organizations, that's one of the main reasons management initiatives do not live up to expectations. Let me illustrate this point with two examples.

Figure 4.3 presents two organizations that have launched performance improvement initiatives. *Situation A* describes an organization that has worked on its strategy, but objectives 'outrun' operational processes, supporting activities, evaluation and control processes, and organizational behaviour processes. In this case, the company has defined a clear mission and an inspiring vision, found answers to the four strategic questions that were raised in Chapter 2 (Whom do we serve? What do we provide? What is our value proposition? What is our operating model?) and set challenging goals. However, the organization lacks efficient operational processes and appropriate supporting processes, and there is no discipline to measure and manage performance. It's clear that this is a situation that – if not addressed in time – creates a lot of frustration among decision-makers. In this organization, there is vision but no action. Imagine a service company that defines its competitive advantage in terms of offering the best service, but lacks adequate well-structured complaint processes and operational guidelines. When clear objectives are set without adequate measurement, it's impossible for managers to judge whether or not the organization is on the right track. The processes are not structured enough to provide reliable information, and managers become confused by biased and conflicting information. For sure, this will create frustration in the company.

Situation B is a different situation. In this organization, results are intensively monitored, but operational processes are hardly defined, and objectives are not clear, so that teams are not sure in which direction the organization wants to go. This situation occurs when a company has set up a Balanced Scorecard project without making clear choices regarding its competitive arena and competitive theme. This situation leads to frustration among the employees of the operational

Situation A		Direction and goal setting processes	Operational processes	Support process	Evaluation and control process	Organizational behaviour process
	Level 1 Entre-preneurial		●	●	●	●
	Level 2 Structured					
	Level 3 Connected	●				
	Level 4 Committed					

Situation B		Direction and goal setting processes	Operational processes	Support process	Evaluation and control process	Organizational behaviour process
	Level 1 Entre-preneurial	●	●			●
	Level 2 Structured					
	Level 3 Connected			●	●	
	Level 4 Committed					

FIGURE 4.3 Problems of maturity misalignment

departments. Similarly, an organization that installs formal and powerful support activities without a clear vision and a process-oriented approach is wasting time and resources. Putting highly sophisticated performance monitoring on badly organized processes is dangerous, because there is no assurance that the measurements reflect reality. For example, following service calls from its customers, a service company measures and internally benchmarks maintenance interventions on the basis of elapsed time between the crucial process steps: customer call, planning the intervention, conducting the intervention, closing the intervention, invoicing customer. However, the processes are not at all streamlined around these process steps. As a result, in the meetings about these monitoring activities, there is more discussion about the interpretation of the measurements than about how to improve these business processes.

Looking at an organization from a maturity perspective provides you with some good insights as to why many performance improvement initiatives fail. Many companies try to apply the new management hypes (which were developed by business schools and consultants) to their organization, often with only mediocre success. For example, some of the holy grails for modern companies today are Balanced Scorecards, empowered employees, knowledge workers, and lean and mean organizations. However, all of these things require an organization to be either connected or committed. Managers often overlook the fact that the organization lacks the management capabilities to successfully launch these initiatives. All this calls for a truly integrated approach towards strategy implementation in which attention is paid to all components of the Strategy Implementation Framework.

In summary, effective strategy implementation requires commitment of an organization. Only then is the organization able to combine a performance orientation with a collaborative and supportive mindset. This requires a structured way of working, a collaborative mindset across departments and a mindset of continuous improvement and values-based management.

Checklist: 'commitment and management maturity'

The following questions may be useful for reflecting about your organization's commitment and management maturity:

1   Is your workforce committed to the strategy of the organization? Do employees know how they contribute to an effective strategy implementation?
2   Is your management maturity level (see Table 4.1) appropriate for tackling the management challenges of your organization? Or do you need to increase your maturity level?
3   What is your maturity ambition? Do you want to create a connected or a committed organization?
4   What are the main barriers to creating such a connected or committed organization?

5   In which of the five management areas do you need to take action to get to the right maturity level? Which actions would you take to increase the maturity level of your organization?

Strategy implementation is about creating both alignment and commitment

In Chapter 3, I presented three well-known configurations – operational excellence, customer intimacy and product leadership – and discussed the challenges of aligning your actions with one of these models. In this chapter, I used the Strategy Implementation Framework to provide you with another typology that classifies organizations on the basis of their management maturity, reflecting different levels of commitment to the strategy. Is there a link between the alignment model presented in Chapter 3 and the maturity model presented in Chapter 4? The answer is 'Yes!' This is graphically illustrated in Figure 4.4.

Figure 4.4 shows that the true product leaders, customer-intimacy firms and operational excellence organizations are at least connected or committed. Entrepreneurial firms or structured firms often have not made clear choices with regard to their value proposition and operating model. Entrepreneurial firms do not see the need to make these choices; they are too much occupied with solving

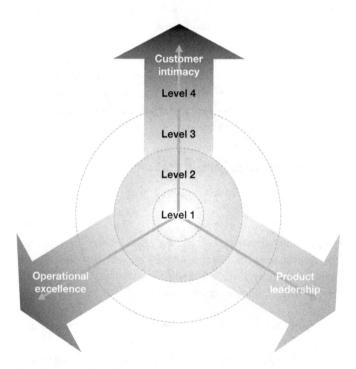

FIGURE 4.4 Linking alignment and commitment

operational issues, or they have not yet specified their competitive arena. Structured organizations find it difficult to make these choices, because they are too inward-focused. They're working on professionalizing and structuring their organization, but they often forget to take the customer's perspective into consideration.

True product leaders, customer-intimacy firms and operational excellence organizations have made these choices explicit, and their managers want their employees to act upon these choices. Obviously, setting up an operational excellence organization is very different from managing a product leader or a customer-intimacy firm. This was discussed extensively in Chapter 3. However, there are also some interesting commonalities between these three configurations. All true product leaders, operational excellence firms and customer-intimacy firms translate strategy down into the organization; they use process management tools to align the various departments around a compelling competitive theme; they also set up support tools and evaluation processes, which are used to check whether the organization is on the right track, but also to identify best practices. The organizational behavioural processes stimulate cross-functional teams and an open and transparent culture, and the leadership style is supportive, favouring participation and empowerment.

That is why I conclude that effective strategy implementation is about creating both alignment and commitment. The Strategy Implementation Framework is a tool that gives you better insights for tackling the challenges of creating both alignment and commitment.

Key learning points

In this chapter, I have argued that a key to successful strategy implementation is creating an organizational environment that translates strategy into actions and results. Effective strategy execution is achieved when a firm integrates a performance-oriented culture with a collaborative and participative mindset. That's how firms engage their workforce to go beyond the call of duty and engage in extra role behaviours to create and sell extraordinary products and services.

I have introduced the concept of management maturity to define different approaches that firms adopt to manage their organization. I identified four maturity levels: the entrepreneurial organization, the structured organization, the connected organization and the committed organization. Winning companies that have achieved a sustainable competitive advantage exhibit many of the characteristics of connected and committed organizations. These are the true product leaders, the true customer-intimate firms, or the true operationally excellent organizations.

In the next parts of the book, I zoom in on the challenges of strategy formulation and implementation for each of those three organizational configurations. I will also present three case studies to illustrate how winning firms implement strategy in practice.

Notes

1 Beer, M. (2009) *High Commitment High Performance: How to Build a Resilient Organization for Sustained Advantage*, Jossey-Bass, San Francisco, CA, p. 29.
2 Vance, R. J. (2006) *Employee Engagement and Commitment*, SHRM Foundation, Alexandria, VA.
3 Welch, J., and Welch, S. (2006) 'Ideas – The Welch Way: How Healthy Is Your Company?', *Business Week*, 8 May.
4 Verweire, K., and Van den Berghe, L. A. A. (eds) (2004) *Integrated Performance Management: A Guide to Strategy Implementation*, Sage, London.
5 The description of the four management maturity stages is based on the following articles: De Cnudde, P., Hindryckx, B., Bauwens, M., Carrette, B., and Verweire, K. (2004) 'Introducing Maturity Alignment: Basic Concepts' in Verweire and Van den Berghe, *Integrated Performance Management*; Greiner, Larry E. (1998) 'Evolution and Revolution as Organizations Grow', *Harvard Business Review*, May–June, 55–67 (this article is a reprint of his famous 1972 *Harvard Business Review* article); Churchill, N. C., and Lewis, V. L. (1983) 'The Five Stages of Small Business Growth', *Harvard Business Review*, May–June, 2–11; Harung, H. S., Heaton, D. P., and Alexander, C. N. (1999) 'Evolution of Organizations in the New Millennium', *The Leadership & Organization Development Journal*, 20 (4), 198–206; Arveson, P., Rohm, H., Wilsey D., Perry, G., Halbach, L., and DeCarlo, J. (2010) *The Strategic Management Maturity Model™*, Balanced Scorecard Institute, Cary, NC, pp. 1–8.
6 Harung *et al.*, 'Evolution of Organizations in the New Millennium', 198–206.
7 Verweire, K., Roelandt, P., De Grande, J., and Van den Berghe, L. (2006) 'What Drives Performance in the Belgian Insurance Industry?', *Research Report*, Vlerick Business School, Gent, Belgium.

PART II

Strategy implementation at product leaders

5

WHAT DOES IT MEAN TO BE A PRODUCT LEADER?

Competing successfully requires firms to make clear strategic choices and to have an aligned and committed organization. One of the most critical strategic choices for any organization is the choice of one of the following operating models: operational excellence, customer intimacy or product leadership. The choice of operating model should be linked to your value proposition, and it drives your company's strategy implementation efforts (see Figure 5.1). I introduced the three operating models briefly in Chapters 2 and 3. In the next three chapters, I will be focusing on *product leadership*.

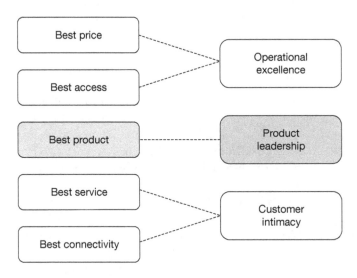

FIGURE 5.1 Product leadership and 'best product'

Almost 20 years ago, Michael Treacy and Fred Wiersema defined product leaders as those companies that convince customers with state-of-the-art products or services. They continually push their products into the realm of the unknown, the untried or the highly desirable. Product leaders' purpose is to discover:

> Discovery put America on the map, men on the moon and the dot-coms in business. . . . Companies driven by discovery will often go far beyond the expected amount of effort to pursue their aims – and often get rewarded for it.[1]

Product leaders pay a lot of attention to developing new products and solutions and look for every possible opportunity to fuel creativity within the organization. In addition to their innovation capabilities, product leaders also have great marketing capabilities: they convince the entire market of the superiority of their products and services.[2]

At first sight, product leadership seems like a straightforward operating model to pursue and implement: you invest in innovation and marketing, and profits will follow. In reality, despite the huge sums spent on innovation and marketing, many companies struggle to implement innovation initiatives successfully. Why is that? I believe that one of the most important reasons is that organizations that aspire to lead their industry through innovation do not always understand what it *means* and what it *takes* to be a product leader. After all, product leadership is about more than investing in marketing and innovation. In this chapter, I will outline the major misconceptions about product leadership and then describe what it really means to be product leader. I will also provide you with more ideas about the value proposition of product leaders. What can companies do to make their products the 'best' in their industry? This chapter should provide you with more conceptual clarity for assessing your product leadership strategy and inspire you to fine-tune and improve it.

Product leaders: who are they?

When I ask my students or participants in an executive seminar to name a few product leaders, chances are that Apple, Google or Pixar will be part of the list. These companies are true innovation leaders: they lead their industry (in profits) because they have a long and successful history of launching new products, services or features, and they are known for their ability to develop and nurture a culture of creativity and innovation.

So far, so good, but when I ask these students whether their own company is a product leader, the answers are less straightforward. Of course, many companies have not made explicit choices with regard to their strategy, but even when the students work in highly innovative companies, many wonder whether their company is a good example of product leadership. Over time, I have become aware that the concept of 'product leadership' is not always clear to everyone, once we move beyond the well-known product leadership cases – there is a lack of understanding about the concept. This is unfortunate, because deep insight into this operating model can help companies improve their performance significantly.

I often hear managers make the following statements – which, in my opinion, are all flawed:

- 'Innovation is important to us, so we are a product leader.'
- 'We operate in an industry where innovation is needed to compete successfully, so that makes us a product leader.'
- 'We are a product leader in our R&D department, but we choose other operating models for our marketing, sales, and operations departments.'
- 'You only find product leaders in manufacturing industries, not in service industries.'

'Innovation is important to us, so we are a product leader'

Most managers think the word innovation is a synonym for product leadership. They argue that, if innovation is a major driver of success or one of their strategic priorities, their company must be a product leader, but that's not necessarily the case. Although all product leaders are innovative, not all innovative companies are product leaders.

The confusion concerning product leadership is due to the lack of understanding of the concept of innovation. The meaning people attach to 'innovation' varies widely, indicating that innovation is not a simple concept. The literature on innovation management has generated a number of classifications and typologies; I find Joe Tidd and John Bessant's classification – which identifies the following '4 Ps of innovation'[3] – the most revealing:

- *Product innovation* refers to changes in the products or services that an organization offers.
- *Process innovation* refers to changes in the ways in which products and services are created and delivered.
- *Position innovation* refers to changes in the context in which products or services are introduced.
- *Paradigm innovation* refers to changes in the underlying mental models that frame what the organization does.

The first two Ps are easy to understand. Product innovation examples include the introduction of newer and better models of Dyson's vacuum cleaners, or the upgrades in a new version of Windows. When IKEA adopted a flat-packaging system for its furniture, the company used process innovation to transport the furniture more cheaply and easily.

Position innovation is a less familiar concept. Sometimes, innovation takes place by repositioning of the product or service in a different context. A company might come up with a product that is meant to be used in a certain manner, but it ends up being used totally differently. An example of position innovation is Levi Strauss jeans – they were originally intended for manual labourers, but, not too long after their development, they were also adopted as a fashion item.[4]

Paradigm innovation has been described extensively in the management literature. People also refer to this as strategic innovation or business model innovation. Clayton Christensen's work on disruptive innovation and Chan Kim and Renée Mauborgne's book, *Blue Ocean Strategy*, deal with this type of innovation. An example of paradigm innovation is [yellow tail], a wine produced by Casella Wines in Australia. In the early 2000s, Casella Wines hit the American market by selling an unpretentious, easy-to-drink, sweet and fruity wine. It came in only two varieties – red and white – and it had a funny kangaroo on the label. Instead of offering wine as wine, Casella created a social drink accessible to everyone: beer drinkers, cocktail drinkers and other non-wine drinkers. Unlike its competitors, Casella Wines did not invest in promotional campaigns and consumer advertising, and, as the production process did not require aging, the necessary working capital was reduced significantly, which allowed the company to invest more in sales. [yellow tail] made retail shop employees ambassadors of its brand by giving them Australian outback clothing. The retail employees were inspired by the branded clothing and, because they themselves did not feel intimated by the new wine, they actively recommended [yellow tail] to their customers. The result: [yellow tail] has been the number one imported wine in the United States in the 2000s.[5] This example shows that Casella did not merely offer a new product; it changed operating practices such as production, marketing and sales, and it challenged the paradigm that wine has to be complex.

A second dimension of the innovation classification scheme is the innovation intensity level. Innovations can be incremental in the changes you make to products or services, or more radical, leading to completely new product and service concepts. Although most books and articles focus on the flashy, radical innovation, we should be aware that most innovations are incremental.

All these different forms of innovation can be plotted in the 'innovation space'. Figure 5.2 indicates that product leaders mainly use product innovation – both incremental and radical – and, to a lesser extent, paradigm and positioning innovation as their innovation strategy.

Product leaders differentiate from their competitors by offering the best product, not only today but also tomorrow. This requires firms to continuously update and upgrade their products and, from time to time, to surprise the market with radically new products. Sometimes, these radical innovations are more than product innovations: they are paradigm innovations. A company such as Apple has not only introduced radically new products – such as the iMac, the iPod and the iPad – it has also radically changed the mobile-phone and music industries. (Apple is a company with several paradigm innovations to its credit, but this is more the exception than the rule.)

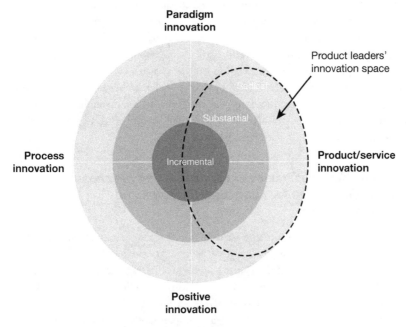

FIGURE 5.2 The innovation space of product leaders

Source: Adapted from Tidd and Bessant (2009)[6]

However, some firms that are labelled 'innovative' are not product leaders. IKEA is such an example; ING Direct USA is another. Both firms have launched a new business model in their respective industry – and so they have both used paradigm innovation to get a foothold in the new market – but they did not (and still don't) offer the best product. Both IKEA and ING Direct are price players, and so their operating model is operational excellence. Of course, these firms innovate: they invest in product innovation, but they invest even more in process innovation. That's the source of their competitive edge and where they dominate their industries.

'We operate in an industry where innovation is needed to compete successfully, so that makes us a product leader'

In industries such as motion-picture production, pharmaceuticals, biotechnology or fashion, being innovative is just a qualification for competing in the market – if you don't innovate, you're dead. However, investing in innovation does not make you a winner in those industries. Many organizations have busy R&D departments working on numerous innovation projects, but how many of these organizations have created truly innovative products or services and outperform their competitors with their innovation strategy? Many firms claim that they are innovative, but only a few really stand out.

In the last 10 years, we've come to realize that winning through product leadership requires more than well-functioning R&D and marketing departments. Coming up with great ideas is the easy part; the hard stuff is selecting the right ideas and following through. Innovation is a management process that pervades the whole company. Although innovation can be a disorderly process, it needs to be managed in an orderly way. Successful product leaders understand this, and they establish a culture of openness, creativity and entrepreneurship throughout the entire organization, not only in the R&D department. This brings us to another misconception about product leadership.

'We are a product leader in our R&D department but choose other operating models for our marketing, sales, and operations departments'

Many managers find it difficult to choose only one of the operating models, because the firm is organized in separate units that all go after their own model. All too often, I hear managers say that their sales organization goes for customer intimacy, their operations department goes for operational excellence, and the R&D department goes for product leadership. Back in Chapter 1, I argued that firms have problems with strategy formulation and implementation because they have defined functional strategies without specifying the overarching business strategy. I see this as one of the most significant problems in organizations today. Strategy – which includes choosing a particular operating model – should be integrative, and it is ineffective if managers concentrate on their functions alone!

Being a product leader is more than stimulating creativity in the R&D department and developing commercialization capabilities in the marketing department. As we will see in the next chapter, product leadership is essentially about managing two very different sets of operational processes – often referred to as the 'fuzzy front end' and the 'speedy back end' – throughout the entire organization. The fuzzy front end deals with the generation of new ideas. This whole process of idea generation is messy and often unpredictable – which is probably why it's called 'fuzzy'! – but that does not mean those activities are unmanageable. Successful product leaders have found ways to get a continuous stream of new ideas from all employees. At the same time, they flesh out and turn these ideas into business propositions and products and services that can be developed, engineered, produced and marketed efficiently in terms of both time and cost. These processes constitute the speedy back end of innovation, and they are geared to bring products on to the market quickly in order to create a first-mover advantage. This requires well-structured production, marketing and sales processes to minimize the time-to-market.

Around these core operational processes in the front and the back ends, product leaders have defined a clear innovation strategy and goals, identified the right performance indicators and set up appropriate innovation support tools. All this is embedded in a culture of entrepreneurship, transparency, openness and creativity.

By continuously managing all of these activities, product leaders are able to dramatically increase the pay-offs from their investments in innovation.

Product leaders maintain a balance between the fuzzy front and the speedy back. In smaller entrepreneurial firms, the emphasis will probably be more on the fuzzy front (i.e. on the creative side). People typically associate product leaders with creativity and entrepreneurship, which is what you find more often in the smaller, entrepreneurial firms, and when you think about James Dyson (Dyson), Guy Laliberté (Cirque du Soleil), or Larry Page and Sergey Brin (Google), you probably think more about their entrepreneurial skills than about their management skills.

Nevertheless, all of the companies I just mentioned are now corporations with thousands of employees and revenues of US$1 billion or more. Running such a large organization requires more than stimulating creativity – it requires a more structured approach towards management. This is not necessarily a bad thing, as structure is needed to continuously surprise the market with new products. It's no coincidence that EA Sports, the Electronic Arts sports video games brand, brings out its new FIFA, NHL and NBA Live games in the August–October period every year. Like many other product leaders, the company has a 'train schedule' that forces its various project teams to approach the innovation projects in a disciplined, rhythmic and controlled way. This is an aspect of innovation that is often overlooked in the management literature. Product leadership is as much about having well-oiled production, marketing and sales organizations as it is about generating wild ideas.

When firms grow, they should be careful not to 'over-structure' the speedy back. Clayton Christensen has vividly described how Medtronic's cardiac pacemaker business ran into trouble as the company became increasingly bureaucratic and rigid.

Case study: the challenges of sustaining product leadership at Medtronic

Medtronic was long known for its technological leadership in the cardiac pacemaker business in the 1950–60s. However, the company began losing market share in the 1970s. Despite its investments in technology and product development, the company failed to produce product designs that could be launched competitively, and the features and functionality of most of the products that were launched lagged behind the competition.

Management realized that the functional organization was a major problem for the company: the functional managers became increasingly absorbed by operating responsibilities in their own divisions, and so they implicitly gave innovation projects a lower priority. Mike Stevens, one of the managers involved, commented as follows:

> *The development people would tell me that they could never get anything to the market because marketing kept changing product descriptions in the middle of the projects. And the marketing people would say that it took so long for engineering to get anything done that, by the time they got around to completing something, the market demands would have changed.*[7]

The company was able to reverse its decline by defining a clearer innovation strategy and implementing a more structured innovation process that cut across the different organizational silos. One of the key elements of the successful turnaround was emphasizing the role of teamwork and empowering the cross-functional innovation teams, which were in the driver's seat when it came to innovation project decisions.

Managing the dilemma between creativity and entrepreneurship on the one hand and structure and formalization on the other hand is key to successful innovation management. In the early phase of a product leader's life cycle, creativity and entrepreneurship naturally flourish, and this drives the growth of the company. However, as product leaders get bigger, they need to adopt more structure and formality in their organization. This is a big challenge for product leaders: they know that structure and formality reduce creativity and entrepreneurship. So organizations such as Google, Pixar and Nike do whatever they can to maintain a 'small organization feel' – which helps them succeed in combining entrepreneurship and creativity with structure and formalization. Product leaders do whatever they can to prevent structure from becoming rigid.

'You only find product leaders in manufacturing industries, not in service industries'

When people think about product leaders, they usually come up with firms from manufacturing industries: software and hardware firms (Apple, Electronic Arts), toy firms (LEGO), fashion firms (Louis Vuitton, Kipling) and so on. But is product leadership a viable operating model for service companies?

The answer is clearly 'yes'. Some of the most prominent product leaders are service companies: McKinsey, Noma Restaurant and Cirque du Soleil all operate in the services business and have become leaders in their markets by adhering to the principles of product leadership. So product leadership could be an appropriate operating model for a service firm that wants to compete successfully.

Nevertheless, it is acknowledged that the barriers to successful product leadership are higher for service companies than for manufacturing firms. Research has shown that service companies seldom invest resources in radical innovation, because it is so difficult to patent services, and thus their innovations can be easily copied. As a consequence, service company managers tend to pay greater attention to incremental innovation. Another complicating factor is that developing a new service is considered to be more complex than developing a new tangible product: service firms often have no R&D department, and customers take a more central role in the innovation process, which complicates the innovation process itself.

Academics have also observed that innovations in service companies have been less successful than innovations in manufacturing companies. One of the main reasons cited is the lack of an effective development process for service innovations and appropriate measures of innovation.[8] However, as we will see later, manufacturing firms also struggle with these issues.

The value proposition of product leaders: what is a 'best product' anyway?

So far, I have presented some common misconceptions about product leadership. Another point that needs further clarification is the notion of 'best product'. In Chapter 2, I argued that successful companies have a winning value proposition. This means that winners have made up-front, deliberate choices with regard to the benefits they are going to offer. Winners explicitly choose in which of the five following value attributes they will dominate and differentiate: product, price, access, service or connectivity.

Product leaders dominate in the 'product' value attribute. They have the best products or services in the market, and they are determined to make products that customers recognize as superior and that deliver real benefit and performance improvements. Simply said, their products are state of the art, truly the best, but what does 'best product' really mean? On which grounds can you claim that your products or services are the best? And what are the particular product benefits that product leaders offer? Figure 5.3 shows that product leaders use five levers to make their product or service the 'best' in the market. These levers are: product quality, features, style and design, innovativeness and emotion. Let us explore these five levers in greater detail.

Product quality

Product leaders differentiate from the competition by offering products that are perceived to be different from their competitors' products. Commoditization is the biggest enemy for product leaders. One of the key elements of their value

FIGURE 5.3 The product levers of product leaders

proposition is that they offer superior product quality: they offer 'the best' rather than 'good enough'. However, just like innovation, quality is a concept that's often not well understood.

Product quality has two dimensions: level and consistency. The quality *level* indicates how well a product is able to perform its functions for a specific target market. Here, the product's quality refers to its *performance quality*. For example, Bose's audio products have superior acoustics and sound. Google has the most comprehensive and fastest search engine in the world. At Louis Vuitton, a tradition of craftsmanship prevails within the manufacturing process, ensuring very high-quality standards.

In addition to quality level, high quality can also mean highly consistent quality. According to marketing specialists Philip Kotler and Gary Armstrong, product quality then refers to *conformance quality*, i.e. freedom from defects and consistency in delivering a targeted level of performance.[9] The Total Quality Movement is referring primarily to conformance quality when it states that 'quality is free'. The idea is that investments in process improvements can reduce variance in output, scrap, rework losses and warranty costs. Toyota's quality image stems from all of the efforts the company has made to increase conformance quality, not performance quality. All companies should strive for conformance quality. In this respect, when it consistently delivers the quality that customers expect, McDonalds can actually offer better (conformance) quality than some three-star restaurants.

From this description, it is clear that product leaders strive for a high level of both performance and conformance quality. Many other companies – including all operational excellence firms – focus only on the latter!

Miele – a manufacturer of global premium domestic appliances and commercial equipment – has a motto that its founders invented more than a hundred years ago: 'Forever Better'. The company prides itself on having the best products, with unsurpassed quality and durability. The average life cycle of Miele's products is more than 6 years longer than that of its competitors' machines. The Miele difference is a combination of quality and reliability, design and innovation, high performance and environmental friendliness. The company applies strict quality control and rigorous testing. Both performance quality and conformance quality are key to the company's long-term success.

Product features

Product features are the characteristics of the product or service. Product leaders ensure that their products have more and better features than the products of their competitors. They often add new features to differentiate their brands and sustain their competitive advantage. Many product leaders are very explicit about their product's features. Porsche publishes extensive technical specifications for each of its models, and Swiss luxury watchmaker Rolex spotlights the exclusive features of its different collections.

Being the first producer to introduce a needed and valued feature is an effective way to compete. Adding new features emphasizes a product's difference from other

products of a similar nature. A second way to make sure you are leading the pack is to improve your product's features – which indicates that you are concerned about continuously satisfying your customers' needs.

Of course, in the end, your product or service has to satisfy customer needs. So, your product's features should translate into customer benefits – which are the reasons customers buy your product or service in the first place. However, features matter, because they provide your customers with hints about how well your product or service will deliver its benefits. Innovative features help companies stand out from their competitors, and the more features your customers find attractive, the higher they value your product or service.

Nike probably provides one of the best illustrations of how to differentiate with product features and benefits. Although some people may dismiss Nike as a marketing brand, it is striking to see how daring the company is in updating its shoes and in constantly innovating. A great example in their product portfolio is Nike Air, a line of shoes originally introduced in 1987. Over the years, the company has frequently introduced new and updated models. The company's marketing stresses the following product features and benefits: lightweight, versatile, cushioning and durable. For example, by displacing heavier midsole materials with Nike Air cushioning, Nike reduces the weight of the shoe, without sacrificing performance. According to Nike, this is important, because the lighter the shoe, the less energy the athlete must expend during performance. Notice how Nike specifies both features and benefits in this example.

Product style and design

Style and design are key differentiating elements actively used by product leaders such as Apple, B&O, Alessi and Ferrari. Kotler and Armstrong define style and design as follows:

> Design is a larger concept than style. Style simply describes the appearance of a product. Styles can be eye-catching or yawn-producing. A sensational style may grab attention and produce pleasant aesthetics, but it does not necessarily make the product perform better. Unlike style, design is more than skin deep – it goes to the very heart of a product. Good design contributes to a product's usefulness as well as to its looks.[10]

Case study: style and design at Apple

Apple is one of the best-known examples of a company using both style and design to make a meaningful difference in the MP3 and the phone market.

The iPod has become the icon of simple design. How did this happen? First, the iPod is aesthetically minimalist. So did Apple just take a rectangular block and add some buttons?

There is much more behind it than can be seen at first glance. The shape of the original iPod is actually based on the golden ratio. With roots in the Fibonacci sequence, the golden ratio is a proportion that is found abundantly in nature, mathematics and ancient Greek art. . . . Apple built a whole visual brand language out of the details, from the radii of the rounded corners to the glossy surface treatment to the absence of exposed screws and the minimal number of buttons. Second, the iPod's user interface is intuitive. You can find your songs quickly. But not only that, it connects to your computer easily. Your computer charges it as well. The attached iTunes software makes it easy to store and manage your music. In fact, it even sells you more music at the click of a button. Apple did not limit its definition of user interface to the small screen on the product. They mapped out all the touch-points you go through when finding, storing and sorting through your music, and looked for opportunities to simplify your life. Stories persist to this day of Steve Jobs returning prototype after proto-type of the iPod to the lab bench because he could not get to his desired song within three clicks.[11]

B&O is another design-driven innovation company. B&O gives designers free reign to create new products that will challenge engineers to find a way to manufacture them. Interestingly, B&O has never employed in-house designers. The philosophy behind this is that B&O does not want designers to be unduly influenced by the limitations of manufacturability.[12] Style and design are mainly used in product industries and less in service industries, although it makes perfect sense to apply design thinking to service companies.

Innovativeness

Many companies spend hundreds of millions advertising that their brands are 'the best' or at least 'significantly improved'. These claims centre around the idea that consumers want products that are differentiated by their efficacy or features. In reality, consumers do not care about efficacy claims they cannot verify in their own kitchens or laundry rooms, or performance claims that can be tested only in a wind tunnel or on the Autobahn.[13] Dominating on product only succeeds if you inspire consumers with true product innovation! Therefore, product leaders need to invest, not only in incremental, but also in radical, product innovation. Academic researchers have proven this point by comparing the effectiveness of an inno-vation strategy with an imitation strategy. There is evidence that, compared with an imitation strategy, an innovation strategy has a greater impact on new product success – not only in Western countries, but also in emerging markets such as China. Leading, rather than responding to, market demand seems to be a more viable strategy – and this is a belief shared by product leadership organizations.[14]

For example, ever since its first performance in 1983, Cirque du Soleil has striven to be different from other circuses by constantly coming up with innovations. From the beginning, Cirque du Soleil's whole concept has been different: it is not just a normal circus. The company adheres to this philosophy today: every show has to be different. The Cirque du Soleil teams are constantly on their toes, always trying to be different. For each new production, there is a new artistic director. The company invests enormous amounts in new costumes and sets. For example, in the show called *O*, acrobats, synchronized swimmers and divers perform in and above a huge pool. For *KA*, Cirque spent US$165 million to build a theatre with two huge moving platforms. Innovation in Cirque du Soleil is driven by artistic considerations, not by market research. The company does not conduct interviews with customers to evaluate the shows, and there are no efforts to update a show. Global Vice President Marketing Mario D'Amico summarizes this approach as follows: 'The culture of this company is not to alter a show to meet market demands. We would rather produce a new show than change an old one.'[15]

Emotion and experience

Many companies have outstanding products in terms of quality and features and yet fail to lead their industry. Product leaders increasingly understand that leading products also inspire and deliver benefits through emotional fulfilment that customers enjoy.

In their book *Built to Love*, Peter Boatwright and Jonathan Cagan recommend using the product itself to create emotions with your customers and not just rely on marketing advertisements and loyalty programmes. According to these two authors, product leaders design their products in such a way that they evoke specific emotions in those who interact with them. In order to create emotions, a product should engage all five of the senses when consumers either see or use the product. In essence, a great product or service energizes and inspires, and makes customers feel good.[16]

To reach their customers emotionally, companies have traditionally built 'experiences' around their products. Many people equate experience with entertainment and entertainment alone, but it is useful to distinguish between two types of experience: the external experience, which is the entertainment factor, and the internal experience, which is more tied to the feeling a customer has about doing business with a particular company. The latter is a more personalized sense of experience.

Later in this book, we will show that the internal experience is what customer-intimate organizations concentrate on – they try to create a connection with their customers by giving them the feeling that they are more than just a number. Product leaders, on the other hand, focus more on the external experience. Hard Rock Café and Rainforest Café pay close attention to the environment in which their products are sold – so they do not just provide food, they provide 'eatertainment' – and these companies are not exceptions: Steve Jobs set up the Apple retail stores to boost sales by improving the retail presentation of Macintosh computers and other Apple products. In a similar way, Louis Vuitton, Nike and Kipling have their own flagship stores to communicate what their brands stand for and to advertise the emotions that go along with their products.

Joseph Pine II and James Gilmore, authors of the book *The Experience Economy*, recommend creating an experience around your products and theming it. Hard Rock Café and Rainforest Café provide good examples of that. Many retailers talk of the shopping experience they provide, but fail to create a theme that ties the disparate merchandising presentations together in a staged experience. Contrast this with the Forum Shops at Caesars Palace, Las Vegas' premier retail, dining and entertainment destination, featuring more than 160 boutiques and shops, as well as thirteen restaurants and specialty food shops. The Forum Shops have held on to their position as the most successful shopping venue in the country through continual progress. The Forum Shops boast a unique concept: an atmosphere that simulates ancient Roman streets. Where else do you find high-fashion stores in such dazzling surroundings, including marble floors, sweeping plaza, flowing fountains, statues and facades? And it pays off: sales per square foot are significantly higher than those of a typical mall.[17]

Some product leaders extend their experiences beyond the purchase moment or the moment that the customer uses the product. They actively involve and stimulate their customers in creating a community or network built around the firm's products. Several researchers have pointed out that organizing high-quality interactions with customers enables an individual customer to co-create unique experiences with the company. Managers should not underestimate the power and the loyalty that such activities generate. The Harley Owners Group can be considered the 'granddaddy of all community-building efforts'. It was set up in 1983 as a way to build longer-lasting and stronger relationships with H-D's customers, by forging ties between the company, its employees and its customers.

In that same industry, Federico Minoli, CEO of Ducati from 1996 to 2001 and from 2003 to 2007, transformed the company by moving from the mechanical to entertainment and by unleashing the power of emotions that his product brought about. Minoli believed that large segments of buyers are more attracted by what the motorcycle evokes and represents than by its intrinsic attributes. So, he set up wholly owned Ducati stores, unique environments that emphasized the distinctive traits of the Ducati brand. In addition, he launched the 'World of Ducati', which consisted of a series of activities such as the opening of a Ducati museum, invitations to join races, events and the Ducati Owners Clubs. After the company launched all those activities, the brand loyalty increased significantly.[18]

LEGO Group is another company that uses a community of enthusiasts to create more emotion around its products. The LEGO Mindstorms products contain both hardware and software to create small, programmable robots, and they are very successful because of the communities that have developed around the users. LEGO organizes a 'FIRST LEGO League Competition' every year, where contestants come to show off their creations and demonstrate the ever-growing capabilities of the product. LEGO extended the concept of co-creation by launching the Mindstorms NXT project, where the company committed to involving its customers more actively in the early design stage of new product development. A LEGO manager commented on this strategy:

We wanted to kick-start the community around the new platform – so, when it came out on the shelf, there was already a lot of buzz on the web. Finally, we had a dream of starting a whole new environment of consumer-generated content. Given the potential, we decided to spearhead some of those activities ourselves.[19]

Case study: a product leader in the service business

I would like to end this chapter by presenting a service company that is a true product leader, offering almost all five of the 'best product' elements. Without any doubt, elBulli can be called one of the best and most innovative restaurants in the world. So, it was remarkable that chef Ferran Adria announced to a shocked audience that he was closing the restaurant in 2012. Nevertheless, elBulli remains an inspiring example of what product leadership can be all about.

The most difficult thing for a customer was to get a reservation. elBulli received up to 1 million reservation requests a year, of which only 8,000 were granted a table. If a guest did succeed in obtaining a reservation, the next challenge was to get to Roses, the little town where elBulli was located, via winding roads and spectacular views. One visitor wrote the following:

We were really in the middle of nowhere, but that just added to the thrill of the experience. It surely would not have been as much fun if the world's best restaurant was just next door or even in a capital city.[20]

Ferran Adria would meet and greet each customer personally, and then the guests would be invited for a tour. The guests could observe the unusual equipment and innovative techniques that the cooks and chefs at elBulli used, and then they were served a cocktail. This was just the start of an incredible meal that consisted of around thirty dishes. The food provoked all of the senses – including the sense of disbelief! An interactive experience between the staff and the patrons was integral to the elBulli experience. For example, many of the dishes came with eating instructions. Customers confirmed that dining at elBulli was certainly a one-of-a-kind experience.[21]

Hopefully, this extreme example will inspire you to think about the various levers you can use to make your product or service the 'best' in the market. elBulli offered a top-quality meal, and Ferran Adria did not merely play upon the sense of taste, but on all five senses, creating a one-of-a-kind experience. He created new food textures: for example, raviolis would be filled with liquid instead of their traditional solid core. Or the customer would receive a serving of soup, but half of the soup was hot, and the other half was cold. Style and design are levers that elBulli used to a lesser extent, but this was compensated for by a high degree of innovativeness. Adria's philosophy was always focused on innovation and creativity: 'We have one rule here: it has to be new. It may be good, but if we have done it before, we let it go.'[22]

Checklist: 'product leadership and best product'

Does your company have a strategy built around product leadership? And have you exploited all five levers to create more benefits for the customer, so that you can claim that your products are really the best? The following questions may be useful for verifying the quality of your value proposition:

1   Is product quality a differentiating element of your products/services? Does your organization apply strict quality control and rigorous testing?
2   Do your products/services have more and better features than your competitors' products/services? Can you prove your claims with hard facts, or were they simply invented by your marketing department?
3   If you offer products, do you use style and design as differentiating elements? Do your products look nice? And are they easy-to-use?
4   How innovative are your products/services? Do you renew your products/services faster than the competition?
5   Last, but not least, do your products/services create emotions with your customers? Which ones? Have you been able to build an experience around your products/services?

Key learning points

In this chapter, I have delved into the concept of product leadership. Product leadership is an operating model that allows firms to lead their industry with state-of-the-art products or services. However, there are many misconceptions about what product leadership is, and that's why I presented four major misconceptions that I often hear when I talk to managers.

In the second section of this chapter, I elaborated on the value proposition of product leaders. I have argued that there are five levers that product leaders can use to make their products or services the best in the market: (1) product quality, (2) features, (3) style and design, (4) innovativeness and (5) emotions. Product leaders can use all five levers to make their products or services distinctive and exceptional.

Now that we have clarified what it means to be a product leader, let us investigate the organizational capabilities that true product leaders share. This is the topic of Chapter 6.

Notes

1 Mourkogiannis, N. (2007) 'On Purpose', *Business Strategy Review*, Spring, 39.
2 Treacy, M., and Wiersema, F. (1993) 'Customer Intimacy and Other Value Disciplines', *Harvard Business Review*, January–February, 84–93.
3 Tidd, J., and Bessant, J. (2009) *Managing Innovation: Integrating Technological, Market and Organizational Change* (4th edn), John Wiley & Sons, Chicester, UK.
4 Inquid (2011) 'Capturing Value with the 4 Ps of Innovation', available at: www.humanitarianinnovation.org/innovation/types (accessed 11 December 2013).

5 Kim, W. C., and Mauborgne, R. (2005) 'Blue Ocean Strategy: From Theory to Practice', *California Management Review*, 47 (3), 105–21.

6 Tidd and Bessant, *Managing Innovation*, p. 13.

7 Christensen, C. M. (1997) 'We've Got Rhythm! Medtronic Corporation's Cardiac Pacemaker Business', *Harvard Business School Case Study*, 9–698–004, p. 3.

8 Oke, A. (2004) 'Barriers to Innovation Management in Service Companies', *Journal of Change Management*, 4 (1), 31–44.

9 Kotler, P., and Armstrong, G. (2001) *Principles of Marketing* (9th edn), Prentice Hall International, Upper Saddle River, NJ, p. 299.

10 Ibid., p. 300.

11 Bush, C., and Hwang, K. (2008) 'Design that Moves Business: Apple's "Overnight" Success', available at: www.sramanamitra.com/2008/11/08/design-that-moves-business-apple%e2%80%99s-%e2%80%9covernight%e2%80%9d-success-part-1/ (accessed 20 April 2009).

12 Austin, R. E., and Beyersdorfer, D. (2007) 'Bang & Olufsen: Design Driven Innovation', *Harvard Business School Case Study*, 9–607–016.

13 Crawford, F., and Mathews, R. (2001) *The Myth of Excellence: Why Great Companies Never Try to Be the Best at Everything*, Crown Business, New York, p. 136.

14 Zhou, K. Z. (2006) 'Innovation, Imitation, and New Product Performance: The Case of China', *Industrial Marketing Management*, 35, 394–402.

15 Pawar, M., and Gupta, V. (2007) 'Innovation at Cirque du Soleil', *ICFAI Case Study*, 307–53–1, pp. 6, 10.

16 Boatwright, P., and Cagan, J. (2010) *Built to Love: Creating Products that Captivate Customers*, Berrett-Koehler, San Francisco, CA.

17 Pine, J. B. II, and Gilmore, J. H. (1998) 'Welcome to the Experience Economy', *Harvard Business Review*, July–August, p. 103.

18 Gavetti, G. (2002) 'Ducati', *Harvard Business School Case Study*, 9–701–132.

19 Brice, F., and Hoang, H. (2007) 'Rebuilding LEGO Group Through Creativity and Community', *Insead Case Study*, 08/2007–5459, p. 9.

20 elBulli.info (2005–12) 'elBulli Review', available at: www.elbulli.info/review.htm (accessed 25 September 2012).

21 Norton, M., Villanueva, J., and, Wathieu, L. (2008) 'elBulli: The Taste of Innovation', *Harvard Business School Case Study*, 9–509–015.

22 elBulli.info, 'elBulli Review'.

6

WHAT DOES IT TAKE TO BE A PRODUCT LEADER?

How product leaders implement strategy

If you want to develop a sustainable competitive advantage, you need to offer products and/or services that keep attracting customers. In their book, *Making Innovation Work*, Davila *et al.* wrote that, 'a blockbuster innovation is not a guarantee of success, just an opportunity. In the long run, the only reliable security for any company is the ability to innovate better and longer than the competition'.[1]

Companies are successful over the longer term only when they are able to consistently produce and deliver good products and/or services. Apple's success does not stem from its newest iMac, but from its ability to continuously offer fashionable, well-designed and easy-to-use computers and other consumer electronics. In this chapter, I present the organizational capabilities that product leaders share. This will provide you with deeper insight into what it takes to be a product leader.

This chapter presents the Product Leadership Pentagon, which is a framework that I use to measure to what extent a company's actions are aligned with the product-leadership model. This Product Leadership Pentagon is derived from the Strategy Implementation Framework (presented in Chapter 3) and describes the activities and processes that you find in highly successful product leaders. You will note that creating alignment is a huge challenge – developing product-leadership competences and capabilities takes a lot of time and effort. However, creating a well-aligned product leader pays off, and I'll present some research to support this statement.

I will also show how product leaders use commitment to create an innovation culture throughout the entire organization. With product leaders, it's not only the R&D department that is responsible for new product and service introductions – innovation is the responsibility of the entire organization!

The Product Leadership Pentagon: identifying the fifteen core activities that constitute product leadership

Strategic alignment – and, thus, effective strategy implementation – means that an organization takes particular actions in support of a particular strategy. What actions do successful product leaders take to ensure that they conquer the market with the best products or services? And how is the orchestrating theme of continuously creating and delivering the best product on the market reflected in the five areas of the Strategy Implementation Framework? The Product Leadership Pentagon presents the fifteen core activities that you find in most successful product leaders (see Figure 6.1).

The Product Leadership Pentagon: research background

The Product Leadership Pentagon is the result of a research project that I conducted with some of my research associates at Vlerick Business School in 2008–09.[2] For

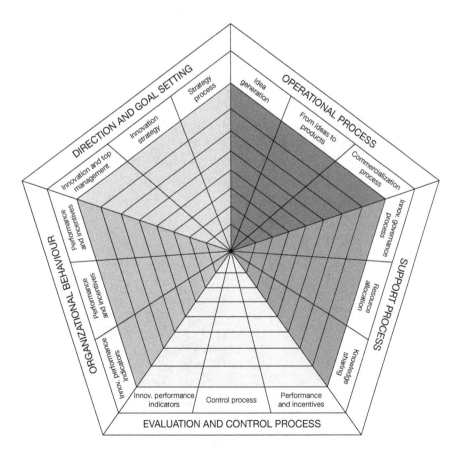

FIGURE 6.1 Product Leadership Pentagon

more than a year, we reviewed the innovation management literature and examined twenty international product-leadership cases in great detail.[3] The literature review and the case analyses allowed us to identify fifteen operational and management practices that were common among product leaders from a variety of industries. Then, we developed a questionnaire to examine how well companies score on each of those fifteen product-leadership practices. We tested this questionnaire with companies that profiled themselves as product leaders – i.e. the managers of the companies agreed that they competed through 'best product' rather than through 'best price', 'best service', 'best access' or 'best connectivity'. I used the questionnaire in my school's executive education programmes and executive MBA programmes. The questionnaires were filled out by at least four managers from the company (or business unit) that pursued a strategy based on product leadership. In this way, we could calculate percentiles for each company on the fifteen items of the Product Leadership Pentagon. (A percentile is the value of a variable below which a certain percentage of observations fall. For example, if a score is in the ninety-first percentile, it is higher than 90 per cent of the other observations.) We also asked those managers to rate their organization's performance on a five-point Likert scale. We asked the managers to benchmark both the revenue growth and profit margin of their company relative to their main competitors.

Over the years, we collected information on 105 product leaders, which included above average, average and below average performers. 'Top performers' grew their top line faster, and had higher profit margins, than their competitors. In our sample, we had six top performers. The six 'bottom performers' scored lower than their competitors on both revenue growth and profit margin. The remaining ninety-three companies were considered 'average performers'.[4]

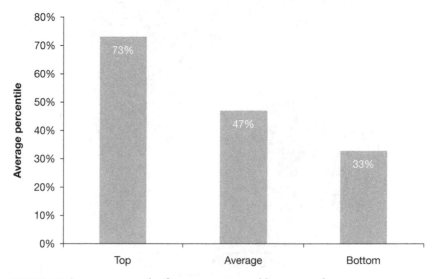

FIGURE 6.2 Average percentiles for top, average and bottom performers

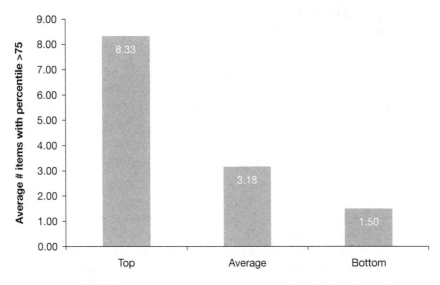

FIGURE 6.3 Number of items with a percentile >75 for top, average and bottom performers

In our research project, we tested whether the top performers had higher levels of alignment than the average and bottom performers. We used two methods to test this hypothesis:

- First, we calculated average percentiles for all fifteen product-leadership items for all three categories of performer. The results, presented in Figure 6.2, indicate that the average percentile for top performers is significantly higher than for average and bottom performers. On average, top performers have scores in the seventy-third percentile, average performers have scores in the forty-seventh percentile, and bottom performers are in the thirty-third percentile.
- Second, we examined how many times a company had an item with a percentile higher than seventy-five. Figure 6.3 shows that, on average, top performers have a percentile that is higher than seventy-five for 8.33 out of the 15 items; for average performers, this figure is 3.18; and, for bottom performers, this figure is only 1.5.

Figures 6.2 and 6.3 indicate that top performers have higher levels of alignment. We evaluated each of the fifteen items and found that the differences between top performers and average and bottom performers were significant for thirteen of the fifteen items. What are the fifteen activities that differentiate successful from less successful product leaders?

Direction and goal setting: a clear innovation strategy and committed top management

How do product leaders use direction- and goal-setting processes to emphasize the important role of innovation in the company? What is top management's role in this process? And how do product leaders translate strategy into targets and objectives?

Innovation and top management

It goes without saying that the top management of any organization plays a crucial role in a successful strategy implementation. Obviously, this also holds true for product leaders. Their top managers believe that innovation is their company's primary source of competitive advantage, and they try to convince everybody in the organization of that message. Innovation and experimentation are a competitive necessity, not just 'nice to have'. Innovation is not another fad of the year or a hollow slogan to put in the company's annual report – it is a belief, a passion, that resides deep in the top managers' heads and hearts. When H-D celebrated its 100th anniversary in 2003, the company was given the 'Outstanding Corporate Innovator Award' because it had made innovation a corporate philosophy through the years.

By definition, innovation is difficult – it requires curiosity, experimentation and openness to change. It's about continuously challenging the status quo. Not everybody likes this, but, for product leaders, this is a fact of life. Creativity, innovation and entrepreneurship are explicit parts of their values and purpose. Product leaders are in business because they want to discover. They have embarked on a route that they have set out for themselves. This is the story of Steve Jobs, James Dyson and Guy Laliberté:

> An essential part of Guy Laliberté's overall philosophy is his commitment to creativity over profits. He wants the Cirque to be a haven for creators, enabling them to develop their ideas to the fullest. ... In keeping with his dedication to creativity, he demands 100 per cent artistic freedom when negotiating sponsor partnerships. That wish to retain control over the creative process is the main reason why Cirque du Soleil has not gone public. According to Laliberté, artistic control allows him to make decisions that do not appear to make business sense.[5]

Uncertainty, risk and occasional failure are all inherent aspects of innovation. The courage to take risks entails being ready to bet one's resources on a new, and often untested, business proposition. Employees usually tend to interpret reprimands for mistakes in innovation as criticisms of their personal initiative and judgement. Therefore, it is top management's responsibility to create an environment where failure is considered part of the learning experience. A 'no-blame' culture, tolerant of experimentation and failure, is essential if long-term innovation programmes are to thrive.

Innovation strategy

Product leaders define the areas in which they want to innovate. The essential role of senior management is to set strategic boundaries that provide innovation with coherence, consistency and cumulativeness. In the late 1990s, Steve Jobs believed that the core technology of consumer devices would no longer be hardware but software. His view was that, the more consumer products evolved, the more they would look like software in boxes. This was a clear message to his staff: 'Fill the portfolio with software innovations. Blend in other innovations, but put the focus on innovative software.'

An innovation strategy answers three major questions: (1) Why do we want to do certain things? (2) Which way should we go? (3) What should be our priorities, now and in the future? Product leaders develop a strategic innovation roadmap that outlines the purpose of the innovation initiatives, the growth targets, and the role of innovation in meeting those targets.

A key element of an innovation strategy is how much to invest in radical innovation. Companies, especially those that are technology-driven, often find themselves in the disjunctive situation of deciding whether to invest in incremental or radical innovation. These different types of innovation require different amounts of investment and need to be managed differently. Investing in incremental innovation will yield short-term gains, whereas the payback period for radical innovations is longer and more risky. Investing only in radical innovation puts the organization in a risky situation: you are betting the organization's future on a very uncertain path.

Case study: the innovation strategy of LEGO Group[6]

The story of LEGO Group provides an excellent example of the importance of having a clear innovation strategy. LEGO Group had always been an icon of innovation and creativity, but, in the late 1990s and the early 2000s, it had gone too far. LEGO's designers produced an impressive set of new products and play experiences, including books, video games, movies, television shows, theme parks, clothing and learning centres. However, these investments left the LEGO Group near bankruptcy in 2003. Jørgen Vig Knudstorp, who was appointed CEO in 2004, and his management team decided to put stricter boundaries around the innovation initiatives. The new goal was to focus 90 per cent of the innovation efforts on the traditional play experiences that the LEGO Group had been known for; 10 per cent of the innovations were to be radical innovations. The company separated the development of the revolutionary play experiences and assigned them to the Concept Lab.

LEGO Group also developed an Innovation Matrix that consisted of eight innovation types, organized in four categories (process, product, communication and business) on the one hand and the degree of innovativeness on the other hand (see Figure 6.4). Filling out the matrix forced a clear identification of where resources were needed, as well as where innovation efforts needed to be coordinated. For example, when developing the second generation of the LEGO robotics kit – MINDSTORMS® NXT – the company realized that the biggest innovation for the company would be how it would collaborate with key MINDSTORMS users in the development process. This new collaborative approach with key customers required a different resource allocation model and monitoring from the traditional product innovations.

The strategy process

In many organizations, top managers see innovation as the key to achieving the company's overall goals. All too often, however, innovation remains a hollow slogan, without any concrete initiatives on the work floor. Especially in turbulent times, top management forgets about the commitments made to innovation. Innovation works only when people at all levels in the organization think about the strategy and provide input to new ideas and initiatives. For that reason, top management needs to spend a lot of time communicating about the innovation strategy, so that everybody is clear about how to contribute. An innovation strategy must grow out of a broadly engaging, deeply creative process of strategic enquiry (not from a two-day strategy retreat attended by a few superannuated divisional directors). A crucial point here is that employees from all levels should be able to discuss and provide input to the innovation strategy. Once the main boundaries are set, management should also communicate what is expected from the different departments.

Product leaders screen the market and share that information internally at regular intervals. For most product leaders, continuously scanning the outside world and building market intelligence are core activities. They realize that you cannot build great products and services if you only look inside. Market intelligence entails understanding customer needs and preferences, but it should also be broader than that: it should encompass insights about future needs, market trends, new technology and other external factors. The information gathered – combined with the opinions of a diverse workforce (youngsters, newcomers, different backgrounds) and awareness of what is happening in the outside world – will increase a company's chances of coming up with revolutionary products and business concepts.[7]

Checklist: 'product leadership and your direction- and goal-setting processes'

To what extent are your direction- and goal-setting processes aligned with the product-leadership operating model? The following questions may help you check whether you have the appropriate direction- and goal-setting processes in place to support a strategy built on entrepreneurship and innovation:

1   Is your top management involved in visioning, launching, steering and coaching innovation efforts? Or is innovation the responsibility of your R&D department?

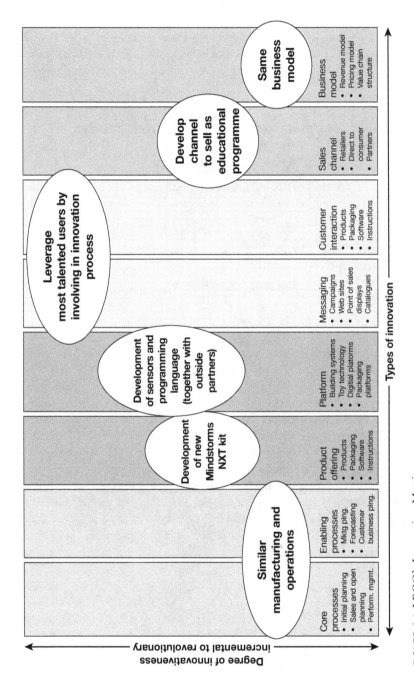

FIGURE 6.4 LEGO's Innovation Matrix

Source: Robertson (2009)[8]

2   Does your company have a clear innovation strategy? Does your company have an innovation roadmap that outlines where to innovate? And have you set innovation targets?

3   Is there a continuous dialogue in the organization on the role of innovation in the company's strategy? Who participates in this dialogue? Is only top management involved, or are employees invited to participate in those discussions as well?

Operational processes: managing the fuzzy front and the speedy back ends of innovation

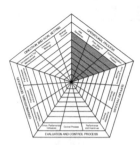

What are the core operational processes of product leaders? What activities and processes have product leaders set up to create great, innovative products and to get to the market? Our research has revealed that product leaders emphasize three core operational processes: idea generation, idea conversion (from ideas to products) and commercialization, both internally and externally.

Idea generation

Too often, top managers see innovation as the product of visionaries. The reality is that most new ideas originate from much lower in the organization. That is why product leaders focus a lot of attention on generating and collecting innovative ideas within and outside the organization. Ideas can come from anywhere in the organization, and that's why encouraging ideas at the grass-roots level is particularly important. The best ideas usually come from those who are closest to the operating details or the market, not from those who are sitting in their ivory tower. Suggestion programmes, planning procedures and management incentives that reward good ideas sound humdrum – but, at the end of the day, they work. Disney's Feature Animation unit was known as a very collaborative and open environment – so open that the leaders relied on all employees to generate story ideas. The company created a competition to generate new ideas, and winners could earn a significant amount of money if their idea was chosen.

Another example comes from Google:

> Googlers can create web pages with their new ideas. The new idea web page is then posted on the intranet so that everyone can test it. According to the company, this process enables quiet Googlers, who are not vocal about their thoughts in meetings, to come out with their ideas by posting them on the intranet. The product development team then explores the relevant ideas. When an idea is selected, its feasibility and user-friendliness are given greater importance than its revenue-generating capacity. Every Friday, in an hour-

long session, Googlers discuss the feasibility of the ideas that have been selected. Each engineer whose idea has been selected is given 10 minutes to defend it. If he/she succeeds in defending the idea, it is turned into a new product or feature, and the Googler who proposed it heads the project.[9]

Although it is important to set up mechanisms for idea generation, it is also imperative that they work productively over time. Management needs to ensure that every single idea deposited in the system is acknowledged and followed up. The company should also show transparency in evaluating and selecting the ideas and provide clear feedback for those ideas that are not selected. Furthermore, the organization should keep track and publish the results of the idea collection process, such as the number of ideas received and implemented and the new business or savings generated. These actions show employees that idea generation (and innovation) is not a one-time event, but a way of working in the organization.

Furthermore, ideas don't have to come solely from your employees. It's important to build external networks to source new ideas as well. Alessi, the iconic Italian design firm, has no in-house designers, but, rather, relationships with 200 external designers. Alessi has realized that its true core competency is in managing this network of designers.

From ideas to products

Innovation is not only about inventing and conceiving new ideas. The new ideas need to be commercialized and turned into financially attractive projects. However, many innovation projects are mismanaged in the innovation project development phase – that's why product leaders have set up a systematic process to turn ideas into products or services. Robert Cooper's Stage-Gate® method is probably the best-known process for moving a new product through the various stages from idea to launch.[10]

Cooper's Stage-Gate® system consists of five stages and five gates (although, for less complex and smaller development projects, companies typically use two or three gates). The discovery stage is the stage where ideas are generated. At Gate 1, the management team decides whether or not the idea is worth investigating in greater detail. If the answer is 'yes', then the idea moves to Stage 1, where a quick technological and business investigation is carried out. If this is encouraging in the second screen (Gate 2), then the team can start to build a business case. The business case includes a much more detailed plan, which involves extensive market and technical research and testing the idea with customers. The first major commitment of financial resources is made at Gate 3. That is where the leadership team decides whether the idea should advance to the development phase. This is the phase in which the actual design and development of the new product occur. At Gate 4, the leaders of the organization review the development efforts and decide whether the product is ready for testing and validation. Financial commitments increase as the company tests the product and its acceptance in the market, and

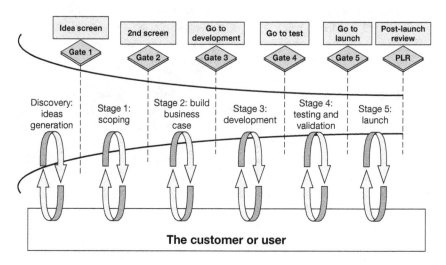

FIGURE 6.5 Cooper's five-stage idea-to-launch Stage-Gate® system

Source: Cooper (2011)[11]

runs trial productions. At Gate 5, the company decides whether to launch the product. This is the phase in which commercialization takes place: it's the beginning of full production, marketing and selling. After launch, the organization tracks the product's performance and decides whether to invest further or withdraw the product from the market.[12]

The Stage-Gate® process is used in many companies – examples include Logitech, Dyson, LEGO Group, Procter & Gamble (P&G), Guinness and H-D – however, not always with great success. Stage-Gate® processes can degenerate into cumbersome, bureaucratic processes that lead to longer lead times (and a higher probability that competitors enter the market with a better product before you do). A key factor for successful application of stage-gating is the separation between the project team and the executive decision-makers. Product leaders' gate decisions should be made by high-level executives. If the decision criteria are clear, this organization can resolve a lot of the bureaucracy. One executive at LEGO described it this way: 'We focused on the gates and deliverables; the rest was left to the teams to sort out on their own.'[13]

Another key element for successful implementation is to instill some rhythm in the product development process; the decisions in the Stage-Gate® process should be made at regular intervals. This ensures that there is a continuous, steady flow of products being launched. Some products are incremental improvements of previous versions; other products are radical innovations that help a company break new ground and sustain its reputation as an innovative firm. At the same time, product leaders reinforce the quality of execution by stimulating a 'do-it-right-the-first-time' attitude. Quality of execution helps shorten the time-to-market, which is a key priority for most product leaders.

The commercialization process: from products to money

Launching products successfully requires you to have strong screening competencies and close connections with your key customers. A passionate and committed customer base is one of the most powerful assets for a firm. Product leaders build deep connections with their customers to get feedback on their products. In addition, they use them as an extra marketing channel for their products or services. H-D was probably one of the first companies to see the power of a strong and committed customer base. The company launched its *The Enthusiast* magazine back in 1916, and it established the Harley Owner Group in 1983.

Large international firms often find it difficult to diffuse new products internally throughout the entire corporation. According to Morten Hansen and Julian Birkinshaw, some organizations have huge problems monetizing good ideas that are generated in the company: decisions about what to bring to the market are made locally, and 'not-invented-here' thinking dominates. These diffusion-poor companies need an idea evangelist to create buzz for a new concept or product within the organization. The idea evangelists are often more senior managers with a lot of credibility and with a huge internal network.[14]

An important pillar within the commercialization process concerns positioning and branding. How many times have we found ourselves in the dilemma of choosing between one brand and another? How many times has the brand we've chosen been the best known? No wonder companies invest millions each year in promoting their brands to position them in the minds of the customers. However, not all product leaders invest massively in marketing and promotion – companies such as elBulli and McKinsey have managed to build their brands without advertising. These kinds of company rely on having their product be 'its own spokesman', making the product or service they offer 'one of a kind'. Companies such as Apple, Nike, Louis Vuitton, B&O and Kipling use their sales outlets to communicate about the high quality and uniqueness of their products.

Checklist: 'product leadership and your operational processes'

To what extent are your operational processes aligned with the product-leadership operating model? The following questions may be useful for checking whether you have the appropriate operational processes in place to manage both the fuzzy front and the speedy back:

1   Does your organization capture enough new ideas from within and outside the organization?
2   Does your organization have a structured stage-gate process that guides resource allocation within your company?
3   Does your organization have a clear marketing strategy that emphasizes the high quality and uniqueness of your products or services?

Support processes: resource allocation and knowledge sharing

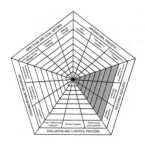

What support processes do product leaders have in place to create an innovative organization? Our research has revealed that product leaders set up an innovation governance process and well-structured resource allocation processes. Furthermore, product leaders pay significant attention to knowledge management to stimulate innovation.

Innovation governance process

Alan G. Lafley, CEO of P&G, once said: 'We are constantly innovating how we innovate.'[15] Firms that aspire to innovate how they innovate must set up an innovation governance process that is audited at regular intervals. Although our research revealed that this is not common practice, such an innovation governance process can really create added value.

Product leaders are able to innovate better and longer than the competition; they build capabilities to continuously launch a stream of new products over many years. Senior management has to consider innovation as a process, not as a unique event. For example, H-D believes that new product development (NPD) is not just about engineering, but that it is a creative process where consistency in approach is critical. To manage this process better, H-D uses an NPD methodology to ensure consistency in actions, provide a mechanism for managing the risks of NPD, establish a common language and terminology for managing NPD, define interface points for the community and foster organizational learning by capturing and measuring repeated activities over time.[16]

Managing the NPD process requires you to have a clear view on the different steps of the innovation process. Figure 6.6 provides an example of such an innovation process model. Then, managers should ensure that every part of the process is managed well, and that there are performance measures and people responsible for tracking progress. A regular audit of the innovation process allows the organization to identify strengths and weaknesses in its NPD activities. Most firms master their innovation process by using innovation steering teams, staffed by senior managers who oversee the various innovation initiatives in the company. Without clear senior management commitment and encouragement, innovation activities lack a sense of importance and urgency.

Resource allocation

Product leaders recognize that continuously developing new products requires significant investments in R&D and NPD. Many product leaders are top investors in R&D: Intel, L'Oréal and 3M invest a fixed amount of their revenues in R&D.

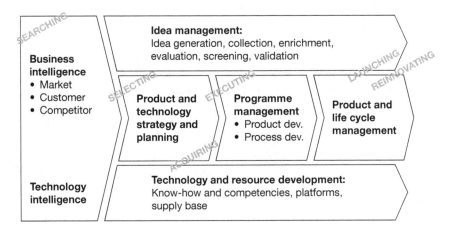

FIGURE 6.6 Innovation process model

Source: Adapted from Deschamps (2008)[17]

These percentages can vary from 3 per cent to more than 30 per cent, depending on the industry in which those product leaders compete.

Product leaders not only allocate financial resources to innovation projects – they also ensure that the innovation projects are staffed with the right people. Some companies have also implemented company policies that ensure that employees have time available to work on their ideas and develop them as business propositions. 3M uses the 15 per cent rule: employees are allowed to spend 15 per cent of their working hours (the equivalent of two coffee breaks plus lunchtime) on independent projects; Google allows its technical employees to spend 20 per cent of their working time on a project of their own choice.

Knowledge sharing

A key differentiating feature of top-performing product leaders is their ability to create and share knowledge within the organization. Truly innovative firms ensure that the flow of communication within the company is intensive, and that people have access to relevant information. Moreover, the information is not limited to best practices, but also includes customer, market and competitor information.

Knowledge-management systems have a reputation for being costly to set up and maintain, and one of the key reasons they fail is the company's inability to get everyone to contribute. This is a lot of hard work: as a manager, you need to instill discipline to get everybody to feed the system. However, knowledge management is more than creating online tools for sharing knowledge; ways to communicate include meetings, cross-functional assignments and brainstorming sessions. Communication also includes storytelling: telling both inspirational and cautionary tales. After all, stories about why ideas fail might be as instructive as stories about success.[18]

Product leaders pay attention to capturing tacit knowledge, which is very difficult to codify and is acquired through personal experience. When people use tacit knowledge to solve problems, the person-to-person approach works best. 3M set up its Technical Forum to encourage its technical staff to share ideas and technologies. In order to introduce its employees to new technologies, 3M invited Nobel Prize winners to forum meetings to discuss their research findings. The Technical Forum also conducted problem-solving sessions at which business divisions brought up their unsolved technical problems, in search of solutions. Bringing engineers and marketing and sales colleagues together facilitates sharing ideas and perspectives on new technologies and business opportunities.

Product leaders also foster external networks across the company. Such external networks encompass a firm's relationships with other organizations, be they suppliers, customers, competitors or other entities. An organization's external network is as important as its internal network for generating new ideas. During the last few years, the concept of 'open innovation' has become increasingly incorporated into firms in order to pull new ideas into the company.

Case study: knowledge management at McKinsey

In July 2006, McKinsey earned recognition as one of the companies committed to growth through innovation and managing enterprise knowledge to create intellectual capital. McKinsey figured in the Most Admired Knowledge Enterprises (MAKE) Report 2006. McKinsey was also inducted into the Global MAKE Hall of Fame for being a Global MAKE finalist for five years in a row. On McKinsey, the MAKE report wrote:

> *McKinsey & Company, founded in 1926, is perhaps the most knowledge-oriented firm within the global management consulting industry. McKinsey is not the largest consulting company in the world but it is among the most profitable and many consider that it has the strongest brand image. McKinsey & Company spends at least 10 per cent of its annual revenues on managing and sharing knowledge.*

McKinsey was largely successful in its efforts to proliferate knowledge across the organization with the use of databases and also by encouraging employees to share knowledge. It focused on exploring knowledge from internal and external sources as well as on distributing and utilizing this knowledge. McKinsey also encouraged sharing of tacit knowledge through personalized knowledge sharing.[19]

Checklist: 'product leadership and your support processes'

To what extent are your support processes aligned with the product-leadership operating model? The following questions will help you assess whether or not your support processes are conducive to managing your innovation efforts:

1   Does your organization have an innovation governance process in place that audits your innovation efforts at regular times?

2   Does your organization have a systematic process in place to allocate both financial and human resources to its various innovation projects?
3   Is the flow of communication within your company intensive, and do people have access to relevant information?

Evaluation and control processes: tracking and rewarding innovation

Performance measurement and management are increasingly important in organizations. Companies measure their performance to ensure that the organization is performing as planned and to identify best practices. Do product leaders also engage in these activities? And is it possible to capture the innovation process in performance metrics and key performance indicators? More generally, how do product leaders use evaluation and control processes to stimulate an environment of creativity, entrepreneurship and innovation?

Innovation performance indicators

Strategy-focused organizations use performance measures to define and communicate the strategy and to monitor strategy execution. Companies following a product-leadership strategy pay special attention to the performance of their innovation efforts. Many organizations use money-based metrics to track their performance, but it is important to use non-financial performance measures as well.

Measurement is fundamental and critical to success with regard to innovation, but a study by McKinsey concludes that few companies are really good at measuring their innovation performance. The study does reveal, however, that the companies that get the highest returns from innovation do use metrics well. These organizations tend to assess innovation more comprehensively than their less-successful peers. They use metrics across the entire innovation process, not just the typical output-related innovation metrics such as revenue growth, customer satisfaction and the percentage of sales from new products or services.[20]

These findings are in line with the recommendations that Tony Davila, Marc Epstein and Robert Shelton make in their book, *Making Innovation Work*. Davila *et al.* use an input–process–output model for innovation and suggest that managers identify performance measures at each stage of the innovation process. The authors have identified more than fifty potential innovation measures and distinguish between input, process and output measures. A company should measure how many resources are devoted to the innovation effort and how this has evolved over time. The inputs are leading measures of success. Process measures track the effectiveness of the innovation process. Output measures measure the results of the innovation efforts. In Table 6.1, I have listed some of the input and output measures that were identified in the McKinsey study, and I have added some process measures that Davila *et al.* recommend.

A firm's typical product development pipeline consists of different projects at different stages in their life cycle. Some projects focus on incremental innovation; others involve radical innovation. When measurement systems are not tailored to the portfolio's mix of incremental and radical innovation, managers lose a key source of information. That translates into lower performance and decreased pay-off from innovation investments.

The goal-setting and performance measurement processes are indeed very different for the two innovation types. Goals for incremental innovation should be specific, and managers will not need to intervene unless there is a significant deviation. These goals are usually quantitative, such as time-to-market, level of resource consumption and incremental changes in product performance. Furthermore, incremental innovation projects should have goals that are clearly achievable and realistic.

On the other hand, radical innovation requires experimentation, trial and error, openness to new ideas and exchange of knowledge. This is only achieved by setting broad goals that allow for flexibility. Because of the inherent uncertainty of radical innovation, these goals generally use more qualitative criteria. Moreover, the goals are 'stretch goals': they demand more than most people would consider to be easy, or even realistic, to attain. This makes the goals inspirational, and the people involved feel as if they are part of something special.

TABLE 6.1 Innovation performance indicators

Input measures	Process measures	Output measures
• Number of ideas or concepts in the pipeline • R&D spending as a percentage of sales • Number of R&D projects • Number of people actively involved in innovation projects	• Percentage of innovation efforts devoted to radical, platform and incremental innovation • Reduction in new product development time/cost • Projects projected within time, budget, product performance targets • Number of new patents granted each year	• Revenue or profit growth due to new products or services • Customer satisfaction with new products or services • Percentage of sales from new products/services in given time period • Number of new products launched • Return on investment (ROI) in new products or services • Changes in market share resulting from new products/services

Source: Adapted from McKinsey (2008) and Davila *et al.* (2006)[21]

Control process

Product leaders use their control process, not just to monitor the long-term performance of the company, but also to learn and experiment. This statement contains two important elements. First, product leaders focus on the long term. This is probably a characteristic of every strategy-focused organization (including the customer-intimate and operational excellence organizations), but it definitely applies to product leaders. As innovation is about dealing with uncertainty, it follows that returns may not emerge quickly, and that there will be a need for 'patient money'. This might not always be easy to provide – especially when shareholder demands for shorter-term gains have to be reconciled with long-term development plans for new products.

Second, the control process is used to facilitate an ongoing discussion between managers that will lead to better innovation and execution. Product leaders use business reviews and planning meetings as privileged forums for discussing and detecting new opportunities, not only for discussing day-to-day operational activities. Innovation leaders instinctively create an environment that values the search for opportunities and the generation of ideas to exploit them. It is management's responsibility to come up with fast decisions to start implementation.

In its 'Entrepreneurial Boot Camps', Alcatel-Lucent brings people and ideas together with the aim of developing and defending a Business Opportunity Plan in front of a jury composed of the Innovation Board (top management from different divisions) and external venture capitalists. The boot camp should yield ideas that will bring business to Alcatel-Lucent within 3–5 years, but that will also yield between €50 million and €100 million in revenues. Management assesses these business opportunity plans by taking their long-term impact into account – they are not merely interested in actions and projects that only have a short-term impact.

Performance and incentives

Management authors recommend rigorously assessing the performance of employees on innovation and rewarding innovators and successful projects at all levels. To our surprise, even top-performing product leaders do not score so well on this item.

Bonuses and financial rewards are an important element of today's management toolbox, but be aware that knowledge workers don't respond to these financial incentives as enthusiastically as you might expect. The key to managing knowledge workers is to treat them as people who are intrinsically motivated. When innovation and creativity come into play, employees feel more motivated by the recognition of their achievements. In turn, this recognition increases their passion for the work they do. If a company decides to give a monetary reward – for example, a bonus or a premium for a successful new product introduction – this can be modest. It's the reward element itself (the recognition) that is important.[22]

3M is very much aware of all this. In addition to monetary rewards, the company has instituted awards to recognize and encourage employee contributions:

> In 1963, 3M formed the Carlton Society (the highest honor) to honor technical employees for their achievements. It also formed The Technical Circle of Excellence and Innovation to honor employees whose innovations had considerable influence on the company's products, processes or programs. 3M has also instituted awards for recognizing the achievements of non-technical personnel. Its Pathfinder Program honors sales, marketing, logistics, finance and production teams for developing innovative methods for launching new products onto the market.[23]

The example of 3M illustrates that recognition of innovation efforts should take place at all levels within the organization. Senior management may recognize innovative design teams and champions, whereas peers typically nominate and recognize teammates for their contributions to the overall effort. In addition, product leaders understand that innovation is a joint effort, not simply the result of the efforts of some 'super-individuals'. For example, Guy Laliberté made sure that the heart of Cirque du Soleil's creative process was its organization, not a particular group of people: Cirque would tolerate neither prima donna artists nor prima donna creators.[24] That is why product leaders choose to reward teams rather than individuals.

Checklist: 'product leadership and your evaluation and control processes'

To what extent are your evaluation and control processes aligned with the product-leadership operating model? The following questions may be useful for checking whether you have the appropriate evaluation and control processes to manage your innovation initiatives adequately:

1   Does your organization have the appropriate performance indicators to measure how well your company is doing at each stage of the innovation process?
2   Does your organization use the control process to monitor long-term performance? And do your performance reviews and business plans include discussions of new opportunities and innovative ventures?
3   Does your organization assess the innovation performance of its employees? And how do you reward your employees? Do you use financial rewards exclusively?

Organizational behaviour: appropriate HR and a culture of entrepreneurship, informality, risk-taking and teamwork

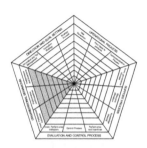

The discussion of incentives and rewards brings us to the final lever of strategy implementation: namely, the people and organization factor. I have called this the organizational behaviour lever. Compared with other strategy-focused organizations, product leaders have very special organization and culture. What particular HR processes do product leaders emphasize? And what organizational structure and culture have they put in place?

HR management

So far, we have mainly discussed innovation strategies and innovation processes. Jean-Philippe Deschamps would call this the top–down innovation mode, but Deschamps discovered that product leaders also promote innovation through a complementary, bottom–up innovation mode. This mode of innovation is fuelled by the ideas and initiatives of individuals within the entire company and is driven by the organization's culture. This process relies on spontaneous and serendipitous ideas, which cannot be micromanaged or mandated. Managers can, however, improve the chances of such ideas occurring by setting up appropriate HR policies and practices.

Creating a creative environment can be done in several ways. Tolerating constructive mavericks is one option. Mavericks challenge 'group think' and, as such, are not always popular in organizations. They tend to be characterized as 'difficult to deal with'. However, product leaders show more patience with these mavericks than most other organizations do. Another option is to institutionalize contacts with outsiders, who bring in fresh ideas.

Product leaders also seek to boost creativity by promoting staff diversity. When everyone in the organization has the same background or views the environment through the same lens, companies are depriving themselves of rich sources of creativity. That is why, in order to enhance organizational creativity, product leaders hire people of different ages, genders, origins and cultures, and educational backgrounds.[25]

Creativity and innovation are very much linked to the environment in which people work. Innovation cannot come from employees who are unhappy and uncomfortable in their workplace. Some product leaders pay special attention to the working environment of their employees. For example, a number of organizations create informal meeting points, such as lobbies and cafeterias, where people can bump into each other and comment on projects they are developing, without having to schedule a meeting. People can discuss ideas while having a cup of coffee or enjoying a sandwich in the cafeteria.

The welfare and health of their employees are equally important for product leaders, who provide side activities to allow employees to relax during or after work hours. Product leaders commit extensively to training and development – which should not be limited to technical training, but which should be a broad portfolio of topics from which people can choose.

Case study: innovative HR practices at Pixar

According to Professor Sir Ken Robinson, internationally-renowned expert in the field of creativity and innovation in business and education, the most distinctive feature of Pixar's organizational culture is the Pixar University (PU) – a continuing programme of lectures, workshops, courses and events offered every day at the Pixar facility. The unit's prime responsibility is to help the employees express their creative ideas, collaborate with each other, and meet project deadlines. As of January 2006, PU offered more than 110 courses, including a complete filmmaking curriculum and classes on painting, drawing, sculpting, and creative writing. Classes are offered in diverse skills such as improvisation, storytelling, and even karate, juggling and belly dancing. Every employee takes at least half a dozen or so courses a year. Participation is not limited to the 'creatives' – it is open to all staff, at every level and in all functions of the company. The courses the employees take do not have to have any direct relation to their work. They take whatever catches their interest. These classes are not regarded as a break from the routine, or perks for a creative workplace, but as an important part of the job itself. The idea is to make art a team sport by having people do it together and fail publicly at it. The company believes that: 'You have to honor failure, because failure is just the negative space around success.' The programme has two major purposes and benefits. First, it provides a constant flow of new ideas and experiences that enrich the employees' lives and minds and make Pixar a more attractive company to work for. The process also feeds the creative culture of the organization as a whole. Second, it promotes direct personal contact and informal communication across the company.[26]

There is an inviting common area in the main atrium in the center of Pixar's headquarters, where employees can meet with each other. It serves as a main reception, eating area and market square. It also has the main café and a number of coffee shops, employee mailboxes and a pool. To get anywhere, or to eat, the employees have to cross this common space:

> *Every employee needs to be able to talk to anybody else. Creativity is not attached to titles; it can come from anywhere. You will have the necessary encounters; you don't have to arrange to see somebody. You will run into someone in the hall; stop and have a discussion about something you have not had time to talk about – and that can change the course of things.*[27]

Organizational culture

All publications on product innovation and product leadership stress the importance of having an innovation culture, but what constitutes an innovation culture? In our research, we found the following four common elements in the typical product leaders' culture:

- First, product leaders share a curiosity for detecting their customers' unarticulated needs and a willingness to try new things to meet those needs. Product leaders are very customer-oriented – they are constantly looking for new opportunities to create extra customer value. In the end, product innovations should lead to better products that expand current performance boundaries or that have unique features that improve the product's performance significantly.
- Second, product leaders have a culture that supports organizational creativity. Product leaders stimulate creativity in many different ways. I talked about this element in the previous section when discussing the HR practices of product leaders.
- Third, there is a 'can-do' climate and an entrepreneurial culture that allow people to experiment in a positive environment in which failure is tolerated. Innovative companies know that failure is as essential to the growth process as success. Daniel Borel, CEO of Logitech, describes this as follows: 'People always say: Good judgment comes from experience! But they forget the fact that experience comes from bad judgment.'[28] Managing employees in a way that encourages innovation requires leaders to acknowledge and reward risk-taking behaviours, not just successful outcomes.
- Finally, product leaders have a culture that rewards winners and that stimulates everybody in the organization to try new things as well. A key element here is that employees are free to communicate and set up collaboration initiatives across departments. Many problems in the innovation process occur through failures in communication, particularly between different functional departments. It is critical to innovation success to develop mechanisms for resolving conflicts and improving the clarity and frequency of communication across departments. Communication and constructive interaction in an innovative company is multidirectional (up, down and lateral) and makes use of multiple communication channels. A company can encourage effective communication in several ways. Team briefings enable team leaders and managers to communicate and consult with their staff. Formal meetings encourage a more formalized approach to communication. Face-to-face communications promote a free and frank exchange of ideas. Other ways of communication – such as e-mail, electronic (or physical) noticeboards, newsletters, phone, fax and videoconferencing – are also used extensively by product leaders.

Logitech is a company with a reputation for consistent product innovations in PC peripherals, and this is fuelled by a particular corporate culture. Key managers need to have a sense of passion, emotion and connection with the product. One manager phrased it as follows: 'I would rather have a smart-alec, fast-moving guy that I have to hold back – and who irritates me on occasion – rather than a guy that is fast asleep.' Logitech has always maintained a strong culture of encouraging personal initiatives and empowering its managers. At the same time, the company stimulates informal learning through coaching and observing. Taking risks is not only tolerated but encouraged: 'In our business, you would rather be right six times out of ten than two out of two.' There is an informal, hands-on management style, and an acceptance of constructive confrontation: 'We are probably about as democratic as a company can get'.[29]

Organizational structure

No matter how well developed the processes are for defining and developing innovative products, they are unlikely to succeed unless the company has an appropriate structure. Achieving this is not easy: it involves minimizing the distance between employees and executives and fostering informality in the management of the company. Research shows that organizations that emphasize loose coupling of groups and a flat hierarchy in their structure are more innovative. Such a structure implies higher levels of autonomy, which facilitates the sharing of expertise, more open and frequent communication, and a tendency to focus on results. A flat hierarchy does not imply that there is no leader or manager. On the contrary! Successful product launches are headed by a dedicated and accountable project leader. Ideally, these team leaders should be dedicated to only one project – but, in reality, most team leaders often have too many projects.

The innovation project teams are staffed by empowered, cross-functional team members. Cross-functional teams contain representatives from all of the disciplines involved in the innovation effort (R&D, design, engineering, manufacturing, marketing and even key customers and vendors). Teams of this kind are not formed simply by grouping people together. Product leaders invest in teambuilding and provide the team members with the necessary training to solve problems and to manage conflicts. Even more important is that these project teams have the freedom to make their own decisions, without having to go through a bureaucratic process. The leader and all team members must be empowered to make project decisions that cannot be overruled by functional heads or senior management. Innovation project leaders should be responsible for the project from beginning to end. Dividing the project into 'functional segments' is definitely not very helpful.

Product leaders ensure that their organization's overall structure is flexible enough to take advantage of new opportunities. Product leaders create smaller units by breaking their staff into teams or clusters. The managers of these departments are true entrepreneurs, not divisional caretakers. In the management literature, we call these organizations 'organic organizations'. The term 'organic' suggests that, like living organisms, organizations change their structures, roles and processes to respond and adapt to their environments. Organic organizations have no problem creating new divisions or redefining the corporate structure to better capitalize on new trends in the market.

Google is probably the best example of a larger firm that is run as an organic organization. Although Google has grown at a rapid pace, the company still prefers to maintain a 'small-organization' feel. Refraining from creating too much hierarchy and structure, Google is a company where ambiguity and chaos are encouraged. An industry insider once described it as follows: 'It's like the Wild West at Google'.[30]

Checklist: 'product leadership and your organizational behaviour processes'

Does your organization manage its people and organization in line with the product-leadership operating model?

1   Does your organization have the appropriate HR policies and systems to stimulate and boost creativity and innovation?
2   Does your company have a culture that encourages employees to take initiative and come up with new initiatives?
3   Is your organization characterized by low levels of formalization, and do you have a flat organizational structure?

Commitment and product leadership

The previous section focused extensively on our Product Leadership Pentagon, a tool that allows firms to assess how well their activities and processes are aligned around the core themes of creativity, entrepreneurship and innovation. Our research indicates that alignment matters: the higher you score on the fifteen core activities of product leadership, the better your company's financial performance.

However, effective strategy implementation not only requires that you align your activities, it also requires commitment from your employees. Commitment means that you create an organizational context that ensures that your employees and managers support and embrace all these strategic activities. In Chapter 4, I described four organizational configurations – the entrepreneurial organization, the structured organization, the connected organization and the committed organization – and I stated that strategy implementation is most effective when an organization has reached the connected or the committed stage.

So, does this hold true for product leaders as well? Are the most effective and successful product leaders connected or committed? Or can the product-leadership model also work in entrepreneurial and structured organizations? Some people argue that the entrepreneurial organization is the ideal organizational context for a product leader. In such an organization, employees are free to explore and try things out; there's a lot of informality, and employees typically enjoy a high degree of freedom to do things the way they want to, as the organization lacks clear procedures.

However, successful product leaders don't just manage the fuzzy front; they also pay a lot of attention to the speedy back end of innovation. Managing this speedy back requires product leaders to implement a structured innovation project development process. At the same time, product leaders have set up an innovation governance process and a resource allocation process to guarantee a continuous flow of new products that can be launched on to the market. Finally, they also have well-developed performance management systems that systematically track their innovation performance. This means that product leaders who want to grow further need to embrace entrepreneurship *and* structure.

Is a structured organization appropriate for running a product leader successfully? Probably not. True product leadership requires at least a connected organization and, preferably, a committed organization. Ultimately, product leadership works best when everybody contributes to the company's innovation efforts. This can only occur successfully, in a coordinated way, when all functional departments understand their role in the innovation process. Product leadership requires the various departments to be connected – which is the essence of a connected organization.

A structured Stage-Gate® process, a well-functioning knowledge management process, cross-functional innovation project teams, a continuous dialogue concerning the innovation strategy, a control process that is oriented towards learning, rewarding innovation at all levels in the organization – these are all crucial ingredients of a successful product-leadership strategy. All these ingredients require a company-wide focus on innovation, which is only achieved when middle managers and employees are actively involved in the strategy implementation process. That's why I argue that the effectiveness of a product-leadership model is highest in connected and committed organizations (see Figure 6.7).

Top managers of product leaders understand this: Ed Catmull from Pixar, Guy Laliberté from Cirque du Soleil and Sergey Brin and Larry Page from Google pay enormous attention to creating the right organizational context for employees to implement the strategy. They understand that their company's management model is one of the most crucial drivers of its success. This is a true source of competitive advantage – difficult to understand and capture, and even more difficult to copy.

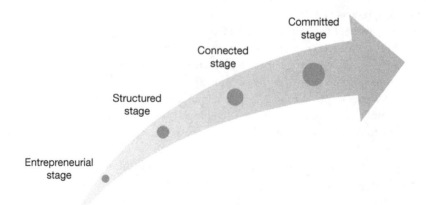

FIGURE 6.7 Effectiveness of the product-leadership model at different maturity stages

Key learning points

This chapter examined what it takes to be a product leader. The Product Leadership Pentagon helps describe the product leader's challenges in implementing strategy. Achieving true product leadership is difficult: product leaders strive to have the best products or services in the market – not only today, but tomorrow as well. Firms can only achieve this if they have the appropriate operational and managerial processes in place to make this value proposition come true. In this chapter, I also identified and described fifteen core processes at which most product leaders excel.

Effective strategy implementation not only requires alignment, it also requires commitment. The fifteen core activities or processes that are captured in the Product Leadership Pentagon must be supported and embraced by the entire organization. This is best achieved when the organization has reached the connected or the committed maturity level.

Becoming a true product leader is a huge challenge, but it is not impossible! In the next chapter, I describe how three entrepreneurs have created a very successful international company, specializing in children's entertainment, based on the principles of product leadership.

Notes

1 Davila, T., Epstein, M. J., and Shelton, R. (2006) *Making Innovation Work: How to Manage It, Measure It, and Profit from It*, Wharton School, Upper Saddle River, NJ.
2 The research project resulted in the following research document: Verweire, K., and Escalier Revollo, J. (2009) 'Sustaining Competitive Advantage Through Product Innovation: How to Achieve Product Leadership in Service Companies', *Flanders DC Research Report*, Vlerick Leuven Gent Management School and Flanders District of Creativity, D/2009/11.885.14.
3 The cases that we examined were: Pixar, Logitech, Intel, Harley-Davidson, LEGO Group, Electronic Arts, Louis Vuitton, Cirque du Soleil, elBulli, McKinsey, Alessi, Google, Dyson, King of Shaves, Medtronic, 3M, Apple, Bose, Bang & Olufsen and Porsche.
4 We set strict criteria for companies to be a 'top performer' or a 'bottom performer'. When we relaxed those conditions, we obtained a classification with sixteen top performers, seventy-five average performers and fourteen bottom performers. The overall conclusions, however, did not change a lot.
5 Kets de Vries, M., and de Vitry d'Avancourt, R. (2007) 'Cirque du Soleil: Attaining "Extreme Creativity"', *Insead Case Study*, 407–032–1, p. 3.
6 Robertson, D., and Crawford, B. (2008) 'Innovation at the LEGO Group (A)', *IMD Case Study*, IMD-3–1978, pp. 1–13; Robertson, D., and Crawford, B. (2008) 'Innovation at the LEGO Group (B)', *IMD Case Study*, IMD-3–1979, pp. 1–25; Robertson, D. (2009) 'Does Your Company Have Good Innovation Governance? Lessons from the LEGO Group," *IMD's Research & Knowledge – Tomorrow's Challenges*, Accessed October 2nd, 2012.
7 Robertson, 'Does Your Company Have Good Innovation Governance?'.
8 Hamel, G. (2000) *Leading the Revolution*, Harvard Business School, Boston, MA.
9 Subhadra, D. S. (2004) 'Google's Organizational Culture', *ICFAR Case Study*, 404–016–1, p. 7.
10 Stage-Gate® is a legally registered trademark of Robert G. Cooper and Jens Arleth.
11 Cooper, R. G. (2011) *Winning at New Products: Creating Value Through Innovation* (4th edn), Basic Books, Perseus Books Group, New York, p. 104.

12 Cooper, *Winning at New Products*; Midgley, D. (2009) *The Innovation Manual: Integrated Strategies and Practical Tools for Bringing Value Innovation to the Market*, John Wiley & Sons, Chichester, UK.

13 Robertson and Crawford, 'Innovation at the LEGO Group (B)', p. 3.

14 Hansen, M. T., and Birkinshaw, J. (2007) 'The Innovation Value Chain', *Harvard Business Review*, June, 121–30.

15 Lafley, A. G. (2008) 'P&G's Innovation Culture', *strategy+business*, Autumn, p. 6.

16 Sarvani, V. (2004) 'Innovations at Harley-Davidson', *ICFAI Center for Management Research Case Study*, 304–103–1, pp. 9–10.

17 Deschamps, J.-P. (2008) *Innovation Leaders: How Senior Executives Stimulate, Steer, and Sustain Innovation*, John Wiley & Sons, Chicester. UK, p. 103.

18 Jamrog, J., Vickers, M., and Bear, D. (2006) 'Building and Sustaining a Culture that Supports Innovation', *Human Resource Planning*, 29 (3), 14.

19 Perepu, I. (2007) 'McKinsey's Knowledge Management Practices', *ICFAI Center for Management Research Case Study*, 907–025–1, pp. 2–3.

20 Chan, V., Musso, C., and Shankar, V. (2008) 'Assessing Innovation Metrics', *McKinsey Global Survey Results*, October, 1–11.

21 Chan *et al.*, 'Assessing Innovation Metrics', p. 4; Davila *et al.*, *Making Innovation Work*, pp. 172–3.

22 Deschamps, *Innovation Leaders*.

23 Subhadra, K., and Dutia, S. (2003) '3M's Organizational Culture', *ICFAI Center for Management Research Case Study*, 403–041–1, p. 7.

24 Casadesus-Masanell, R., and Aucoin, M. (2010) 'Cirque du Soleil – The High-Wire Act of Building Sustainable Partnerships', *Harvard Business School Case Study*, 9–709–411, p. 4.

25 Ibid.

26 Purkayastha, D. (2006) 'Pixar's Incredible Culture', *ICFAI Center for Management Research Case Study*, 406–077–1, p. 12.

27 Warren, C. (2004) 'Innovation Inc.', *American Way Magazine*, 15 December, available at: www.americanwaymag.com/animation-incredibles-and-syndrome-monsters-inc-woody-the-tom-hanks (accessed 23 October 2012).

28 Pahwa, A., and Deschamps, J.-P. (2003) 'Innovation Leadership at Logitech', *IMD Case Study*, IMD-3–1337, p. 9.

29 Ibid., pp. 9, 11.

30 Khanna, R., and Chhaochharia, S. (2008) 'Google's Leadership: The Cutting Edge', *ICFAI Center for Management Research Case*, 408–051–1, pp. 6–8.

7

STRATEGY IMPLEMENTATION IN PRACTICE

Studio 100: a showcase in show business[1]

> Since its foundation in 1996, Studio 100 has continued to pursue one goal: to create quality time for children and their mums and dads, their brothers and sisters and friends. Studio 100 is a great success story. A success story we are expanding worldwide, with partners who share the same vision: making children's dreams come true.
>
> (Studio 100 website, 2012)[2]

In the two previous chapters, I have described what it means, and what it takes, to be a product leader. I used many examples of well-known companies that are (or have been) top-performing product leaders, but I'm often asked how companies become product leaders? Where should firms start? And how do firms build product leadership capabilities over time?

So, allow me to present the wonderful story of Studio 100. Studio 100 started as an entrepreneurial initiative by three programme makers in 1996. Gradually, the company evolved into an international corporation, with more than 1,000 employees, dozens of popular characters and one of the largest independent catalogues of children's TV series in the world. The company's revenues increased from €5.6 million in 1996 to €170.2 million in 2011. This chapter describes Studio 100's strategic choices, actions and organizational context. It shows how a clear strategy and consistent implementation are important drivers of Studio 100's success.

In the first section, I present the range of activities that Studio 100 has set up over the years and the strategic choices the company has made. Then, I describe the particular actions the managers have taken to manage the business. I conclude this chapter by looking at the strategy commitment of Studio 100's managers and employees.

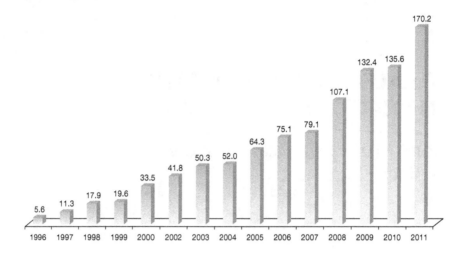

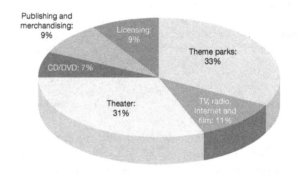

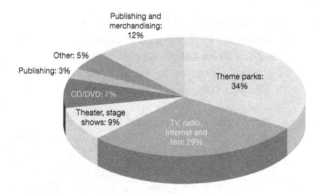

FIGURE 7.1 (a) Studio 100's revenue evolution (€ million). (b) 2007 sales per activity. (c) 2011 sales per activity

Source: Company information

The shaping of an international entertainment company

The early years

Hans Bourlon, Gert Verhulst and Danny Verbiest were three programme makers at Belgium's national television station (BRT). Gert Verhulst was a continuity announcer who wanted to make announcements for children's television programmes more appealing by having an animal puppet presenting next to him. Danny Verbiest was the puppet player who created the puppet dog, Samson. Samson and Gert became very popular in Flanders, the northern part of Belgium, and they starred in their own television and theatre shows in 1990. The three programme makers decided to leave BRT to create their own production house, so that they could build a business around the characters they had created. They started the company without any help from investors and bought an office in Schelle, a town close to Antwerp (Belgium), where they created new characters, recorded television shows and rehearsed for the theatre shows. The company started with seven people, in an office building that was much too large.

Soon after the company was founded, Studio 100 created a new format called *Plop the Gnome* – the show was broadcast on the Flemish commercial television station and was a big success too. In the years that followed, Studio 100 created other formats, including *Pirate Pete*, *Bumba* and *Big & Betsy* (see Figure 7.2), which were broadcast in Flanders and the Netherlands on the major television channels.[3] Studio 100 also created stage shows and movies and became the market leader in theatre shows for children and families in Belgium and the Netherlands. These shows were based on the Studio 100 characters or on classic fairy tales, such as *Pinocchio*, *Robin Hood*, or *Snow White*. In addition, Studio 100 released two or three movies per year – each one was an original adventure related to one of the well-known Studio 100 characters.

Today, the characters that were introduced on television more than 10 years ago are still shown on prime time in Belgium and the Netherlands. The success of Studio 100's characters can be attributed to the fact that the characters are timeless: they enact the good versus the bad, and there is always a happy ending. Another reason for the success is the omnipresence of the Studio 100 characters: they record songs, they appear in books, newspapers and magazines, and they go live on stage in theatres, concerts or musicals. This means that the Studio 100 characters are part of the daily life of Belgian and Dutch children and their parents and grandparents. A final element is that Studio 100's characters are very Flemish and Dutch. This provides the company with a significant advantage over many international production companies, as many Belgian and Dutch audiences prefer local TV programming.

Theme parks

Studio 100 launched some new initiatives at the end of the 1990s. One of these was the opening of a theme park, called 'Plopsaland'. Hans Bourlon and Gert

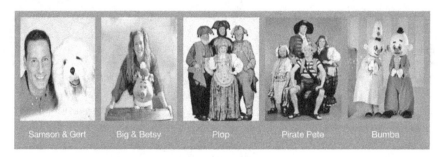

Samson & Gert   Big & Betsy   Plop   Pirate Pete   Bumba

FIGURE 7.2 Some early Studio 100 formats

Verhulst decided to buy an old theme park near the town of De Panne on the Belgian coast and thematize it around the popular Studio 100 characters. The company also invested a lot in extra catering and parking and added new attractions every year.

Looking back at this move, Hans Bourlon admits the creation of Plopsaland was a crazy idea – it was a risky move, but also an immediate success. Studio 100 opened the park in April 2000. In the first year, it attracted 575,000 visitors. Today, with some thirty-five attractions and more than 1.1 million visitors per year, Plopsaland is one of the most frequented parks in Belgium, the Netherlands and Luxembourg. Hans Bourlon comments on this strategic move:

> To be honest, none of the plans about Plopsaland made any sense. We never imagined that we would have so many visitors . . . and three more theme parks some 8 years later. . . . But that's how it goes in our company – we're always open to new things.

The success of Plopsaland De Panne led to the creation of other theme parks. In 2005, Studio 100 opened the first indoor theme park in Flanders: Plopsa Indoor. This park is open 300 days per year and offers some twenty attractions. A third park has been added to the list – Plopsa Coo – located at the Coo waterfalls, a popular tourist attraction in the southern part of Belgium. Besides the spectacular falls, Plopsa Coo also offers fifteen attractions and a wildlife park. In April 2010, Studio 100 opened its first theme park in the Netherlands (in Coevoorden), and, in that same year, the company bought Holiday Park in Germany as well.

A girl band

In 2002, Studio 100 acquired *K3*, a Flemish girl band. K3 had been founded in 1999, but, when they became fully part of Studio 100 in 2002, their popularity exploded. The three girls of K3 (their names all begin with 'K') are solely responsible for creating a new phenomenon in the Belgian and Dutch market: toddler pop. K3 has released thirty-five singles and, with the continuous release of their music videos, six successful feature films and many sold-out concerts, the group is unstoppable. *The World of K3*, a weekly magazine TV show, has towering ratings, and the girls are superstars, adored by the public and feted by the media. What's more, K3 have their own line of clothing and accessories. There are comic books, magazines, posters and daily newspaper adventures, and MP3 players come preloaded with K3 songs.

Merchandising and licensing

Merchandising and licensing are extremely important for Studio 100: in 2011, 12 per cent of the €170.2 million in turnover came from these activities. The company has developed a multitrack merchandising strategy, aimed at maximizing revenue streams while keeping tight control over image and brand. A significant part of the revenues comes from merchandising. Depending on the character, one or two merchandising lines are designed and developed in-house each year and sold to wholesalers and retailers. About twenty people manage the contracts with the licence holders in Belgium, the Netherlands, France and Germany. Every activity that connects Studio 100 with the outside world – and that could affect the company's image – is formalized and controlled. The company receives numerous requests for licensing its characters, and the reputation of the characters results in significant sales for the licence holders, but, of course, Studio 100 wins too. Tom Grymonprez, commercial director, explains:

> We ask ourselves a series of questions. Is there a fit with our company? What about the quality of the product? Where is the product to be sold? And last but not least: does the product fit in the world of our target audience? You will not see Bumba toy guns in the product assortment.

More formats

Studio 100 has continuously added new formats to its product portfolio. In 2002, the company introduced *Spring*, targeting the 'older tweens'. In the years that followed, Studio 100 further expanded and created *TopStars*, *Mega Mindy*, *Anubis House*, *Amika*, *Galaxy Park*, *Rox*, *Dobus*, *Bobo* and *Hotel 13* (see Figure 7.3 for some examples). After the television series came the CDs, games, merchandising, movies and musicals. In this way, Studio 100 has become the largest provider of family and children's entertainment in Benelux. Features common to all of these programmes have been the high production quality, the clear focus on the target children's audience – segmented by age and gender (see Figure 7.4) – and the family-friendly entertainment value.

In addition, Studio 100 is not afraid to apply some radical changes to existing formats. This has given a boost to the formats that had reached the saturation phase. A great example is how the musical *The Three Piglets* recharged K3's career. Hans Bourlon reflects:

One day, we were searching for a way to boost the career of K3, our girl band. One of our employees, who was sitting at the conference table, said: 'Turn them into piglets and make them the main characters in a new musical called *The 3 Piglets*.' We couldn't stop laughing. But one year later, the *The 3 Piglets* musical was completely sold out. It was a major success. You don't get such ideas out of a market study. If we had asked the public via market research to say what they expected the next K3 show to be like, we would have simply ended up with a 'greatest hits' extravaganza.

FIGURE 7.3 Some later Studio 100 formats

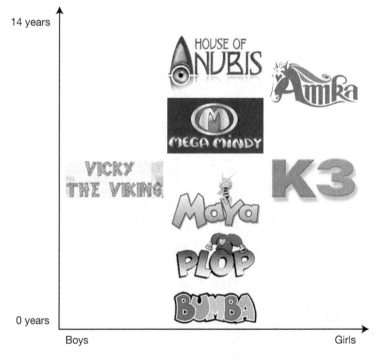

FIGURE 7.4 Market segmentation of Studio 100

Source: Company information

Some challenges

Still, despite the company's many successes, Studio 100 has faced significant challenges over the years. New initiatives have not always been successful. 'Radio Bembem', the radio station project for children, was discontinued, and, sometimes, key people leave: in December 2004, Danny Verbiest, the founder who had lent his voice to Samson for 15 years, decided to retire and sell his shares. In 2009, Belgium was stunned when Kathleen – K3's 'blonde' singer – decided to quit the band. The company turned a problem into an opportunity: it created a reality show – *K2 searching for K3* – in which the group recruited a new third member.

Expansion 'abroad'

In 2005, Studio 100 achieved another milestone: for the first time, TV content was produced in a language other than Dutch – namely, French, for the market of southern Belgium (Wallonia). In that year, the company aired remakes of the *Plop* shows on Wallonian television. The shows were now called *Le Lutin Plop* and featured characters such as 'Lutin Dordebou' ('Lazybones the Gnome'), 'Lutin Pipolette' ('Chatterbox the Gnome') and 'Lutin Bric' ('Handyman the Gnome'). Studio 100 also did remakes of all the Samson and Gert shows, which were translated into French as *Fred & Samson*. The main driver for offering television shows in French was to convince the Belgian national retail chains to distribute the merchandized material in Wallonia, but, as Wallonia is rather small, the profits from this expansion were limited. Would they be able to expand internationally? Studio 100 had always been successful because its characters were Dutch and Flemish. Could they simply export these characters to different (foreign) markets?

Expansion into Germany

Studio 100 decided to bet high on international expansion, and so it recruited Jo Daris as Director of International Business. The company also looked for additional funding and founded Studio 100 Media in Munich in 2007. This unit distributes TV series worldwide and was the first Studio 100 entry into the German market. However, Jo Daris soon discovered that the international television stations were hardly interested in the stories of Plop the Gnome, Pirate Pete and Mega Mindy. Jo Daris comments:

> The people at Studio 100 are used to having everything they touch turn into gold. This time, however, many eggs were touched, but none of them turned to gold. It was very difficult to convince the buyers at the television stations that our characters could be successful in countries other than Belgium and the Netherlands.

Nevertheless, the company continued with its internationalization. In 2008, the international expansion process was accelerated by the acquisition of the German EM Entertainment Group. Studio 100 paid €41 million for EM Entertainment and got an enormous distribution network – EM delivers children's programmes to more than 120 countries. It would have taken decades for Studio 100 to build such a distribution network. Even more than that: EM Entertainment also has an impressive independent catalogue of content, with characters such as *Maya the Bee*, *Vicky the Viking*, *Heidi*, *Lassie* and *Pippi Longstocking*. What if Studio 100 could use its competences to revitalize and commercialize these well-known international characters?

Studio 100 Animation

With the acquisition of EM Entertainment, Studio 100 also became the owner of Flying Bark, an Australian animation studio. In that same year, Studio 100 opened an animation studio in Paris. Studio 100 Animation develops, finances and produces series and feature films in 2D and 3D. The Paris studio mainly produces TV series, whereas feature films are the mainstay of production in Sydney.[4] Studio 100 is working on remakes of classics such as *Maya the Bee* and *Heidi*.

Germany is now the spearhead for Studio 100's international expansion – in November 2010, the company purchased the German leisure park Holiday Park. Studio 100 transformed this park into a theme park, where German children can meet their favourite characters – such as Tabaluga, Maya the Bee and Vicky the Viking – much like what happened in Belgium with Plopsaland.

Further internationalization

Studio 100 internationalized in other markets as well. It started a co-production, called *Big & Small*, with Kindle Entertainment, 3J's Productions, the BBC and Treehouse TV. The show is a live-action comedy, filmed in the UK with British actors. Because of the show's high quality, Studio 100 has managed to get a foot in the door with the BBC, a distribution channel that is envied by many competitors. In the meantime, Studio 100 has set up another co-production with the BBC, called *Kerwhizz*.

Studio 100 also has expanded into the US. The company remade *House of Anubis*, which was originally a teen drama mystery television series for the Belgian and Dutch markets. The company sold the series to Nickelodeon, an American children's channel, which made a very successful German remake of the series and later a US remake. Again, the series was a success, in Germany as well as in the UK and the US, and this helped boost merchandising and publishing revenues in those countries significantly.

Studio 100's strategic choices

The corporate picture

Studio 100 has become an international family-entertainment corporation, active in a variety of business lines: the development and exploitation of characters, theme parks, media and animation (see Figure 7.5). All these units have their own executive teams and profit-and-loss accounts (see Table 7.1), but they are managed by a strong central unit.

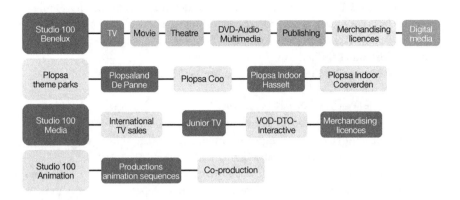

FIGURE 7.5 Studio 100 visualized

Source: Company information

TABLE 7.1 Financials of Studio 100 (2006–11)

	2006	2007	2008	2009	2010	2011
Revenues (€1,000)	**75.125**	**79.128**	**107.099**	**132.419**	**135.572**	**170.205**
– Benelux				71.091	67.548	83.500
– Plopsa				38.749	43.681	58.300
– Media				14.965	19.484	22.700
– Animation				7.609	4.859	5.500
– Business Development & corporate				5	0	
Recurring EBITDA (€1,000)	**13.995**	**14.846**	**17.842**	**28.199**	**30.090**	**38.085**
– Benelux	6.914	4.750	7.420	10.645	7.177	6.150
– Plopsa	8.081	10.276	11.488	15.889	17.168	24.571
– Media			3.474	4.652	5.820	6.493
– Animation			-1.973	-226	2.659	4.350
– Business Development & corporate	-1.000	-422	-2.567	-2.761	-2.735	-3.478
EBITDA in % of sales	*18.6*	*18.8*	*16.7*	*31.1*	*29.9*	*22.4*
Net result (€1,000)	**6.159**	**2.036**	**55**	**7.316**	**4.611**	**329**
Profit margin, %	*8.2*	*2.6*	*0.1*	*5.5*	*3.4*	*0.0*

Source: Company information

The *theme park* business has always been considered a separate activity – unlike the other business lines, this is not a creative business. The staff is composed largely of temporary workers, and the culture of a theme park is very different from the culture of the other business units within the group.

The other three businesses, however, are much more closely related:

- Content is created in *Studio 100 Benelux*, which represents the original business model, in which characters show up on television and in live-action shows and are then exploited through various channels (stage shows, DVD, audio, publishing, website and merchandizing and licensing).
- *Studio 100 Media* focuses on selling and distributing the Studio 100 programmes to TV broadcasters worldwide. The company has long-term relationships with privileged media, licensing, distribution and project partners.
- *Studio 100 Animation* is a rather new activity in the group, as it develops, finances and produces animated series and feature films. The development of new series and concepts is undertaken in close collaboration with Studio 100 Benelux. However, Animation's business model is different from the traditional Studio 100 business model: it is more complex, more global, and the process of bringing a character to television takes much longer. An important advantage of animations is that they can be truly international products that need little tailoring for local markets. They allow for proper exploitation of economies of scale and can be sold in very large volumes, once they are successful.

Studio 100: a well-aligned product leader

The core business of Studio 100 – creating content and exploiting that content through various channels – is run by applying a number of the principles of the product-leadership model. In all of its business lines, Studio 100 tries to create quality time with top-quality programmes and/or top-quality products. Furthermore, the company comes up with new concepts and new formats all the time. The ability to continuously produce high-quality, innovative content and products requires well-developed product-leadership capabilities. The Belgian business community has recognized this: Gert Verhulst and Hans Bourlon were named Managers of the Year in 2008, and the company was named Company of the Year in Belgium in 2009. Nevertheless, Hans Bourlon hates the word 'management':

> A company starts to get into trouble when it merely organizes, plans and structures what is already there – which is what I call 'management'. My biggest fear is that we will lose that creative drive which is very much present in our company. If we start to do 'more of the same' and exploit rather than explore, then that will be the end of Studio 100.

However, when we take a closer look at how Studio 100 is managed, you see a nice example of how a company balances creativity and innovation with structure and management. Let us examine – for each of the five levers of my Strategy Implementation Framework – what Studio 100 has done to stimulate creativity, entrepreneurship and innovation.

Direction and goal setting: a clear innovation strategy and committed top management

Creativity, entrepreneurship and innovation as core values

The DNA of Studio 100 can be described as 'boundless creativity and innovation'. The essence of Studio 100 is about discovery: creating new ideas, every day, over and over again, starting from a blank sheet of paper. What makes Studio 100 unique is the fact that the shareholders and founders of the company are still involved in the conceptual and creative side of the business. This does not often happen in media companies: the creative minds usually stay as far away as possible from the business brains. However, in Studio 100, doing business and being creative are inextricably linked, and therein lies the company's strength, but there's a clear understanding that creativity comes first – it's the creative impulses that keep driving the company forward.

Creativity helps the company cope with difficult times. Expanding a business is full of unexpected changes and indefinite opportunities. When the company was founded, the sale of CDs was its biggest success. Ten years later, the audio market had collapsed, but, by then, the shows in the theme parks and theatres had become the money-makers. Now, Bourlon and Verhulst believe that animation has a huge growth potential.

Portfolio management

Over the years, Studio 100 has started to build competences in portfolio management. The various characters have their own strategies and life cycles. Formats targeted to older children, such as *House of Anubis* or *Mega Mindy*, are more prone to fads and have the potential to generate substantial cash flows in short time frames. Formats directed towards younger children, such as Bumba or Plop, have longer life cycles and the potential to generate steady cash flows over longer periods of time. An important part of Studio 100's strategy is to create the right mix of formats and characters that serve different target age groups for boys and girls. In this way, shorter-term, potentially more volatile, cash flows are counterbalanced with longer-term, steady cash flows (see Figure 7.6). Bourlon, however, admits that his approach towards innovation is still more intuitive.

Communication

In a fast-growing company, it's important to keep employees informed about strategic projects and the organization's key challenges. Studio 100 organizes

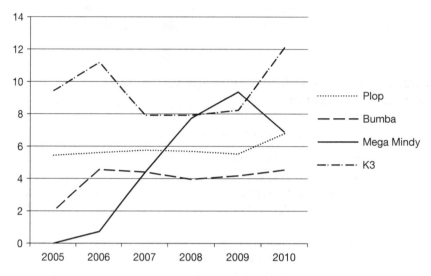

FIGURE 7.6 Illustrative life cycles of characters (revenues in € million)

Source: Company information

strategy road shows every 2–3 months. In these meetings (which can last an entire afternoon), management presents what, and how well, the company is doing, formulates questions and presents where it has doubts. Furthermore, people are given about 15 minutes to present what they are doing. Of course, this is also the forum for presenting new commercial projects. New products and formats are marketed extensively, internally and externally. In addition to these formal meetings, both Gert Verhulst and Hans Bourlon provide employees with a lot of input and market information.

Operational processes: managing the fuzzy front and the speedy back ends of innovation

Idea generation

Gert Verhulst and Hans Bourlon see it as their major task to push creativity down into the organization. Although both managers are still heavily involved with the new projects, they 'manage' new ideas, rather than create and develop the ideas themselves. This means challenging their people, providing feedback, giving advice and coaching. Leading a creative environment means detecting and recognizing strong ideas and promoting them within the company. Hans Bourlon explains:

> It goes without saying that we are always open to new ideas, although it is obvious that, first of all, people are expected to do what we pay them for.

But overall, I think that people with great ideas have the opportunity to develop them. For example, our cost controller has developed a new quiz programme. And our webmaster has produced a nice board game.

From ideas to business

However, generating ideas is only the first step. It's equally important to make everyone in the organization believe in a great idea and go for it. Verhulst and Bourlon stimulate people to generate and work out ideas as a team. The power of Studio 100 is its integrated business model. TV and music are the primary platforms for launching new characters. The company then builds the content and characters further in multimedia, such as theme parks, theatre shows, movies, CDs, books, merchandising and licensing. All of these elements are crucial in Studio 100's business model, and this requires teams from different departments to work together seamlessly. The Studio 100 marketing department plays a very important role in this process. In many media companies, the marketing department is a separate entity, cut off from the creative process. At Studio 100, the two sides have to work together. Creative ideas are supported only when they can be com-mercialized. Studio 100 is business-driven and has clear goals, and that makes it different from many other creative companies, which do not make plans but simply carry on, relying on a hazy form of artistry. . . .

Creativity and entrepreneurship are at the core of Studio 100, but, over time, the creative process has become more structured. For example, the creation of a new character goes through three phases. In the first phase, the baseline for the character is developed. Gert Verhulst and Hans Bourlon are frequently involved in this phase. The deepening of the characters takes place in a second phase. Small cells are responsible for creating the derivatives (such as games, publishing, shows, movies, etc.) that are based on the core character. The last phase is the development of the character. In this phase, the characters are stable, have proven themselves and are simply further developed through, for instance, licensing and merchandising. At this point, every employee can contribute ideas or concepts. Although this is welcomed in phases 1 and 2 as well, creativity experts play a part in the early phases. (Figure 7.7 provides an overview of these phases for Plop the Gnome.)

Support processes: resource allocation and knowledge sharing

Innovation governance and resource allocation

Studio 100 does not have a formal innovation governance process. This role is taken up by the two founders, who know most of the employees, and their com-petences, personally. The two managers allocate resources to the various projects, but manage this process in a rather informal way.

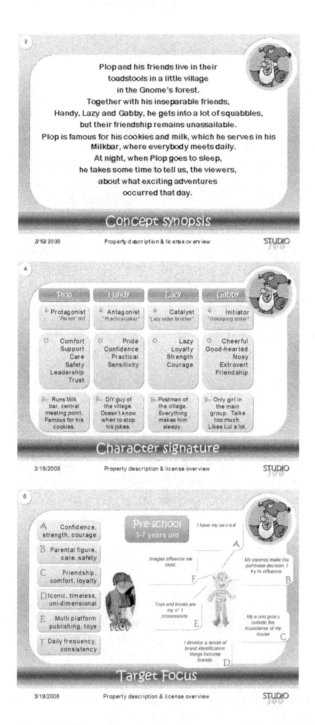

FIGURE 7.7 The product development process in Studio 100: Plop the Gnome

Source: Company information

Knowledge management

Studio 100 focuses a lot of attention on knowledge management. Both top managers provide the employees with a lot of input and market information. Again, the company does not use formal systems to ensure an intensive flow of communication; instead, Studio 100 has created a flat organization where people from different teams work together seamlessly. Bourlon and Verhulst are the drivers of the knowledge management efforts within the company:

> Every morning, I search the websites of a few newspapers for articles that are related to Studio 100 in one way or another. And I forward these articles to employees that can use them. Everything you see in the world can be a source of inspiration for a story, a new concept or project. Our employees need to know what is on television these days, what are big hits, and what interests people have at this moment. Information should be available to the people who need it.

Evaluation and control processes: tracking and rewarding innovation

Control

For a long time, the two founders have mainly focused on creating a culture of entrepreneurship and innovation. Gradually, they have introduced more formal systems to manage innovation, but the informality still prevails. This also applies to the company's evaluation and control system. The company follows up the financials of all the various formats and pays attention to managing the life cycles of its formats. When the sales of a format start to decrease, Studio 100 thinks about launching new initiatives to revitalize it. For example, the musical *The 3 Piglets* gave the career of K3 a new boost and helped to increase sales of this format.

In Studio 100, the command-and-control style that you find in many companies has given way to a softer control, with more emphasis on output control. Although the firm uses clear performance measures to track the progress of specific projects, most attention is paid to a more personal form of control and coaching. Some projects are monitored extensively by the top managers; for others, there is the confidence that the organization will bring the projects to a good conclusion.

In brief, one could say that, for Studio 100, control is primarily accomplished by creating an appropriate culture in the organization – a culture built around entrepreneurship and empowerment.

Performance and incentives

Everybody in Studio 100 is paid a fixed amount, even the sales people. This reward system is quite conservative, and yet it highlights the philosophy that all factors in the creation and sale of qualitative products are equally important. When somebody – say, an actor – asks for more than fair pay, this might be a reason to change the format and exclude the actor. These discussions occur from time to time. In order to counter these problems, Studio 100 tries to create a group feeling where everybody feels at home and earns well. The company offers people a long-term perspective, although some people feel they should receive part of the income of their successful project. However, Studio 100 is very strict here: you do not get a bonus for contributing to a successful project – although an employee can receive extra pay if he/she contributes *more*. Motivated, creative and committed employees obviously get more promotion opportunities. In 2009, Studio 100 introduced an option plan for all employees, but Hans Bourlon doubts whether this was really necessary. He's not convinced that money really drives commitment.

Organizational behaviour processes: Studio 100's innovation culture and structure

HR management

Creativity is stimulated, above all, by providing people with a warm nest, an environment that gives them the opportunity to slowly rise and shine. The Studio 100 management team sees this as one of its major tasks. There is a lot of energy in the air at Studio 100. Very often, you can hear music in the corridors: an orchestra is rehearsing, ballet lessons are in session, or some of the characters are learning new songs.

Studio 100 pays a lot of attention to attracting the right people. In a fast-growing company, it's vital to have the right people on board. The company looks for energized and engaged people, and it deliberately chooses *not* to attract famous actors for a particular character. The total picture must be right. You cannot play Pirate Pete for one year, earn a lot of money and then leave the company.

The company has no trade unions, because there have never been candidates. Studio 100 has flexible working hours and does whatever it possibly can to create an energizing and positive environment. The company organizes power yoga sessions, there are quiz teams, and so on. The real writing often takes place late in the evening, in groups, and certainly not in suits. In short, you won't find the classic 9-to-5 clerk at Studio 100.

Creativity embedded in the organization's structure

Creative companies stimulate imagination and out-of-the-box thinking – which means that there's a certain amount of chaos in the organization – and Studio 100 is no exception. The organization is quite flexible and fluid. The company has set up creative cells that create new characters and monitor the correct interpretation of, and alignment with, the character over all of the different departments (television, merchandizing, theatre, marketing, and so on). Both the creative cells and the departments have a direct link to the executive management team. This makes decision lines very short, and it results in a balanced organization. This structure also offers the best guarantees that the main ideas and philosophies of the top are transferred to every part of the organization.

According to Jo Daris, the most synergy is created when employees – whatever their function or department – meet each other continuously. An open workspace promotes all that. Indeed, there are some offices in the Studio 100 building, but most of the space goes to studios, rehearsal rooms, ballet rooms and the clothing department where the costumes are made. That is where the employees write songs, create new shows, invent new attractions for the theme parks and make stage sets. On the tables, you will find models of the theme park attractions or scenery, and rhyming dictionaries are more commonly used than calculators. At noon, the restaurant looks like carnival: pirates, gnomes, piglets and mermaids are all sitting at one table. While they are having lunch, new ideas bubble up. The food is provided for free.

Studio 100's Product Leadership Pentagon

We've been discussing how Studio 100 has been able to create a culture of innovation and entrepreneurship throughout the entire organization. Figure 7.8 shows how well the company scores on the Product Leadership Pentagon, the tool that I presented in Chapter 6.

Studio 100's Product Leadership Pentagon was obtained by benchmarking the scores of Studio 100 on a product-leadership questionnaire with the scores of 107 other product leaders from different industries and different countries.[5] The fifteen scores that are presented are percentiles: they indicate the percentage of companies whose scores were equal to, or lower than, Studio 100's for that particular item. A more shaded pentagon means that a company applies more of the product-leadership actions; in other words, it is more aligned.

Figure 7.8 indicates that, overall, Studio 100 is a well-aligned product leader: it has high scores (i.e. scores of 75 or more) on nine out of fifteen product-leadership items. This is rather exceptional. Few firms in my database have such good scores. The Product Leadership Pentagon indicates, however, that there is still room for improvement in stimulating innovation, mainly in the support and evaluation and control processes. Overall, however, the company is an example of true product leadership, and I believe this explains why the company has been able continuously to develop and launch new products over time.

Studio 100 and strategy commitment

In the previous section, I have described the various operational and management activities that Studio 100 has introduced over the last 15 years to stimulate creativity, entrepreneurship and innovation. Whereas Hans Bourlon and Gert Verhulst stress the entrepreneurial and innovative culture in all their communications – they

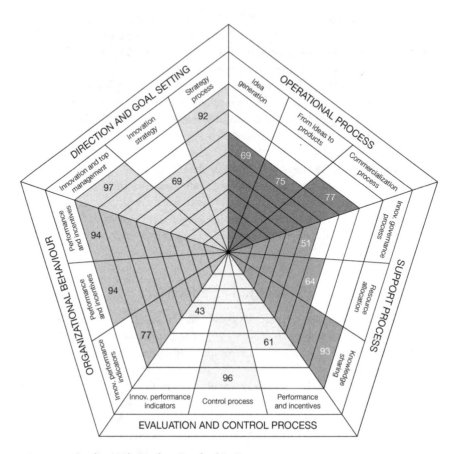

FIGURE 7.8 Studio 100's Product Leadership Pentagon

mainly emphasize the 'fuzzy front' of Studio 100 – I have highlighted the company's efforts to put more structure into the innovation process. This process is not finalized yet, as can be deduced from Figure 7.9: the company has not reached the connected maturity stage that you find in most highly successful product leaders.

I obtained Studio 100's maturity profile based on a Maturity Assessment Toolkit that was filled in by one of the founders and two top managers. The maturity self-assessment toolkit examines the level of maturity of forty-six operational and management practices in a company.[6]

Figure 7.9 indicates that Studio 100 operates as a 'structured organization', except for its direction- and goal-setting processes, where the company has reached the 'connected' stage. What does all this mean?

Hans Bourlon and Gert Verhulst are still the main orchestrators of the company's innovation efforts, and they are still actively involved in all of the organization's operational activities, but this is gradually changing over time. In connected organizations, middle management assumes a more active role in managing the entire organization, while top management ensures that middle managers do not become overly concentrated on their own silo. This is the case in Studio 100; the company has strong values that all employees live by. The top managers involve middle managers in the strategy formation process, and even employees can provide input into the strategy discussions. Over time, the strategic planning process has become more formal, but there is still room to test and try out new ideas that emerge spontaneously. All these activities indicate that Studio 100's *direction- and goal-setting* processes are connected: they are well established and actively used by the top and middle managers, and they span the whole organization.

For the other areas of the Strategy Implementation Framework, the Maturity Assessment Toolkit indicates that Studio 100 has the characteristics of a 'structured organization'. This means that, for example, activities within departments are defined and planned, and that there are well-defined expectations for each task. A few key processes are documented, and the company pays systematic attention to product quality and, sometimes, process quality. This definitely applies to Studio 100's *operational processes*, but many of the process improvement initiatives are focused on the processes within the departments, not *across* the departments. Furthermore, many of the process improvements are more reactive than proactive, which is another prerequisite for having 'connected' operational processes.

The company has 'structured' *support processes*, indicating that it has started to have more formal communication, resource allocation and appropriate IT tools. However, from the case description, it is clear that this is not a priority for the top managers. The organization does not use its support tools to establish connections between the departments; rather, these tools are used within the various departments.

	Direction and goal setting processes	Operational processes	Support process	Evaluation and control process	Organizational behaviour process
Level 1 Entre-preneurial					
Level 2 Structured		●	●	●	●
Level 3 Connected	●				
Level 4 Committed					

FIGURE 7.9 Maturity profile of Studio 100

Studio 100's *evaluation and control processes* are also 'structured'. The company's control system is directed to managing the financials and the operations. The control system does not include more sophisticated innovation metrics; it checks whether action plans lead to the desired results. The company has a risk management system, but the focus of the evaluation and control processes is on controlling, not on learning, which is typical for a structured organization.

Studio 100 has a very collaborative and flat organization, and so one would expect that its organizational behaviour processes are at least 'connected'. A lot of things do point in that direction: for example, responsibilities and authorities reside with the employees, and the management style is a coaching management style (not a telling or selling style). Building teams and a strong culture are top priorities. However, in order to be truly 'connected' or 'committed', Studio 100 must build more formality into its organizational behaviour processes. The company has no formal performance targets or evaluations for its managers and employees, and there is no formal reward system in the company. That's why the company is classified as 'structured' on the organizational behaviour dimension as well.

Key learning points

The case of Studio 100 demonstrates how three entrepreneurs were able to build an entertainment company from scratch and grow it into an international entertainment corporation. From the beginning, the company's key values have been 'boundless creativity and innovation', and that explains how the company has created so many new formats and has built activities in a wide variety of businesses, such as TV shows, theatre, music, theme parks, animation, licensing and publishing, and so on. The essential features of all these initiatives are high quality and innovativeness, and the company has implicitly used a strategy with product leadership as the core operating model.

Over time, Hans Bourlon and Gert Verhulst have initiated many actions in line with the product-leadership model. Studio 100's Product Leadership Pentagon illustrates this (see Figure 7.8) – it shows that the company has done a lot to align actions and activities to the core themes of innovation and entrepreneurship.

The top managers of Studio 100 have also launched a series of actions to commit the entire organization to its strategy. The company has not yet reached the 'connected' maturity stage – it's still a 'structured organization' (see Figure 7.9). In Chapter 4, I argued that two of the problems with structured organizations are the lack of entrepreneurship and the emergence of a silo mentality, but I do not think this will be a problem for Studio 100. The opposite might well be the case: moving towards the next maturity stage will require the organization to balance entrepreneurship and creativity with more structure and formality, so that the middle managers can play a more active strategic role in managing the organization. For me, that's Studio 100's key challenge for the future.

Notes

1   This case study is based on a Vlerick Business School case study, 'Studio 100: A Showcase in Show Business', written by Kurt Verweire and MBA students Kristoff Lievens, Nicolas Van Boven and Pascal Vercruysse, in 2009, and a report written by MBA students Annick Bolland, Leonardo Fininzola e Silva, Stefan Keereman, Jef Laurijssen, Werner Roelandt and Alex Waterinkx (2009): 'Studio 100 – Growth strategy', for the Vlerick Business School strategy course.

2   Studio 100 website, available at: www.studio100.tv/ (accessed 22 November 2012).

3   People in Flanders and the Netherlands speak Dutch. That is why Studio 100 has quickly reached out to the Dutch market. In the southern part of Belgian, the main language is French.

4   Studio 100 (2011) *Preliminary Offering Memorandum*, Studio 100, p. 68.

5   I obtained input for my product-leadership questionnaire from one of the founders and two other top managers of Studio 100.

6   The Maturity Assessment Toolkit was developed by Vlerick Business School and Suez Group/Electrabel and consists of forty-six items that check the maturity of an organization's direction- and goal-setting processes (nine items), operational processes (nine items), support processes (ten items), evaluation and control processes (nine items) and organizational behaviour processes (nine items). The Maturity Assessment Toolkit ranks the scores of all items per lever of the Strategy Implementation Framework and presents the thirty-third percentile for each of the five levers. The Maturity Assessment Toolkit provides a rather detailed, yet comprehensive, picture of an organization's management model.

PART III

Strategy implementation at operational excellence companies

8

WHAT DOES IT MEAN TO BE OPERATIONALLY EXCELLENT?

Whereas the previous chapters introduced you to the challenges of implementing a strategy built around product leadership, the next three chapters focus on the operational-excellence operating model. Just like product leadership, operational excellence seems to be a straightforward concept – but, in reality, it is often *mis*understood. And that's a pity, because effective strategy implementation only occurs when everybody understands what the organization is trying to achieve.

In this chapter, I will explain what it means to be operationally excellent. When is operational excellence the appropriate operating model for your organization? And what are the commitments that you make when you declare that you are pursuing this model?

I start this chapter by tackling the most important misconceptions about operational excellence, and I provide a more strategic view on this important topic. I will link operational excellence to Crawford and Mathews's Consumer Relevancy Framework, which I presented in Chapter 2. More specifically, I will show that the implementation of a strategy based on operational excellence allows firms to be the cheapest or the fastest in their market. I will also show that there are three formats of operational excellence. Many people associate operational excellence with the traditional 'cost leadership' model, but there are other operational excellence formats that firms may adopt if they aspire to grow successfully.

Operational excellence: what's in a name?

Operational excellence is a common term in (strategic) management. Many people regard it as a management philosophy of the workplace that stresses the application of a variety of principles, systems and tools towards the sustainable improvement of key performance indicators. Much of this philosophy is based on the continuous improvement methodologies that were introduced into the quality literature in the 1980s.

However, this is a dangerous misinterpretation of operational excellence. This definition associates operational excellence with efficiency improvement initiatives that are applied primarily in an organization's operations department or back office. In my opinion, operational excellence is a strategic choice – a management philosophy, with a distinctive operating model and particular management systems – that pervades the entire organization, not only the operations department.

For example, Toyota's Production System (TPS) extends beyond the shop floor and is found in the boardroom, the sales offices, the product development department and even throughout the entire supply chain. One of the most influential books on operational excellence – *Lean Thinking* – emphasized that lean thinking is about the entire organization working together to give customers what they want, while eliminating waste in the value stream and striving for perfection.[1]

This interpretation of operational excellence is very much in line with the definition of Michael Treacy and Fred Wiersema, who defined operational excellence as:

> A specific strategic approach to the production and delivery of products and services. The objective of a company following this strategy is to lead its industry in price and convenience. Companies pursuing operational excellence are indefatigable in seeking ways to minimize overhead costs, to eliminate intermediate production steps, to reduce transaction and other 'friction' costs, and to optimize business processes across functional and organizational boundaries. They focus on delivering their products or services to customers at competitive prices and with minimal inconvenience.[2]

Treacy and Wiersema's definition focuses mainly on the production and delivery of products and services – today, people would extend this definition of operational excellence to the product development stage as well.

Treacy and Wiersema's definition also links nicely to Crawford and Mathews's Consumer Relevancy Framework (presented in Chapter 2). Crawford and Mathews argued that winning companies have a winning value proposition: they decide to be the best ('dominate') in one of five attributes – product, price, access, service or connectivity – and they often select a secondary attribute that is strongly complementary to the first and helps to further 'differentiate' them from their competitors. At the same time, they realize that they must not fall below the industry par for the other three value attributes; they must avoid slipping into the consumer underworld.

Using these concepts, I define operationally excellent firms as companies that dominate on the 'price' or 'access' dimension (see Figure 8.1). Companies pursuing operational excellence manage their costs continuously, and they optimize their business processes across the entire organization. This allows them to lead their industry by being the cheapest and/or the fastest or easiest to deal with.

Many people still think of operational excellence organizations as the typical low-cost providers, such as Walmart, Aldi and Ryanair, but, in this chapter, I will

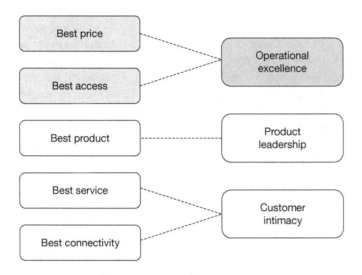

FIGURE 8.1 The value proposition of operational excellence organizations

show that operational excellence exists in various formats. However, the underlying principles of operational excellence are strikingly similar, irrespective of the format you have chosen. In the remainder of this chapter, I will present three different formats of operational excellence. I will provide you with examples of each format and introduce some key concepts behind their successful deployment. Two of the companies focus on providing the 'best price' to their customers, and the third company's format is built around 'best access'.

The value proposition of operationally excellent firms: what is 'best price'?

Operational excellence and cost leadership

The most obvious definition of operational excellence is to equate it with cost leadership, as introduced by Michael Porter in the early 1980s. This means relentlessly reducing and minimizing costs in order to offer the lowest prices to the customers. Examples of such operationally excellent companies are: Aldi, Walmart, easyJet and Hotels Formule 1 (now called HotelF1 in France), the super-low-budget unit of French Accor Group. These firms constitute the first category of operational excellence firms, which I call the '*pure price players*'.

Ryanair is probably one of the most extreme cost leaders in the world. Ryanair strives to make its offering as lean as possible in order to guarantee the lowest possible price for its customers. The elimination of seatback pockets, blankets and airsickness bags, the no-refund policy and the limited airport transportation are only some examples of Ryanair's focus on cost cutting.

Although this 'no-frills' concept is common to most low-cost airlines, Ryanair is unique in its no-nonsense way of communicating this to the public. Quotes from its flamboyant CEO, Michael O'Leary – such as 'At the moment, the ice is free – but if we could find a way of putting a price on it, we would' – demonstrate that Ryanair is constantly challenging the boundaries of what customers perceive as 'good enough'. Unlike other airlines, Ryanair involves its customers in this quest by launching online polls on its website. Polls that ask people if they would mind standing in the airplane or being charged for using the toilets often initiate public discussions, which create free publicity for Ryanair. For example, Figure 8.2 shows what I found on Ryanair's website.

Ryanair News

News Release

09.07.09

FREE FLIGHT - WOULD YOU STAND?

Ryanair, the World's favourite airline, today (9th July) launched an online poll to ask if passengers would 'stand' on short flights if it meant they could travel for FREE, or pay 50% less than seated passengers. Ryanair is gauging passenger demand for its 'vertical seating' which will allow passengers to travel – for free – in a secure upright position on short flights of approximately one hour.

Ryanair's corporate song – I'm still standing »

FIGURE 8.2 Ryanair: Would you stand?

Source: Ryanair website[3]

Offering a no-frills product or service at a very low price is also how companies such as Aldi and Hotels Formule 1 have become market leaders. These companies look for cost-saving opportunities every day. Strategic management has always emphasized cost advantage as a primary basis for competitive advantage in an industry. This focus on cost reflects the traditional emphasis that economists place on price as the principal medium of competition, and competing on price depends on cost efficiency, which has always been – and still is – a popular theme among managers, especially in periods of crisis. That's why many strategy textbooks devote a full chapter to 'cost advantage' and 'cost leadership'.

Sources of cost advantage

What do firms do to lower their cost base? Here is a list of the potential sources of cost advantage:[4]

- *Economies of scale* exist wherever proportionate increases in the amounts of inputs employed in a production process result in lower unit costs. They can arise from divisibilities of the resources or from advantages due to specialization.
- *Economies of learning*, sometimes called *economies of experience*, originate when repetition allows firms to develop both individual skills and organizational routines. Part of Honda's success in the motorcycle industry can be explained by the presence of economies of experience.
- *Process technology and process design* are a third source of cost advantage. McDonald's, ING Direct USA and Toyota are examples of companies that have demonstrated that superior process management can lead to significant cost advantages.
- *Product design* can lead to a cost advantage if the organization designs products for ease of production rather than simply for functionality and aesthetics. Many car companies have significantly cut product development costs by working with platforms rather than with car models. As you will see later, IKEA is a master of product design (and other elements of operational excellence).
- *Capacity utilization* is an important cost driver in businesses with high fixed costs. easyJet, Southwest Airlines and Ryanair are able to operate at lower costs, partly because they have a significantly higher capacity utilization than most of their competitors.
- *Input costs* are important cost factors for particular industries. If an organization is able to obtain inputs to the production process at lower costs – e.g. through bargaining power, or by accessing low-cost sources of supply – it might obtain a cost advantage relative to the competitors.
- A last source of cost advantage originates from *residual efficiency*. According to Robert Grant, residual efficiency depends on a firm's ability to eliminate organizational slack: that is, surplus costs that keep the firm from operating at maximum efficiency. These costs are often referred to as 'organizational fat'.

Nucor Corporation, a global steel company, is noted for its streamlined organization structure but also for its frugality in travel and entertainment expenses.[5]

The pure price players use many of these sources of cost advantage to become true cost leaders in their industries. Cost leadership leads to price leadership, and that's how the pure price leaders are able to grow both the top and the bottom line. For example, Ryanair has been able to increase its revenues from €2.7 billion in 2007 to €4.3 billion in 2011 – an annual growth rate of more than 12 per cent – in a very tough industry. The company transported 75.8 million passengers in 2011, more than twice the number of British Airways passengers (34.1 million). From 2007 to 2011, the company had an average profit margin of more than 10 per cent – which is very high compared with the profit margins of British Airways (1.1 per cent), Lufthansa (2.2 per cent) and Scandinavian Airlines (-5.4 per cent).

The meaning of 'best price'

For pure price players, price is the most important attribute for attracting new customers. Pure price players set very low prices for all of their products. However, having the best price does not necessarily mean having the absolutely lowest price. Rather, it means consistently offering customers fair and honest prices. Fred Crawford and Ryan Mathews found that customers want a price that is visible and consistent – a price that does not appear to have been artificially increased or decreased at the expense of other, related items they need to purchase.[6] Here, Ryanair obviously makes some mistakes. Many people find that Ryanair is not clear about the extra charges: in a 'consumer-watchdog' survey in 2008, the company scored worst for unfair 'extra' costs. Despite these criticisms, Ryanair's number of passengers has increased every year.

The pure price players should be aware that price has become a multidimensional attribute that goes far beyond the simple notion of lowest price. Those dimensions are: honesty, consistency, fairness, reliability, a range of acceptable prices and price impression. This is nicely illustrated in the following Walmart and Aldi case studies.

Case study: price leadership at Walmart

Perhaps no consumer business understands this new definition of the price attribute better than Walmart. Through its consistent, honest pricing, the giant retailer has succeeded in setting the lowest-price impression among customers and has become a trusted purchasing agent for those shoppers. People automatically think of Walmart as the price leader. In reality, however, Walmart's prices were higher than those of its competitors on one-third of the items checked. On those items for which its prices were lower . . . average savings were only $0.37 per item. So, consumers have come to perceive Walmart to be the 'lowest', even when that *is often not the case. Its 'Every-Day-Low-Price' focus reassures customers that no pricing games are being played. Of course, you have to have low prices to create the impression of lowest price. But the bottom line is that consumers simply feel they won't get ripped off in Walmart, lending credence to our belief that price impression is, in fact, more important than price itself. How did they do it: they listened to consumers, delivered what they wanted, and, in the process, established a relationship based on trust. Only then was Walmart able to leverage that relationship to become viewed as the price leader.*[7]

Case study: price leadership at Aldi

Aldi is another example of a company that understands the essence of price leadership.

The company's basic principle is to sell products at prices lower than anywhere else, in contrast with many other retailers whose goal is to get the highest possible prices without endangering the company's competitiveness. . . . No one disputes the fact that Aldi sets prices in the food retail trade. Aldi strives for lower costs, but never at the expense of quality. Everything Aldi sells is benchmarked against leading branded products. As a principle, when different qualities are involved, purchase price differences are not the sole factor in the decision-making process. A higher purchase price is accepted for higher quality.

Another element of Aldi's sales system is a limited product range, with a focus on goods which reflect basic consumer needs. Aldi buyers concentrate on essentials: specifically, their customers' needs. Vendor conditions do not play any role at all in the product range strategy. It is often argued that 'sales psychology' is the basis for Aldi's decisions regarding merchandise placement. The interiors are kept so simple on purpose, simply to create the illusion of being cost-conscious. This is wrong. Aldi does not focus on appearances. Aldi's focus is on costs and, in addition, making the customer an honest offer without any 'show'. Customers are not supposed to believe Aldi is low-price − Aldi is low-price.[8]

When pursuing a cost advantage over rivals, managers must take care to include features and services that buyers consider essential. Even if it is priced lower than competing products, a product that is too frills-free can turn buyers off. Focus on cost and price alone is, therefore, very dangerous. Operationally excellent companies understand this very well: they often complement low price with ease of purchase and great quality.

The importance of quality

For almost all operational excellence companies, quality is as important as offering a great price. In Chapter 5, I showed that product quality has two dimensions: level and consistency. The quality level refers to the performance quality and indicates how well a product is able to perform its functions for a specific target market. For product leaders, performance quality is key − for example, Miele strives to offer the highest-quality domestic appliances in the industry. A second dimension of product quality is conformance quality, which is defined as freedom from defects and consistency in delivering a targeted level of performance. The Total Quality Movement is referring mainly to conformance quality when it states that 'quality is free'. The idea is that investments in quality can reduce variance in output, scrap, rework losses and warranty costs. Toyota's quality image stems from all the efforts the company has made to increase conformance quality, not performance quality. Conformance quality is key for operationally excellent firms.

Many operationally excellent firms have embraced the Total Quality Management (TQM) philosophy. From the 1970s onwards, Japanese firms – with Toyota leading the pack – demonstrated that low price does not always have to mean low quality. Although TQM has lost some of its appeal in recent years, operationally excellent companies are still guided by the basic TQM principles.

One of the most important principles is that TQM starts from the customer perspective. Quality is not pursued for quality's sake! Better quality should be defined by the customer, and everybody in the organization should be aware of what the customers' needs and requirements are. An organization attains customer focus when all employees know both the internal and the external customers and their requirements. TQM stresses the importance of internal customers, who should be treated as well as external customers. Then, quality is everybody's responsibility, not just the concern of front-office people or production people.

Another principle is that TQM considers all of the costs of quality, not only the costs of a bad product or service. This includes prevention costs, appraisal costs (such as costs of inspection) and failure costs. Companies that invest wisely in quality will see the total cost of quality reduce over time. It is important to get things right the first time. Measurement is crucial, and many operationally excellent firms adopt a culture of continuous improvement.

TQM adopts a systems approach to management. An organization's success in achieving its quality objectives is driven by identifying, understanding and managing all interrelated processes as a system. Interrelationships are not restricted to departments within the organization, but extend to suppliers (and customers). Operationally excellent firms concentrate on supply chain management more than customer-intimacy and product-leadership firms.

These quality principles have also led to a different notion of the cost of products and services for customers. Customers (both retail and corporate) are aware that the purchase price represents only part of the total cost of owning a product or service.[9] That's why management accounting professionals have developed the Total Cost of Ownership (TCO) concept – a financial estimate that helps consumers and company managers determine direct and indirect costs of a product or service.

So, what is 'low price' anyway? Is it low purchasing price? Or is it low TCO? A company such as Toyota has focused on the latter. The following statement shows how Toyota positions itself on its website to business-to-business (B2B) customers.

Case study: Toyota and TCO

International Fleet Managers have identified Total Cost of Ownership (TCO) as the most important purchase criterion. The major part of TCO is depreciation, which can account for over 50 per cent of the total operating cost. However, Toyota's strong focus on quality, durability and reliability contributes significantly to a good residual value position, relative to our closest competitors. According to the independent Schwacke Automobile Index, Toyota fleet cars are ranked among the top models in terms of residual value. Therefore, Toyota can offer a competitive TCO in the European fleet market. Toyota is also renowned for manufacturing some of the world's most reliable cars. This simply means the cars spend less unscheduled time in the workshop, and more time on the road, resulting in a lower actual cost of maintenance over the vehicle's life. Toyota continuously takes TCO into account in the design process, the product planning, and the development stage of their cars. TCO is truly embedded in its fleet strategy.[10]

Toyota is able to give its customers a good, reliable product at a good price – which is not, however, the lowest purchase price. Some strategy authors interpret this as a combination of low cost and differentiation. I believe that many operationally excellent firms focus on TCO rather than on purchase price. Automotive.com, one of the Internet's leading car buying portals and consumer information websites, has published a list of the lowest cost of ownership cars in 2011. Toyota is represented three times in the Top 10.

Operational excellence and business process management

Operationally excellent firms have also embraced business process management (BPM) methodologies to offer their products and services quickly and conveniently. 'Fast, easy, painless' is a common slogan among operationally excellent companies. Building on the foundations laid down by TQM, BPM is a management approach to supporting the design, administration, configuration, deployment and analysis

TABLE 8.1 Lowest cost of ownership vehicles, 2011

1	Nissan Versa
2	Toyota Yaris
3	Hyundai Accent
4	Honda Civic
5	Smart Fortwo
6	Scion xD
7	Honda Fit
8	Toyota Corolla
9	Toyota Prius
10	Ford Fiesta

Source: Automotive.com[11]

of business processes. BPM considers processes to be strategic assets of an organization that must be understood, managed and improved. It emphasizes process improvements and automation as drivers of a firm's performance. Just as with TQM, BPM forces companies to adopt an attitude of continuous improvement.

Two business improvement philosophies are particularly popular: 'Lean' and 'Six Sigma'. Lean is a management philosophy, derived largely from the TPS, that has been extensively described in the literature. Through the adoption of Lean thinking, a company tries to eliminate all activities that do not create added value. Companies that adopt the principles of Lean management use empirical methods and measurements to decide what matters, rather than uncritically accepting pre-existing ideas. They also involve their employees in these efficiency improvement initiatives. The Lean concept has been applied to industries as diverse as insurance and healthcare, and it is currently considered to be critical in departments other than production.

Six Sigma is a related management philosophy, originally developed by Motorola in the mid 1980s. Recognizing that variation hinders the ability to deliver high-quality products and services reliably, Six Sigma seeks to minimize variability in the business processes and to improve the quality of process outputs by identifying and removing the causes of defects (errors). Management authors consider Lean and Six Sigma complementary: Lean is about speed and low cost; Six Sigma is about defect-free service.

Applying BPM, Lean and Six Sigma creates a business process orientation throughout the entire company. Today, operational excellence means process excellence – and most operationally excellent companies see BPM and improvement as the major drivers of higher customer satisfaction, product quality, delivery speed . . . and cost! Process management skills are among the most critical core competences in most operationally excellent firms. I will discuss this in more detail later, in the next chapter.

Operational excellence format 2: the 'price-plus players'

Companies such as Zara, Amazon and IKEA have been able to move away from the image that low price and good quality are the only things that matter in a value proposition. Offering their customers more than a combination of quality, price and hassle-free service, these firms have adopted the 'price-plus' operational excellence model.

Case study: Zara and fast fashion

Zara is an exceptional story in the corporate world, and its case study has been taught in almost every business school.

Zara sells what has been referred to as 'fast fashion', 'disposable fashion', 'fashion on demand' and 'fashion that you wear 10 times'. The company copies runway fashions, producing quality goods and selling them at affordable, market-based prices. Zara determines the existing market price for a product, and then establishes a price below the lowest competitor's price for a similar product.[12]

Figure 8.3 compares Zara's prices with the prices of a competitor.

Before Zara became a global powerhouse, true fashion was synonymous with expensive and exclusive apparel. The largest fashion retailers (such as H&M) worked together with fashion icons on a biannual basis to determine what collections would be sold in their stores 6 months later. If the collections were successful, so were the stores. However, if the collections did not catch on, the store's season sales would make a loss. GAP was such a leading retailer that saw its sales decline for 5 consecutive years owing to bad design choices. Zara has a different view on fashion. As trends change quickly, Zara cannot afford to produce high quantities of inventory. That's why its collections evolve every 6 months and are often limited. This creates a sense of scarcity. Zara's customers know that if they do not buy what they like now, they may not find it again when they come back.

The cheap

Frock coat (119)
White shirt (25) ZARA
Black necktie (65) HACKETT
Woolen trousers (45)
Black boots (55), both ZARA

The expensive

Black cashmere frock coat (950)
White tuxedo shirt (190)
Black necktie (86)
Woolen trousers (380) RALPH LAUREN
Black boots (500) UNGARO

FIGURE 8.3 The cheap (*lo barato*) versus the expensive (*lo caro*)

Source: Linguri and Kumar (2005)[13]

Though Zara positions itself as 'affordable to the masses', it also creates a perception of luxury.[14] In order to provide affordable high fashion, Zara has reconfigured its entire value chain to curb, and sometimes eliminate, unnecessary activities. There is no expensive advertising, nor are there any expensive designers in the company. Instead, the company invests in setting up a vertically integrated value chain that develops, produces and sells clothes quickly. The company controls its products from the design decision to the point of sale, which enables it to keep costs low. Zara has also embraced Lean throughout the company. It takes Zara 2 weeks from design to delivery to stores all over the world. For competitors, this process takes months.

IKEA is another example of a company that has reconfigured its value chain to become a 'price-plus' operational excellence firm.

Case study: IKEA and price plus

IKEA offers a wide range of well-designed, functional home furnishing products. The range includes everything from sofas and beds to textiles and cookware. The targeted market segment is the group of young buyers in search of stylish and fashionable furniture and household accessories at a low cost. The IKEA motto is: 'The best way to sell a product is to show how it functions.' One of IKEA's strengths is its ability to steer the purchasing process in the shops. IKEA involves its customers in a real shopping experience and provides everything that is needed for convenient shopping: pencils, notepads, tape measures, store guides, catalogues, shopping bags and trolleys. IKEA really wants to attract as many people as possible to its stores. At the entrance to every store, there is a playroom for children, where parents can leave their children under the supervision of IKEA employees, free of charge. Many people also come to the stores for the inexpensive food and the many Swedish delicacies that are served in the restaurant.[15]

Figure 8.4 indicates that IKEA and Zara both dominate on price. Cutting costs where many of their competitors spend huge sums of money, they operate on a

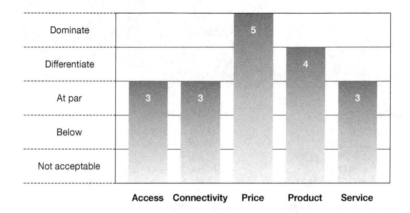

FIGURE 8.4 The value proposition of IKEA and Zara

lower cost base than the competition. But both companies are more than that: they differentiate from other price players with their products. Zara has used the principles of Lean, not just to offer good quality, but also to offer innovative clothes. In a similar way, IKEA attracts customers with trendy and stylish designs, often copied from the more expensive furniture producers. Although IKEA and Zara do not invest in expensive designers, design is of strategic importance to both companies. For example, IKEA has centralized its design operations in its head-quarters in Sweden. IKEA products bear the label 'Design and Quality, IKEA of Sweden'. Product design is centralized because it is a key driver of lower production and logistics costs. Design is probably even more important for Zara, as the company leads through fast fashion. Zara has very short production runs, and rapid changes in design cause consumers to believe that Zara's clothes embody the latest trends in fashion. In order to provide fast fashion, Zara works with 300 in-house fashion designers, a substantial investment for a low-cost provider.

Firms pursuing a 'price-plus' model are not less operationally excellent than the pure price leaders. These companies use the same management models and philosophies to run their organizations; they both focus on minimum total cost, good quality and BPM.

Checklist: 'operational excellence and best price'

Does your company embrace operational excellence to meet your growth targets? Is your strategy based on offering the best price to your customers? The following questions may be useful for checking the quality of your value proposition:

1   Do you offer (very) low prices for all your products or services? How often do you review your prices?
2   Does your communication to your customers stress fairness and honesty in your pricing? Are your prices readily visible? Are they simple, clear and intuitively correct? Are they consistent? Or are they artificially inflated or deflated?
3   Do you stress the quality of your products or services in your value proposition? Do you go as far as stressing the TCO in your offer to the customer?
4   What do you do to offer your products or services hassle-free? Or is 'fast, easy, painless' just a nice slogan, without real meaning?
5   If you differentiate on a second attribute other than access, is your offer really attractive and inspiring? Is it unique? Or do you offer what your competitors offer?

Best access: how do you turn a hassle into a positive experience?

The underrated importance of access

Many operationally excellent firms pay a lot of attention to price as the dominant element in their value proposition. They try to win in their market by offering low prices for good-quality products or services. However, offering your products in a fast, easy and painless way – which is what access is all about – is an equally powerful value proposition that too few companies employ.

Access is an important attribute to customers. Offering 'best access' means eliminating all the transaction costs for your customers. Have you ever had to wait endlessly when you contacted your supplier's call centre? Or have you ever been in a store in which it takes you hours to find what you need? Well, that's what access is all about.

Many people associate access with geographical proximity. Access used to be all about real estate (a gas station on every street corner, ATMs in every kind of retail setting . . .). Today, however, access has more to do with psychological access – the perception of being able to easily and successfully navigate the physical plant of a business (whatever it is: banking, supermarket, car dealer) and find what you are looking for. The concept of access is equally important in a B2B context – many B2B firms find accessibility more important than best price or best product. FedEx Corporation became a leading express delivery company by providing unique services such as time-definite delivery of consignment, overnight consignment delivery, Internet consignment tracking system, money-back guarantees and proof of delivery service.[16]

Amazon and Dollar General, two retailers, illustrate the new meaning of access. Amazon is an operationally excellent company that has built its entire business model on accessibility. The company's website is easy to locate and navigate and includes many value-added services, demonstrating that the new definition of access encompasses more than shopping. Amazon not only provides access to books or CDs, it also provides access to a community through such services as book reviews by other customers. In the physical world, Dollar General has also successfully captured this new notion of access by focusing on ease of internal navigation in its nearly 5,000 stores: 'We need to be quick-in and quick-out', says Bob Carpenter, the company's chief administrative officer:

> Our stores have to be about 6,500 to 7,500 square feet in size, because when you walk into the store, you should be able to stand in the door and see every part of the store – nothing blocking your view, so that you can see what you want, get it and go out.[17]

Access and service quality

Access is a value attribute that fewer firms have used, but it's been around for a long time – specifically, since the 1980s, when service quality emerged as a major issue for service firms. When quality management boomed, service companies found it difficult to apply the product quality concepts to their organization. In contrast to manufacturing, service organizations produce a product that is intangible – and its intangibility makes defining service quality difficult. In addition to tangible factors, service quality is often defined by perceptual factors. Despite these challenges, academic researchers introduced SERVQUAL – an instrument for measuring customer perceptions of service quality that has been widely used by service organizations from many different industries. SERVQUAL measures the gap between customer expectations and experience; the instrument uses twenty-two items that capture five quality dimensions:

- *Tangibles* comprise the appearance of physical facilities, such as the room furnishings and the appearance of personnel.
- *Reliability* characterizes the seller's ability to supply the outputs at the stated level dependably and accurately.
- *Responsiveness* relates to the organization's willingness to help customers and provide prompt service.
- *Assurance* refers to the seller's ability to deliver the output, specifically in terms of the knowledge, politeness and courtesy of the employees and their ability to convey trust and confidence.
- *Empathy* indicates the seller's willingness and ability to provide individualized attention and to respond to individual customer desires.[18]

Operational excellence companies that dominate on access focus on 'reliability' and 'responsiveness' as the main elements of their value proposition. In general, these companies tell their customers exactly when services will be performed (responsiveness), give prompt service (responsiveness), are always willing to help (responsiveness), will do what they promise (reliability), will perform the service right the first time (reliability), will provide their services at the time they promise to do so (reliability), and will insist on error-free records (reliability). On the other hand, customer-intimacy firms will strive to excel on the items 'assurance' and 'empathy'.

Operational excellence and customer centricity

Although most operational excellence firms stress a combination of price, quality and hassle-free service in their value proposition, there are some that have used the principles of operational excellence to dominate on access without offering a low price. Companies such as Dell, the French insurance broker Sofaxis and Belron® (the world's leading automotive glass repair and replacement company) are all examples of the access–plus operational excellence model.

Case study: customer centricity and operational excellence at Belron®

Belron® is an international automotive glass repair and replacement corporation with business units in more than thirty countries. All these business units differentiate themselves from the competition by becoming world-famous for customer service. This ability to consistently deliver a great customer experience has enabled the company to grow continuously over the last 10 years. Belron® focuses on two kinds of customers.

For motorists/vehicle owners, Belron® offers a 24/7 service in which the company strives to serve every customer when and where they'd like their glass fixed. The customer can choose to go to any Belron® location, or have a mechanic come to them. The company can repair a chip or crack, and it also has all necessary spare parts in stock for replacement. It offers fast and good-quality service with warranty. Belron® even handles insurance claims.

For corporate customers – regarded as partners, which include the major insurance and fleet companies – Belron® offers significant cost savings (for repair service, as one example), enabling the company to build long-lasting relationships based on trust, quality of service and same-page thinking.

Case study: an access-plus player in the French insurance brokerage industry

Sofaxis is France's leading provider of insurance for local-authority and hospital staff. It helps companies deal with their people management problems by offering group personnel insurance (such as death, sickness and accidents at work) and individual insurance (additional health insurance, additional pension schemes, accident and death coverage for elected representatives). Sofaxis differentiates itself from its competitors by offering, not only insurance coverage, but related services as well, such as advice on HR issues, absenteeism benchmarks, medical control and reintegration of personnel. In this way, the company has moved from managing the coverage of risks of absenteeism in local authorities towards the prevention of such risks. The company is insurer to one out of every two local governments and one out of every three hospitals, or three-quarters of all local-authority and hospital staff. Sofaxis is praised by its customers for its expertise in HR and for its exceptionally fast service. The company has always tried to maintain its original spirit of 'natural quality'. Its original quality slogans are still applicable: 'Answer the phone before the third ring!' and 'When a customer has a problem, resolve it that day'.[19]

Many people would regard these three companies as great examples of customer-intimate companies. But they're not! Companies such as Dell, Belron® and Sofaxis are customer-centric, but not customer intimate.

Most managers confuse customer centricity with customer intimacy. The two concepts, however, are very different. Customer centricity means that a company focuses on the needs and behaviours of its customers, rather than having an internal orientation. Customer centricity is about 'outside–in' thinking: it's about standing in the customer's shoes and viewing everything the company does through the customer's eyes. All too often, companies pay too much attention to their own bottom line and they neglect the customer.

Obviously, customer-intimacy firms are customer-centric: they integrate the customer's perspective into all their activities. That is also the case for operational excellence companies. Operational excellence companies also start from the customer perspective – this is one of the main principles of TQM. Better quality should be defined by the customer, and everybody in the organization should be aware of what the customers' needs and requirements are. Therefore, the difference between operational excellence and customer-intimacy firms is not their approach to strategy – they both adopt an outside–in perspective, and they are both customer-centric. The difference is in their value proposition: customer-intimacy firms win in the market through a service and relationship orientation. They offer great services to their *best* customers and reward the loyalty of these customers in many ways.

Operational excellence companies win by offering the best price or by turning a hassle into a positive experience. Operationally excellent companies do not have best customers: all customers are best customers, and all these customers receive the same great service. Note that 'service' here means a fast, easy and hassle-free service experience. Recall that Crawford and Mathews defined service as 'what a company does in addition before, during, and after the sale'. Companies such as Dell, Belron® and Sofaxis focus more on offering a fast and easy service experience. They are reliable and responsive, but customers usually receive the same standard treatment (the exception being the unhappy customers, who are often going through a service recovery programme). Some access-plus players offer extra services to some of their customers (see Figure 8.5). For true customer-intimate firms such as Château*form'*, Four Seasons Hotels and SIA, there is no standard treatment. Customer-intimacy firms go for the specific, not the generic.

How are those companies able to combine the efficiency of operational excellence with such a service orientation? Belron® and Sofaxis are highly process-oriented organizations that instill a quality mindset throughout the entire organization – very typical for operationally excellent organizations. They have been able to achieve their reputation for service in the market because of a hassle-free, convenient service experience. In comparison with a standard car repair shop, Belron®'s operating companies offer only two services, nothing else. This very narrow focus gives them the aura of being specialists in the market, while it also allows them to streamline and optimize all their internal processes, which drives

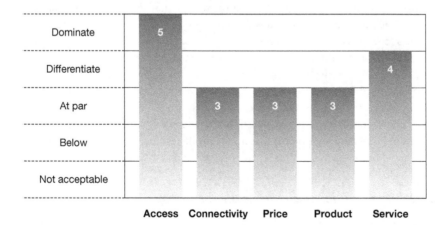

FIGURE 8.5 The value proposition of Dell, Belron® and Sofaxis

costs down and accelerates the speed of service for the customer. Sofaxis is also very focused, with a very specific target group and a limited product offering. It does not insure property, liability or any other risks; it only insures people-related risks.

Operational excellence and mass customization

However, Dell has gone one step further than Sofaxis and Belron®. Through its direct model, Dell builds every desktop, laptop and server to order (instead of in product batches to a forecast) and customizes every computer to be exactly what the customer wants. Dell has been able to blend low cost with customization. Based on this case, management scholars and consultants have argued that firms with a hybrid strategy – a combination of low cost and differentiation – are no longer considered to be 'stuck in the middle'; firms no longer have to choose. Here, I disagree, however. Let me explain why.

Advances in IT, flexible manufacturing systems, and management methods have allowed producers to customize large volumes of goods or services at low cost. In this way, customers can reap the benefits of customized products with relatively low prices. This trend is called 'mass customization' – and it's very difficult to achieve. Firms that aspire to become mass customizers must excel at TQM. In that way, mass customization is a logical extension of what operationally excellent firms are working on: cost management, process management and quality management. Mass customization adds one important element to all this: it adds customization to mass production.

The key to low-cost, efficient, high-volume customization is *modularity*. When you think about modularity, think of LEGO blocks. What can you build with LEGO blocks? The answer is: 'anything that you want'. You have that large number of modules with different sizes, shapes and colours and this simple, elegant system for snapping them together. That is what mass customizers do to their operations. They create modularity in their production and have a modular product design.[20]

Mass customizers pay a lot of attention to product design; 80 per cent of a product's lifetime cumulative cost is designed into the product and is very difficult to remove later. At the same time, mass customizers design products or services specifically to meet the needs of a particular customer. Some companies involve the customer even at the design stage; other mass customizers enable a final product to be assembled from a predetermined set of standard components. I won't go into much greater detail on this topic – there are different mass-customization strategies, and the challenges of mass customization are extensively described in specialized literature – but my main point is that mass customizers use concepts of operational excellence, not customer intimacy, to compete in the marketplace.

Checklist: 'operational excellence and best access'

Does your company aim to win in the market by offering a hassle-free purchase and delivery experience?

1   Do you stress the importance of access in your value proposition? How convenient is it to do business with you? Are your conditions much more favourable than those of your competitors?

2   How reliable are you as a supplier? Do you have the best rates for order fulfilment? Do you perform the service right the first time?

3   How responsive are you as a supplier? Do you have a well-trained customer support or service operations staff to help customers quickly? Are you always willing to help, or do you have a long list of excuses that your service staff use every day?

4   Are you really customer-centric? Do you take the customer's perspective in all that you do?

5   Have you built modularity into your offering, so that customers get a customized product or service?

Key learning points

Understanding operational excellence is key for companies that want to develop and implement a successful business strategy centred around 'best price' or 'best access'. However, the concept's meaning has evolved over time. Treacy and Wiersema defined 'operational excellence' as a specific strategic approach to the production and delivery of products and services that helps companies to lead their industry in price and convenience. Managers typically think of the pure price players when they think about operationally excellent companies. In this chapter, I have explained that there are two other formats of operational excellence: the price-plus model and the access-plus model.

Although operationally excellent firms might differ in how they position thems-elves in the market – the three formats all pursue a different value proposition (see Table 8.2) – the operating and management models of these firms share a number of common characteristics. Companies that pursue an operational-excellence opera-ting model pay significant attention to principles of cost management, quality management and process management. A small number of operationally excellent companies have become mass customizers.

TABLE 8.2 Operational excellence formats and value attributes

	Format 1: pure price players	Format 2: price-plus players	Format 3: access-plus players
Dominating value attribute	Price/access	Price	Access
Differentiating value attribute	Access/price	Product, service or connectivity	Service, connectivity or product
Examples	ING Direct USA Ryanair/easyJet	IKEA Zara	Dell Belron®

In the next chapter, I will explain what it takes to be an operationally excellent company.

Notes

1 Womack, J. P., and Jones, D. T. (1996) *Lean Thinking*, Simon & Schuster, New York.
2 Treacy, M., and Wiersema, F. (1993) 'Customer Intimacy and Other Value Disciplines', *Harvard Business Review*, January–February, 85.
3 Ryanair website, available at: www.ryanair.com/en/news/free-flight-would-you-stand (accessed 27 May 2013).
4 Grant, R. M. (2008) *Contemporary Strategy Analysis* (6th edn), Blackwell, Malden, MA, pp. 228–35.
5 Ibid.
6 Crawford, F., and Mathews, R. (2001) *The Myth of Excellence: Why Great Companies Never Try to Be the Best at Everything*, Crown Business, New York, p. 43.
7 Ibid., pp. 47–9.
8 Brandes, D. (2005) 'Is Aldi Really that Special?', *ECR Journal*, 5 (1), 32.
9 Degraeve, Z., and Roodhooft, F. (2001) 'A Smarter Way to Buy', *Harvard Business Review*, June, pp. 22–3.
10 Toyota website, previously available at: www.toyotainbusiness.com/fleet_content/cost/tco/index.aspx (accessed 15 July 2011; no longer available).
11 Automotive.com website, available at: www.automotive.com/best-cars/lowest-cost-of-ownership-vehicles/page10.html (accessed 15 July 2011).
12 Ireland, R. D., Hoskisson, R. E., and Hitt, M. A. (2009) *The Management of Strategy: Concepts and Cases* (8th edn), South-Western Cengage Learning, Mason, OH, p. 144.
13 Linguri, S., and Kumar, N. (2005) 'ZARA: Responsive, High Speed, Affordable Fashion', *London Business School Case Study*, 305–8-1, p. 18.
14 Reyntjens, W., Delalieux, F., Vermeir, S., Ooreel, F., and Uhoda, J. (2011) 'Zara Operational Excellence Strategy', *Assignment for Vlerick Course Strategic Management*, Vlerick Business School.
15 Maertens, N., Tack, J., De Tant, G., Goethals, B. and Ancaer, Y. (2011) 'IKEA: Operational Excellence', *Assignment for Vlerick Course Strategic Management*, Vlerick Business School.
16 Sinha, A. (2009) 'FedEx: The Cutting Edge', *IBS Research Center Case Study*, 606–034–1, pp. 1–27.
17 Crawford and Mathews, *The Myth of Excellence*, p. 113.
18 Parasuraman, A., Zeithaml, Valarie A., and Berry, Leonard L. (1991) 'Refinement and reassessment of the SERVQUAL scale', *Journal of Retailing*, 67 (4), 420–50.
19 Dexia Sofaxis (2002) 'European Quality Award – Dexia Sofaxis 2002 Submission', *Dexia Sofaxis Report*, Bourges, France.
20 Pine, J. B. II (1993) *Mass Customization: The New Frontier in Business Competition*, Harvard Business School, Boston, MA.

9

WHAT DOES IT TAKE TO BE OPERATIONALLY EXCELLENT?

How operationally excellent firms implement strategy

Setting direction and creating clarity about it are crucial for success. Firms that want to implement a strategy built around operational excellence need to know what they will promise to their customers. For operational excellence firms, this is often more than just offering a low price. That was the topic of Chapter 8.

This chapter focuses on the actions and behaviours that are required to implement a strategy built around operational excellence. Achieving true operational excellence is difficult and complex, as Liker and Morgan noticed when they studied the Toyota Way: 'The journey is far more complex than applying a few tools or holding classes. It truly is a cultural transformation. You need to start on the learning journey and then keep going and never stop.'[1] But, if you choose operational excellence as your operating model, and you take actions that support that strategy, you start to develop a competitive advantage that can last for years. In analogy with the Product Leadership Pentagon, we developed an Operational Excellence Pentagon, which I will present in this chapter. This pentagon prescribes what actions to take to create a well-aligned operational excellence organization.

At the same time, winning companies are able to create commitment throughout the entire organization – and I also find this characteristic in many successful operationally excellent companies. So, in this chapter, I will outline how operationally excellent firms commit their organization to turn their strategy into results.

The Operational Excellence Pentagon: identifying the fifteen core activities that constitute true operational excellence

Strategy implementation means creating alignment and having a committed workforce that is going the extra mile to implement your strategy. This is one of the core premises of this book. For operationally excellent firms, alignment

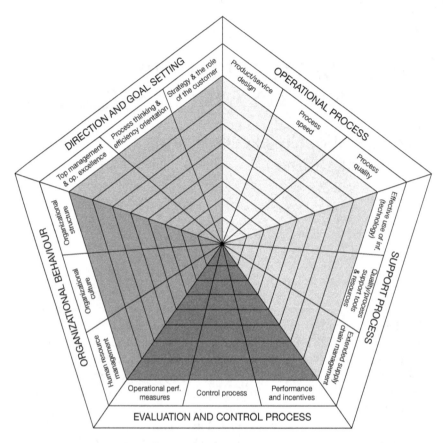

FIGURE 9.1 Operational Excellence Pentagon

means setting up a whole range of actions around the core competitive themes of efficiency, low price and great access. Although I have identified three different formats of operational excellence, the management and operational systems of all of these firms are strikingly similar. The Operational Excellence Pentagon presents the fifteen core activities that constitute true operational excellence.

The Operational Excellence Pentagon: research background

In 2011, I embarked on a research project with my research team to find out how the concept of operational excellence has evolved in the first decade of the new millennium and what the main management practices of these operational excellence firms are.[2] We read many academic papers, management books and reports, analysed about twenty case studies of well-known operational excellence firms in great detail, and developed a questionnaire to collect data on operational excellence practices and performance.[3]

We collected data from ninety-eight management teams of business units pursuing an operational excellence strategy. The data allowed us to calculate percentiles for each company on the fifteen items of the Operational Excellence Pentagon. We also asked these managers to benchmark their company's revenue growth and profitability relative to their competitors. Using the performance data, we classified firms as top performers (eight), average performers (eighty-three) and bottom performers (seven).

We linked our alignment data with the performance data to find out whether there was a correlation between alignment and financial performance. First, we calculated average percentiles for top, average and bottom performers (see Figure 9.2). Then, we examined how many times a company had an item with a percentile higher than seventy-five. The maximum score is fifteen. We calculated average scores for the top, average and bottom performers (see Figure 9.3).

As in our product-leadership sample, the results indicate that the top performers – companies that grow their revenues faster than their competitors and that have a higher profitability – are more aligned than the average and bottom performers. Figure 9.2 shows that top performers have scores in the sixty-fourth percentile, whereas the percentiles for the average performers and the bottom performers are forty-eight and thirty-six, respectively. Figure 9.3 indicates that, on average, top performers have 6.38 out of 15 items with a percentile higher than seventy-five. The scores for average and bottom performers are 3.48 and 1.86, respectively. Further analyses reveal that there is a significant correlation between the financial performance and the two alignment measures.

Let us examine the core activities of the most successful operationally excellent firms in greater detail.

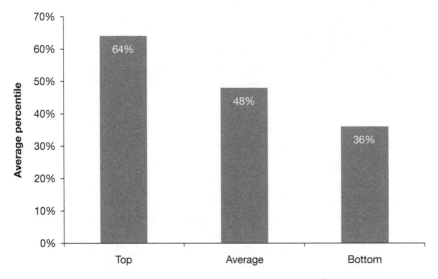

FIGURE 9.2 Average percentiles for top, average and bottom performers

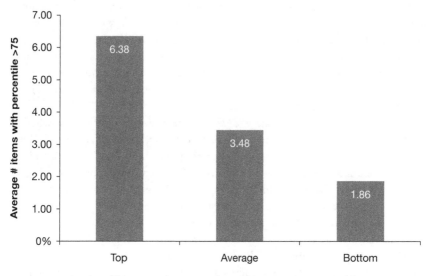

FIGURE 9.3 Number of items with percentile >75 for top, average and bottom performers

Direction and goal setting: a long-term focus on process excellence supported by top management

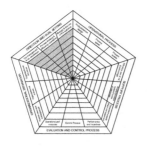

Direction and goal setting involves all of the processes and actions that lead to the formulation and communication of the organization's mission and vision, and the translation of concrete strategies into clear performance goals. How do operational excellence companies use direction- and goal-setting activities to achieve process excellence that allows them to offer a value proposition based on quality, convenience and price?

Top management and operational excellence

A clear process orientation is a key differentiating characteristic that sets operationally excellent firms apart from other companies. Processes are the beating heart of every company that strives to be operationally excellent. A process can be defined as a specific group of activities and subordinate tasks that result in the performance of a service that is of value to the customer.[4]

In order to achieve process excellence, it is crucial that top management be completely aligned on the company's process orientation and that they actively and visibly support this. Too much results orientation at this level is harmful, because results-oriented managers typically want to see quick financial wins. Process-oriented managers are more patient, and they firmly believe that investments in people and processes will pay off and lead to the desired performance. These managers realize that, in order to move faster, you first need the right operating systems. Toyota's ultimate goal is to be Number 1, not in sales or volume, but in quality on a sustained basis: 'Unless we enhance quality today, we cannot hope for growth in the future.'[5]

The story goes that, when he opened his first McDonald's in 1955 in Des Plaines, Illinois, Ray Kroc made the operating system his passion and the company's anchor. Whereas competitors focused on recruiting franchisees (whom they promptly ignored) and identifying the cheapest suppliers, Kroc focused on quality and building a unique operating system.[6]

In an operational excellence firm, top management needs to have a thorough understanding of the company's operational processes. They need to be familiar with the daily work in order to solve problems and take the right decisions. At Toyota, this principle is called *genchi genbutsu* – which means that you cannot be sure you really understand any part of a business problem unless you go and see it for yourself firsthand.

Process thinking and efficiency orientation

No matter what their formula for combining price, reliability and hassle-free service is, minimizing total cost and improving efficiency are important goals for every unit in the company. Operationally excellent companies assign a strategic role to the operations function, and they consider these operational goals to be the company goals. The goal is not just to reduce costs and to have higher profit margins: operationally excellent firms emphasize efficiency, because it is a source of competitive advantage. That's why these firms expect every department to contribute to some of the five operations performance objectives: quality, speed, dependability, flexibility and cost.

Figure 9.4 tells us that a well-functioning operations department helps companies provide better quality, speed, lower costs, more on-time deliveries and more flexibility to their customers. Having better quality also improves the speed, cost and dependability for internanl customers. Better quality means fewer mistakes, which means costs are saved, speed of response increases, and dependability (which means 'being on time') increases. For operationally excellent firms, these operations goals have become company-wide goals that are translated into every department.

The management literature emphasizes the role of process quality and process speed in a company's competitive advantage. Operations specialists define product or process quality as 'conformance to specifications'. The fewer defects a process produces, the less rework and reconfiguration are required, which results in higher efficiency and speedier processes – with 'zero defect' as the ultimate goal. A popular methodology that is often used to achieve this objective of process quality is

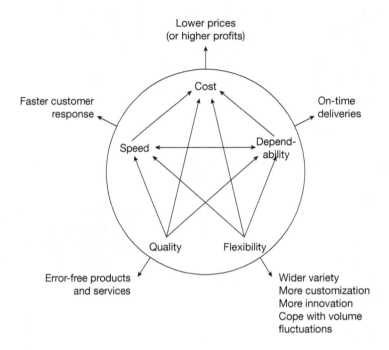

Lower prices
(or higher profits)

Cost

Faster customer
response

On-time
deliveries

Speed

Depend-
ability

Quality   Flexibility

Error-free products
and services

Wider variety
More customization
More innovation
Cope with volume
fluctuations

FIGURE 9.4 The five operations performance objectives

Source: Slack *et al.* (2010)[7]

Six Sigma. Corporations such as Motorola and GE were among the first to launch company-wide Six Sigma programmes.

Process speed is another important performance objective. This concerns the time elapsed between customers (both internal and external) requesting products or services and receiving them. Eliminating waste in all its forms is the basis for accelerating process speed. Shorter lead times and flexible production lines result in higher quality, better customer responsiveness, better productivity and better utilization of equipment and space. The Lean management philosophy – mainly derived from the TPS – forms the basis for achieving this end and has been adopted by many companies from a variety of industries, even service industries.

Strategy and the role of the customer

So, it is clear that, in operationally excellent firms, the process and efficiency orientation helps to deliver customer value, not just profits. Therefore, consistently bringing the 'voice of the customer' into the company's processes – and actively acting upon it – is a crucial element in maintaining operational excellence leadership. This principle is not new – it's one of the core principles of TQM. The following case study is an example of how eBay uses customer input:

Case study: customer input at eBay

We rely on the feedback of our users for almost all changes to the site. Our users know the site really well – some are on the site up to eight hours a day. As our Collectibles team was looking to restructure the ever-expanding category, we tapped the expertise of our users on how they use the site. The result is a Collectibles page that is much like a portal tailored to the collector. The updated structure is more convenient and easy to use, while better reflecting the trading areas that are important to our users.[8]

In addition to drawing on customers and their internal organization for input, operationally excellent firms also pursue close partnerships with their suppliers and distributors. Providing high-quality products and services conveniently at attractive prices is impossible without focusing on quality and efficiency throughout the entire supply chain. Operationally excellent firms use long-term partnerships – not market transactions – to get better inputs faster. Partnerships are pursued because, in many cases, vertical integration of the entire supply chain is not feasible or desirable, and pure market supply relationships do not provide the degree of closeness and involvement that's needed.

Checklist: 'operational excellence and your direction- and goal-setting processes'

Are your direction- and goal-setting processes aligned with the operational-excellence operating model? You can use the following questions to check whether you have the appropriate direction- and goal-setting processes in place to support a strategy that allows you to be the most efficient company in your industry:

1   Does your top management have a process view of the organization? Do they emphasize process excellence as a key priority for the entire organization? Is your top management team aligned on the company's process orientation? Do they actively and visibly support this?
2   Does the operations function play a crucial role in your strategy? Do you recognize some of the operations performance goals in your overall strategic goals? To what extent are all of the people in your organization familiar with these strategic goals?
3   Why are you pursuing efficiency initiatives? Is there a clear advantage for your customers? To what extent do you bring in the voice of the customer? And do you also involve your suppliers and distributors in your efficiency and process orientation?

Operational processes: a strategic role for the operations function

Operational processes involve all activities, from the creation to the delivery of a product or service. In the Lean terminology, this is called the 'value stream'. What are the core operational processes for operationally excellent firms? Our research revealed that operationally excellent firms pay a lot of attention to product or service design, process speed and product and process quality.

Product/service design

Product and service design is a crucial part of the operational processes in operationally excellent firms, as it largely determines the costs of products and services. In fact, product/service design not only determines the materials and resources needed to produce the product or deliver the service, but it also determines factors such as machine changeover times and other important, process-related costs. By the time a product reaches the production stage, 95 per cent of its cost has already been defined – so it's very difficult to remove this cost at a later stage.[9]

Complexity has a significant impact on a company's bottom line. This is also true in the design stage. Operationally excellent firms are very careful not to provide excessive offerings, as this increases complexity. Operationally excellent firms use standardization, commonality and modularization to reduce that complexity. Standardizing products, services, processes and materials allows companies to restrict variety to that which has real value for the end customer. This is a message well understood by Zara, which uses many standardized input materials for most of its products.

Another way to reduce complexity is to use common elements across multiple products and services. The more different products and services can be based on common components, the less complex it is to produce them.

Modularization makes use of standardized sub-components of a product or service that can be put together in many different ways. These standardized modules, or sub-assemblies, can be produced in higher volume, thereby reducing their cost. The Dell model was a high-volume, assemble-to-order model of an inherently modular product. Not only do standardization, commonality and modularization help to reduce costs, they also improve quality, flexibility, speed and responsiveness.

Recently, management thinkers have applied Lean concepts to the product development function. The goal is to reduce development cycle times and costs by having cross-functional teams thinking and working on new products and considering the implications of new products, not just for the R&D department, but for the entire value chain.

Process speed

As discussed earlier, process speed and efficiency are core priorities in any operationally excellent organization. The main techniques and practices that are used to achieve these targets come under the umbrella of 'Lean manufacturing and Lean (services) management'. The goal of Lean is to accelerate the velocity of any process by reducing waste in all its forms. Based on the famous TPS, lean manufacturing was defined as:

> A way of thinking that focuses on making the product flow through value-adding processes without interruption (one-piece flow), a 'pull' system that cascades back from customer demand by replenishing only what the next operation takes away at short intervals, and a culture in which everyone is striving continuously to improve.[10]

It is important to note that Lean is used in customer-intimacy firms and product leaders as well, but there it is often restricted to the manufacturing or operations department. This is different in operational excellence firms. Taiichi Ohno, the founder of TPS, puts it like this: 'All we are doing is looking at the time line from the moment the customer gives us an order to the point when we collect the cash.'[11] In other words, Lean is applied across a company's entire value chain.

Lean is a well-known concept in the management literature, and so I will concentrate here on the most important elements of Lean management, which Jeffrey Liker has summarized well in his book, *The Toyota Way: 14 Management Principles from the World's Greatest Manufacturer*. Lean is about eliminating 'non-value-added waste' in your processes. Although some waste may be needed – e.g. buffer inventory to keep the bottleneck machine operating at maximum capacity – most waste in a process does not add any value for the customer and needs to be removed. The Lean literature identifies eight types of non-value-added waste, of which overproduction, excess inventory and waiting time are considered to be the most important.

A fundamental concept in establishing Lean processes is the achievement of 'flow' – which is defined as the progressive achievement of the activities that are required to deliver a product or service as it proceeds along the value stream. Simply stated, flow means that you see products or materials moving. In a services environment, companies try to establish a flow of information (instead of raw materials and parts). Achieving flow in a company's processes requires a clear process orientation, as opposed to the traditional department structure. Only when processes are the determining factor in organizing work can flow be identified, visualized and continuously improved.

Case study: 'flow' at Walmart

No company has been more efficient at improving its supply chain than Walmart. In 2007, the movement of goods was supported by 129 distribution centres and close to 7,100 tractors and 44,500 trailers. Each centre was a well-oiled machine: on one side of the building, trailer trucks dropped off boxes of goods from thousands of suppliers. These were then fed onto a conveyor belt at each dock. These smaller belts fed onto a bigger belt, like streams feeding into a powerful river. As the Walmart river flowed along, an electric eye read the bar code on each box on its way to the other side of the building. There, the river parted again into a hundred streams. Electric arms from each stream reached out and guided the boxes toward an awaiting truck, ready to transfer the products to a particular Walmart store somewhere in the country. Suppliers had to adapt their packaging and delivery routines to fit Walmart's supply chain. The message to suppliers was clear: You have a 30-second delivery window. Either you are there, or you are out.[12]

A second key element in the achievement of process speed is 'pull' production. When supply does not match demand, either inventory builds up or there is a shortage of the requested goods or services. With a pull production system, goods and services are only produced when there is demand for them. This is the opposite of a push production system, where the production of goods and services is based on a schedule – according to projected customer demand – that has been made in advance. The essence of pull production is to let the downstream stages in a process, operation or supply network pull items through the system, rather than having the items pushed through the system by the supplying stages.

Pulling materials, parts and components through the company's processes eliminates inventories, because everything that is produced is based on customer demand. This is the ideal state of pull production and just-in-time manufacturing: it means giving the customer (who could also be an internal customer) what he or she wants, when it is wanted and in the demanded amount or quantity. Ideally, this translates into true one-piece flow. In practice, however, it is almost impossible to achieve this – some inventory is usually needed to achieve flow and to keep processes running at optimal speed. At Toyota, this principle is called 'flow where you can, pull where you must'.

In addition to waste elimination and pull production, a third element in increasing process speed is capacity management. The capacity of an operation can be defined as 'the maximum level of value-added activity that a process can achieve under normal operating conditions'. It is a misconception that companies need to operate at maximum capacity (keeping their assets working all the time) to build efficient and effective processes. Most likely, each step in the process has a different maximum capacity. One process step will have the smallest capacity and will limit the speed at which the other steps are able to operate. This weakest link – called the bottleneck or constraint – limits and determines the pace of the other process steps and the possible throughput of the process. There is no point in pushing the other steps to their capacity limits, as this will only build up inventory.

Another important capacity consideration is the creation of a level production schedule. When production follows customer demand (which is the case with pull production), there is always the risk of peaks and lows, which lead to huge jumps in production workload, with employees being overloaded or almost idle, respectively. This type of waste needs to be overcome by ensuring a level production schedule. The operations management literature has developed techniques to achieve more level production schedules, although the best situation is to have a level demand.

Product and process quality

In addition to working on product/process design and optimizing process speed, operationally excellent firms focus intently on managing product and process quality. To deliver on the promise of consistently high and reliable quality, operational excellence companies strive for zero defects in their processes. Whereas traditional quality thinkers assume that there is an optimum amount of quality effort, operationally excellent firms believe that mistakes and failures can never be tolerated, and they strive to reduce all quality costs by preventing defects from occurring in the first place.

In order to manage product and process quality, operationally excellent firms use many of the TQM principles that I presented earlier: defining quality from a customer's perspective, emphasizing the prevention of quality problems and making everybody in the organization responsible for quality. In pursuing the goal of zero-defect processes, companies need to make sure that any quality problems and defects are detected and fixed immediately, before they enter into a following process step. When a problem occurs, the process (or a part of it) needs to be stopped, to solve the problem and prevent more defects from being produced. At Toyota, this principle is known as *Jidoka*, and the following case study shows how this works:

Case study: Jidoka at Toyota

> *In the case of machines, we build devices into them that detect abnormalities and automatically stop the machine upon such an occurrence. In the case of humans, we give them the power to push buttons or pull cords – called 'andon cords' – which can bring our entire assembly line to a halt. Every team member has the responsibility to stop the line every time they see something that is out of standard. That is how we put the responsibility for quality in the hands of our team members. They feel the responsibility – they feel the power. They know they count.*
>
> *(Alex Warren, former Executive Vice President,*
> *Toyota Motor Corporation, Kentucky)*[13]

The principle is simple, but very effective: bring problems to the surface, make them visible through easily noticeable devices and techniques, and go to work immediately on countermeasures.

In addition, operationally excellent companies apply techniques and methods to reduce the variety of components that affect quality in their processes. Variety kills efficiency in a company's production processes. Unless the company is able to mass-customize its products or services, operationally excellent companies reject variety, because it burdens the business with costs.

Furthermore, operationally excellent companies try to reduce the variability in their manufacturing and business processes. The most popular methodology that is used to reduce variability is called Six Sigma, which can be defined as: 'a disciplined methodology of defining, measuring, analysing, improving and controlling the quality in every one of the company's products, processes and transactions, with the ultimate goal of virtually eliminating all defects'.[14] The methodology uses a number of measures and statistical techniques to assess the performance of processes and expresses this in terms of defects per million opportunities (DPM). Six Sigma quality reflects 3.4 DPM, which approximates zero defects. Implementing a full Six Sigma programme involves a huge organizational change, but this is essentially about launching a process orientation with a quality mindset.

Standardization is a crucial feature in the operational processes of every company wishing to achieve an operational excellence status. Besides being a key product design ingredient and a contributor to the creation of process flow, standardization of work is also an essential element of process quality. 'Standardization of work' might make one think of very tightly defined work specifications and an environment in which workers are regarded as machines that need to be made as efficient as possible, through the manipulations of engineers and autocratic managers, but that is not the kind of standardization of work that helps operational excellence companies achieve their quality targets. These firms involve their people in defining the standardized work. Implementing standardization thus implies finding a balance between providing employees with standardized assets, tools and rigid procedures and providing the freedom to innovate and be creative to meet the challenging targets for cost, quality and delivery in a consistent way. It requires standards to be specific enough to be useful guides, but also general enough to allow for some flexibility.

Case study: the importance of standards at McDonald's

Standardization at McDonald's can be viewed as 'freedom within a framework'. The framework strengthens McDonald's operational excellence and brand around the world by setting standards for, among other things, product ingredients, restaurant cleanliness and the use of the Golden Arches logo. McDonald's determines store layout and specifies seating, lighting fixtures, music, napkins and cleaning soap. Company procedures even cover bag folding and presentation.[15]

McDonald's has developed an operations manual of 750 detailed pages. It describes how operators should make milkshakes, grill hamburgers and fry potatoes. It specifies exact cooking times and temperature settings and precise portions for all food items.[16] Freedom applies to everything else, based on the belief that those closest to the customer are best positioned to make decisions.[17]

Checklist: 'operational excellence and your operational processes'

To what extent are your operational processes aligned with the operational excellence model? The following questions may help you verify whether you have the appropriate operational processes in place:

1   Does your organization pay attention to the design of its products or services? What do you do to reduce complexity in the design phase? Do you involve people from different areas and functions, including suppliers, in the design phase? Do you apply lean thinking in the design phase?
2   Has your company introduced lean management in all its departments? Does lean thinking extend beyond the operations or manufacturing department?
3   How important is product and process quality in your organization? What methods does your company use to improve quality? Do you use TQM or Six Sigma principles to improve the product/process quality in your organization?

Support processes: streamlining tasks and operations and supporting quality-driven efforts throughout the supply chain

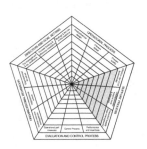

What support processes do operationally excellent organizations use to increase coordination and process speed and quality? My research has revealed that operationally excellent organizations make extensive use of IT to improve coordination across departments and streamline tasks. Furthermore, I find that operationally excellent organizations use all sort of tools and resources to support quality-driven efforts throughout the supply chain.

Effective use of information (technology)

Operationally excellent firms use information (technology) for several purposes. They use it to automate routine work. Through the use of technology and information systems, repetitive, labour-intensive processes can be automated to provide lower costs and more consistent quality. Computer-controlled manufacturing operations have replaced workers for routine machining, processing and assembly operations. Computerized stock control systems help update stock records, reflecting the position, status and possible change of value in stock every time a transaction takes place. Computerized point-of-sale systems are used to collect item-level data in real time. Whatever the automation application, operationally excellent companies are frontrunners in the application of these tools and systems.

Operationally excellent organizations are particularly adept at using data and information from all levels and all parts of the organization in order to steer, coordinate, measure, review and, ultimately, improve processes and performance. The enterprise resource planning (ERP) system – an integrated software system – is a company cornerstone, facilitating information flows between various business functions such as operations, HR management and finance. However, ERP systems can integrate organizations substantially only if they are implemented within a sound business process architecture,[18] and that is one of the capabilities of true operational excellence firms. For example, Amazon and Charles Schwab (the American brokerage and banking company) were pioneers in investing heavily in interfaces and internal systems to build integrated front- and back-end systems to serve customers better.

Operationally excellent organizations use information sharing to support the flow of end-to-end, core processes. Information from both inside and outside the organization is captured, stored and then shared across departments and chain members. Information is constantly available throughout the chain, and the sharing of information enables overall supply chain performance to be constantly improved.[19] Some firms share this information with their customers, who perceive this as an extra service offered by their supplier.

Quality and process support tools and resources

Achieving conformance quality requires a lot of work on the work floor and the creation of a particular organizational culture. Operationally excellent organizations invest in expertise to execute those business projects with great success. They allocate experts to work on processes together with line managers. Some companies have a 'Lean Office', whereas others work with Black Belts and Green Belts to run Six Sigma projects. Whatever their title, these seasoned professionals serve as catalysts to help operating units continuously improve in order to reach the company's goals. For example, when faced with the challenge of entering emerging markets, IKEA called in expatriates schooled in the best practices and nuances of the global IKEA organization.

Apart from the HR support, operationally excellent firms make extensive use of quality and process management tools and methodologies to embed the continuous improvement of processes and quality. There are many different improvement methodologies that operationally excellent companies use to help teams go through a process of intense problem-solving, to identify the root causes of defects and to put countermeasures in place after problems occur. Approaches range from four-step methodologies, such as PDCA (plan, do, check and act), to five steps, such as DMAIC (define, measure, analyse, improve and control) or DMEDI (define, measure, explore, develop and implement). Others use seven or eight steps, such as Toyota's seven-step 'practical problem-solving' process, as well as the eight-discipline 'team-oriented problem-solving' (TOPS) approach. All this shows that becoming operationally excellent requires discipline and a systematic approach to improving the organization's process capabilities.

Extended supply chain management

When discussing the direction- and goal-setting processes of operationally excellent firms, I talked about the important role of partnerships between suppliers and customers to increase overall supply chain efficiency. Operationally excellent organizations coordinate daily activities with suppliers and distributors in order to ensure that value is delivered to the customer. This often means intense sharing of information, software and hardware. For example, Walmart was one of the first companies to open up access to its sales data when it shared those data with its main suppliers (such as P&G). In exchange, Walmart expected the suppliers to proactively monitor and replenish products on a continual basis. Ultimately, such information sharing helps suppliers and distributors to obtain an overview of what is happening throughout the chain – leading to improvements in supply chain performance.

Quite often, operationally excellent firms set a series of challenging targets for quality, cycle time and process cost with their suppliers. In return, they provide extensive support to their key suppliers and distributors to help them achieve these targets. Support ranges from sharing information and providing managerial and employee expertise and knowledge to direct financial assistance. An example of this is Dell:

Case study: how Dell connects with its suppliers

Dell wants its suppliers to see data on product quality every minute of every day in order to encourage its suppliers to quickly detect problems and improve product quality. The Internet further facilitates the connections between Dell's design teams and its technology suppliers. Engineers from different companies can share the same design database, sets of notes, product road maps, specifications and metrics, so that they can work together from designing new products to launching them to the end-customer.[20]

Some operationally excellent firms intervene in the business of their supplier and work at the operating level to help the supplier develop specific skills. Toyota and IKEA do this extensively. For example, IKEA provides both technical advice and financial support to help suppliers find the best and cheapest raw materials, and it also provides support in building and managing manufacturing facilities.

Checklist: 'operational excellence and your support processes'

Do your support processes reinforce your operational excellence strategy?

1   To what extent does your organization use automation to make processes faster, cheaper or more reliable than those of your competitors? Does your organization have an enterprise-wide integrated information platform that helps coordinate and streamline processes and workflows?

2   Does your organization have a team of seasoned professionals to build process capabilities in the organization? Do these experts use process tools and methodologies to attack and eliminate waste and variability in processes and in quality?
3   Do you set efficiency targets for your suppliers or distributors? And do you provide support to your suppliers or distributors to increase overall supply chain efficiency?

Evaluation and control processes: measuring and tracking process excellence and quality

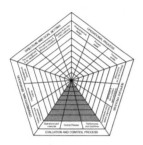

Evaluation and control processes are designed to ensure that the organization performs as planned. How do operationally excellent organizations use evaluation and control processes to create the necessary alignment within the organization? What do they measure? And how do they control their operations? Review of the literature and case-study research reveal that the evaluation and control processes of operationally excellent firms are different from those of most other organizations.

Operational performance measures

Operational excellence organizations stress rigorous efficiency, quality and cost control throughout the entire organization, and they use specific performance measures to check whether the company is on the right track. Operationally excellent organizations are masters of the performance measurement game: they continuously check customer satisfaction by measuring various aspects of the five operations performance objectives (see Table 9.1).

In their publications on the Balanced Scorecard, Bob Kaplan and David Norton have regularly presented strategy maps and key performance indicators for operational excellence firms. These authors recognize that implementing a strategy built around operational excellence requires firms to track different performance indicators to those tracked by product leaders and customer-intimate organizations.

Not only do operationally excellent organizations differ in the measures they use, they also measure a lot – measuring has become second nature to them. Carglass® Belux – the Belgian business unit of Belron®, the world's largest automotive glass repair and replacement corporation – measures customer satisfaction 80,000 times per year. The company uses a short survey that tracks ten elements of the service experience, such as ease of contact, friendliness, punctuality, quality, and so on. The company distributes the scores of each branch on a weekly basis and monitors this extensively. The goal of all these measurement activities is to

TABLE 9.1 Examples of operations performance measures

Quality	Speed	Dependability
• Number of defects per unit • Level of complaints customer • Scrap level • Warranty claims • Mean time between failures	• Customer query time • Order lead time • Frequency of delivery • Actual versus theoretical throughput time • Cycle time	• Percentage of orders delivered late • Proportion of products in stock • Mean deviation from promised arrival • Schedule adherence

Flexibility	Cost	
• Time needed to develop new products/services • Range of products/ services • Machine changeover time • Average batch size • Average capacity/ maximum capacity	• Minimum delivery time/ average delivery time • Utilization of resources • Labour productivity • Efficiency • Cost per operation hour	

Source: Slack *et al.* (2010)[21]

find ways to further improve speed and quality across the entire supply chain. At DHL, one of the leading global contract logistics players, lead time (along with other important key performance indicators) is continuously measured and projected in real time on big, flat screens, throughout the facility.

Control process

The control processes of an operationally excellent organization can best be summarized by Deming's famous Plan–Do–Check–Act cycle. Operationally excellent firms have defined standards for their most important processes. They set stretch goals for these processes and then check whether the targets have been achieved. Their well-developed control process is a core element of their management system, and it is audited regularly. Operationally excellent firms also maintain their operational measurement system better than their competitors do. This calls for 'double-loop learning' – the process by which managers question their underlying assumptions and reflect on whether the theory under which they have been operating is still consistent with current observations.

In addition to using performance information for continuous improvement, operationally excellent organizations excel at selecting and ensuring the effective use of key comparative data and information, to challenge operational and strategic decision-making and to promote process innovation. These data are obtained by benchmarking – identifying processes and results that represent best practices and performance for similar activities.

Performance and incentives

In operationally excellent firms, cost control is key, but that doesn't mean that operationally excellent firms pay low wages. On the contrary. Companies such as Aldi, Nucor Corporation and ING Direct USA pay higher wages than the industry average. The fact that their employees are expected to perform to high standards justifies the higher salaries.

Operationally excellent organizations encourage teamwork and the generation by teams of ideas and solutions to problems. They recognize that often it is the integrated set of ideas about plant layout, assembly-line operations or office procedures that make the major savings, rather than isolated, incremental ideas. When the ideas are generated by teams, implementation becomes much easier for all concerned. Recognition programmes can take the form of non-cash and/or a cash complement to reward outstanding team-based contributions.

Apart from individual contingent and team pay, financial reward schemes within operationally excellent organizations also typically include profit-sharing and gain-sharing to recognize collective effort. Gain-sharing is based, not only on successful organizational performance, but also on the specific improvements made in organizational performance (which are measured using productivity indicators) and improvements related to quality, delivery and cost-reduction performance measures. In this way, bonuses can be related specifically to performance improvements that are within the employees' control.[22]

Nucor Corporation, a large steel producer, places performance-based compensation at the heart of its organization culture.

Case study: Nucor's performance-oriented culture

Nucor has a very special organization culture. The company does not believe in hierarchy, and its motto is: 'Employees [called "teammates"], not managers, drive our success'. That's why the company has only five layers of management for about 12,000 people. Nucor's egalitarian culture places a premium on teamwork and idea-sharing between teammates and managers.

To maintain its culture, the company pays a lot of attention to recruiting and training the right people, and it has developed a unique performance-based compensation system. On average, two-thirds of a Nucor steelworker's pay is based on a production bonus. The company believes that teammates perform better when they have the opportunity to earn according to their productivity. There is healthy competition among facilities and shifts, balanced with a long history of cooperation and idea-sharing. Peer pressure is also strong: teammates do their best to avoid letting their team down, as this would mean a lower bonus for everyone concerned. Overall, teammates enjoy pay above the industry average, as the company has the highest productivity figures in the industry. This performance-based culture leads to a continuous search for improvement: every teammate is driven by a constant desire to improve the business processes. This constant dissatisfaction with the status quo leads to changes that drive growth by continually improving efficiency, effectiveness and flexibility.[23]

Checklist: 'operational excellence and your evaluation and control processes'

To what extent are your evaluation and control processes aligned with the operational-excellence operating model? The following questions can help you verify whether you have the appropriate evaluation and control processes in place to create a truly process-oriented organization:

1   Does your company measure cost, speed, flexibility, dependability and/or quality? How frequently do you measure these items?
2   Does your company have a well-established control process? Do you set challenging targets for your most important (operational) processes? Do you set up improvement initiatives if the targets are not achieved? Do you benchmark with best-in-class companies?
3   Does your organization reward process excellence? Do you use both financial and non-financial rewards? Do you reward teams or individuals?

Organizational behaviour: creating a business process orientation throughout the entire organization

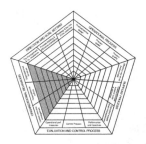

The organizational behaviour processes are important processes in strategy implementation. What kind of structure and culture do operationally excellent organizations put in place to achieve process excellence? And how can you use HR systems and policies to stimulate an operational excellence culture?

HR management

Delivering good-quality products or services at great prices, in a fast, easy way, does not occur without the support of good people. Operationally excellent organizations understand that they need to pay significant attention to HR management practices, as many people often associate operational excellence organizations with over-structured, rigid bureaucracies.

As I have mentioned already, standardization is an important element in every operationally excellent firm. Moreover, the employees understand the importance of a process orientation and standardized work. Everybody – from upper management to shop-floor workers – has a thorough understanding of the company's processes and how their own work fits into the overall picture. Every employee has at least some basic familiarity with all of the process steps and is likely to perform several of them. Given the clear process orientation pursued by these firms, employees also have a thorough understanding of the importance of flow and standardization to ensure speed and quality in the company's processes. Deep knowledge and understanding of the firm's processes are often the result of the high employee retention rates at operationally excellent companies. Not only do the employees understand the company's processes, they are also closely involved in their standardization. In the search for continuous improvement, every employee needs actively to practice the standardization of his/her work. Only then will an organization succeed in building company-wide engagement and support for this process orientation.

Apart from encouraging excellent individual activity, operationally excellent organizations strive to realize the advantages of their process orientation by means of team-based work. It has been shown consistently that teams are more effective in solving problems than individuals. Operationally excellent organizations understand that an effective, high-performing team is not simply the result of combining a group of people, but, rather, the result of careful selection, investment in training and team-building, and experience.[24]

Case study: teamwork at Southwest Airlines

At Southwest Airlines, even the process of recruiting is a team effort. Southwest is extraordinarily selective in its recruiting. To ensure fit, the company emphasizes peer recruiting, e.g. pilots hire other pilots.

> *Teamwork is critical – so, people who say 'I' too much in the recruitment interview do not get hired. The process consists of an application, a phone screening interview, a group interview, three additional interviews (two with line employees), and a consensus and a vote. During the interview process, an applicant will come into contact with other Southwest employees. These people are also invited to give their assessments of whether the person would fit into the company. The entire process focuses on a positive attitude and teamwork.*
>
> *Southwest works because people pull together to do what they need to do to get a plane turned around. That's a part of the Southwest culture. And if it means that the pilots need to load bags, they do so. The culture promotes informal teamwork, and employees routinely help each other out.[25]*
>
> *As a result, Southwest employees understand the overall work process and the links between their own jobs and the jobs performed by their counterparts in other functions.*

To encourage a 'deep' understanding of flow and standardized work, a company also needs to continuously train its people. Training programmes are established, not only for new recruits, but for all employees, including top management. Of course, the content of the training differs according to the target audience: the training spectrum can range from technical training to teach employees how to perform a job correctly, to sessions that acquaint employees with the company's processes, to leadership courses for Black-Belt Six Sigma experts. Furthermore, refresher training courses (to keep employees familiar with job-related requirements and processes) and retraining (for employees who have made mistakes in their work) need to be provided as well.[26]

Organization culture

An organization's ability to improve its operations depends to a large extent on its organizational culture. In operationally excellent firms, you find a culture that supports process excellence and that has drilled down to the entire organization. Key elements of such a process excellence culture include attention to cross-functionality and customer orientation, along with process and system thinking. This process view contrasts sharply with the functional view that you find in many organizations (this is illustrated in Table 9.2). A process-oriented culture is essential for achieving continuous improvement, a typical element found in every strategy-focused organization.

Another important element of any operational excellence culture is an obsession with quality – which is everyone's responsibility. In striving for zero defects, operationally excellent companies aim to get quality right the first time. Compared with a system of inspecting and repairing quality problems at a later stage in the process, 'in-station' quality (preventing problems from being passed down the line) is much more effective and less costly. To achieve in-station quality, employees are empowered to closely monitor – and take responsibility for – the quality of their work. To further support them in this crucial responsibility, they also receive extensive training to ensure that everybody knows how to deal with quality problems.

Organization structure

True operational excellence organizations emphasize processes, as opposed to hierarchies, as the main operating units. These processes should be defined, starting

TABLE 9.2 Comparison between a process view and a functional view

Process view	Functional view
• Emphasis on improving 'how work is done'	• Emphasis on which products or services are delivered
• Cross-functional coordination, teamwork stressed	• Frequent hand-offs among functions that remain largely uncoordinated
• 'Systems view', i.e. entire process is managed	• Pieces of the process are managed
• Customer orientation	• Internal/company orientation

Source: McCormack and Johnson (2001)[27]

with the customer's request and ending with the delivery of the product or service and the finishing of all related activities. This can be done by value stream mapping, a very popular lean management technique. Firms that view the business this way are said to have adopted a business process orientation.

Kevin McCormack and William Johnson have conducted several research projects to define what a business process orientation is all about. They have identified three factors that constitute a business process orientation: (1) process management and measurement, (2) process-oriented jobs and (3) a process view.[28] I have discussed the first element in the section on evaluation and control processes, and so the following paragraphs discuss the concepts of process-oriented jobs and process view.

McCormack and Johnson define process-oriented jobs as jobs that are multidimensional, include frequent problem-solving and involve a lot of learning. They define a process view as a view of the business as a series of linked processes that are well defined and documented. All three factors are significantly correlated with interdepartmental connectedness and overall business performance. McCormack and Johnson conclude that companies that are structured into broad process teams – rather than narrow functional departments – have fewer internal conflicts and a stronger team spirit. The fact that a process orientation is needed to create a more efficient organization is an important message for operationally excellent companies.

Firms can stimulate more process orientation by appointing process owners and process managers: a process owner is responsible for a particular core business process, and a process manager is in charge of, and responsible for, particular sub-processes. The process owner is responsible for designing processes, enabling process execution and following up on process performance. Many process owners are supported by a process improvement team. It is important to note that process owners have overall supply chain authority, as they are responsible for an entire process (which often cuts across typical organizational departments).

When firms have not yet created a process-based organization, they might use cross-functional teams that work in tight coordination to facilitate process improvement, as most processes cut across traditional functional or departmental boundaries. Through the creation of cross-functional teams that work together on their processes and realize real synergies from working together, these processes can be continuously improved.[29]

Checklist: 'operational excellence and your organizational behaviour processes'

Does your organization manage its people and organization in line with the operational-excellence operating model? The following questions can help you assess whether your support processes are conducive to managing your process excellence efforts:

1 Does your organization have the appropriate HR systems and policies to stimulate a process orientation across the company? Does your organization promote effective teamwork?

2 Does your organization emphasize process excellence in all that it does? Is there a focus on zero-defect quality? Is continuous improvement a key element of your organization's culture?

3 Has your company adopted a business process orientation? Does your company view the business as a series of linked processes? Do you have process owners and process managers in place who are responsible for tracking process performance and process improvement?

Operational excellence and commitment

So far, I have been outlining in detail how to create a well-aligned operational excellence organization. I have presented fifteen core activities that I've found in most successful operationally excellent firms. However, strategy implementation is not only about creating alignment around an orchestrating theme. It is also about making your middle managers and employees committed to bringing strategy to life. This last section explains why true operational excellence can only be achieved when an organization is connected or committed.

In Chapter 4, I presented four organizational configurations: the entrepreneurial organization, the structured organization, the connected organization and the committed organization. The four organizations represent four different stages of organizational development and management maturity.

The *entrepreneurial firm* is characterized by a continuous search for new opportunities, but it lacks the structure and professionalism to continuously deliver good, reliable products or services. This sounds like the opposite of operational excellence, but we need to be aware that all great operational excellence corporations – such as IKEA, Nucor, Toyota and Tata Group – all started as entrepreneurial ventures. Entrepreneurial firms may offer customers products or services at low prices, quickly and conveniently. The price advantage may come from doing things fundamentally differently or from a lack of (overhead) costs that larger, more mature firms incur. However, as the entrepreneurial firms become successful, they will grow in size and scale . . . and in costs.

As they grow, entrepreneurial firms need to adopt a more *structured* organizational configuration. Many of the management and operating tools that I have presented in this chapter are used to add more structure to your organization. This is a challenge that every strategy-focused organization will face, regardless of the operating model the company has (implicitly) chosen. However, operational excellence companies go much further in applying these tools than their customer-intimacy or product-leadership competitors do.

True operational excellence requires at least a *connected organization*. In structured organizations, a functional mindset prevails, whereas connected organizations have adopted a business process orientation in which end-to-end processes – not functional departments – are managed. Teamwork is important, and employees from different functions discuss strategy and implementation initiatives. Furthermore, the performance measures are holistic, providing a picture of how well the company (not just the functional unit) is doing.

As we saw in Chapter 4, the *committed organization* is the ultimate stage of organizational development (albeit a stage that few companies have reached). In my research database, the committed operational excellence organizations are among the most successful firms in my research sample (see Figure 9.5).

Examples include some business units of the Toyota Corporation, ING Direct USA, Sofaxis and Carglass®. In those organizations, all employees feel responsible for the strategy, and they actively contribute to it. Everybody is looking for opportunities to reduce costs and price for the customer. Each customer contact is a moment of truth and judgement, and everybody contributes to delivering a hassle-free, high-quality service experience. This cannot be enforced through hierarchy and authority – it requires personal commitment from every employee. Operationally excellent organizations are designed to enable the high levels of employee involvement and commitment that are required to support the efforts of continuously improving cost, quality and timeliness. Such organizations mobilize employees to contribute to continuous improvement, while simultaneously providing the necessary structures and formalized procedures to avoid chaos and ensure efficiency.

How do operational excellence companies create commitment in an environment that is characterized by formalization, standardization and structure? When people speak about bureaucracies, they inevitably think about red tape, over-controlling bosses and apathetic employees. On the other hand, companies need appropriately designed, formalized procedures and structures to ensure order,

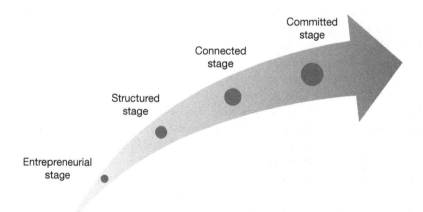

FIGURE 9.5 Effectiveness of the operational excellence model at different maturity stages

efficiency, quality and timeliness. This holds even more for operational excellence firms, as this is the core of their value proposition – that is, where they make the difference relative to their competitors. Paul Adler has introduced an interesting concept to solve this dilemma: 'the enabling bureaucracy'.[30]

Adler's research suggests that the negative consequences of bureaucracy – rigidity, alienation and low commitment – may be widespread, but they are not inherent in bureaucracy. Adler defines two types of bureaucracy: coercive bureaucracy and enabling bureaucracy. The first type of bureaucracy is the familiar one, in which a company installs hierarchical authority and procedures manuals to ensure that incompetent and irresponsible employees do the right thing. The *enabling bureaucracy*, however, starts from a very different perspective:

> Bureaucratic structures and systems function to support the work of the doers rather than to bolster the authority of the higher-ups. The hierarchy is one of expertise rather than positional power, and the different levels in that hierarchy collaborate. The procedures are designed with the participation of the users in order to identify best practices and opportunities for improvement. And staffs function as partners with line groups.[31]

It is clear that Adler suggests adopting enabling, rather than coercive, social structures. In his research, Adler refers extensively to NUMMI (a Californian joint venture between Toyota and GM, run by Toyota) and MIEL (Motorola's Indian Electronics subsidiary) as examples of enabling bureaucracies. At the same time, the two companies are regarded as employing best practices in quality management and operational excellence.

Key learning points

This chapter has presented what it takes to be operationally excellent. As I said in the introduction to this chapter, the journey is difficult and complex . . . but not impossible. Operational excellence requires that everybody understands the organization's strategy, and that every unit takes actions to implement the strategy. In operationally excellent firms, the orchestrating theme is to maximize efficiency through a process and quality mindset. These firms launch actions to translate strategy into clear goals for everyone (direction and goal setting), to increase process speed and product and process quality (operational processes), to streamline tasks and operations throughout the entire supply chain (support processes), to measure and track process excellence (evaluation and control processes) and to create more business process orientation (organizational behaviour processes).

It is important to involve your people in this journey; otherwise, you end up with a coercive bureaucracy. Paul Adler showed that it's possible to create formal structures and still have a committed workforce. The challenge is to find the subtle balance between structure and creativity, between direction and involvement, and between control and learning. In the next chapter, I show how ING Direct USA became a leading American bank by adopting many of the principles presented here.

Notes

1 Liker, J. K., and Morgan, J. M. (2006) 'The Toyota Way in Services: The Case of Lean Product Development', *Academy of Management Perspectives*, May, 18.
2 Verweire, K., De Grande, J., and Greef, G. (2011) 'Operational Excellence: What Does It Mean? What Does It Take?', *Vlerick Business School Research Report*, Vlerick Business School, pp. 1–98.
3 We examined the following case studies: Aldi, Lidl, Amazon, Walmart, Toyota, FedEx, Charles Schwab, ING Direct USA, Fidelity, IKEA, Nucor Corporation, Ryanair, easyJet, Shouldice Hospital, Southwest Airlines, Tata Group, Belron® (Carglass®), Zara and McDonald's.
4 McCormack, K. P., and Johnson, W. C. (2001) *Business Process Orientation: Gaining the E-Business Competitive Advantage*, St. Lucie Press, Boca Raton, FL, p. 5.
5 Stewart, T. A., and Raman, A. P. (2007) 'Managing for the Long Term: Lessons from Toyota's Long Drive', *Harvard Business Review*, July–August, 77.
6 Upton, D., and Margolis, J. (1992) 'McDonald's Corporation', *Harvard Business School Case Study*, 9–693–028, p. 2.
7 Slack, N., Chambers, S., and Johnston, R. (2010) *Operations Management* (6th edn), Pearson Education, Harlow, UK, p. 40.
8 George, M. L. (2003) *Lean Six Sigma for Service: How to Use Lean Speed and Six Sigma Quality to Improve Services and Transactions*, Mc-Graw Hill, New York, pp. 82–3.
9 Anderson, D. M. (2004) *Build-to-Order and Mass-Customization: The Ultimate Supply Chain Management and Lean Manufacturing Strategy for Low-Cost On-Demand Production Without Forecasts Or Inventory*, CIM Press, Cambria, CA.
10 Liker, J. K. (2004) *The Toyota Way: 14 Management Principles From the World's Greatest Manufacturer*, McGraw-Hill, New York, p. 7.
11 Ibid., p. 7.
12 Nie, W., and Léger, K. (2008) 'Walmart: Should It Change? Can It Change?', *IMD Business School Case Study*, IMD-3-1883, p. 7.
13 Liker, *The Toyota Way*, p. 129.
14 Slack *et al.*, *Operations Management*, p. 554.
15 Parry, Mark E. (2004) 'McDonald's: The Hamburger Price Wars', *Darden Business Publishing Case Study*, UVA-M-0687, p. 2.
16 Upton and Margolis, 'McDonald's Corporation', p. 3.
17 Goldberg, R. A., and Droste Yagan, J. (2007) 'McDonald's Corporation: Managing a Sustainable Supply Chain', *Harvard Business School Case Study*, 9–907–414, p. 3.
18 Beretta, S. (2002) 'Unleashing the Integration Potential of ERP Systems: The Role of Process-Based Performance Measurement Systems', *Business Process Management Journal*, 8 (3), 254–77.
19 Slack *et al.*, *Operations Management*.
20 Simatupang, T. M., and Sridharan, R. (2008) 'Design for Supply Chain Collaboration', *Business Process Management Journal*, 14 (3), 406–7.
21 Slack *et al.*, *Operations Management*, p. 608.
22 Armstrong, M., and Stephens, T. (2005) *Employee Reward Management and Practice*, Kogan Page, London.
23 Company website, available at: www.nucor.com, and Vasanthi, V., and Chowdary, N. V. (2006) 'Nucor Corp.'s Performance-Driven Organizational Culture: Employee-Driven Competitive Advantage?', *IBSCDC Case Study*, 306–336–1.
24 Brown, S., Lamming, R., Bessant, J., and Jones, P. (2000) *Strategic Operations Management*, Elsevier Butterworth Heinemann, Amsterdam.
25 O'Reilly, C., and Pfeffer, J. (1995) 'Southwest Airlines (A)', *Stanford Graduate School of Business Case Study*, HR-1A, pp. 5, 9, 13.
26 Bigelow, M. (2002) 'How to Achieve Operational Excellence', *Quality Progress*, October, 70.
27 McCormack *et al.*, *Business Process Orientation*, p. 5.

28 Ibid.
29 Johnston, R., and Clark, G. (2005) *Service Operations Management: Improving Service Delivery*, Pearson Education, Harlow, UK, p. 393.
30 Adler, P. S. (1999) 'Building Better Bureaucracies', *Academy of Management Executive*, 13 (4), 36–47.
31 Ibid., p. 38.

10

STRATEGY IMPLEMENTATION IN PRACTICE

ING Direct USA – a rebel in the US banking industry

> With the right culture, the problems of commitment, alignment, and motivation go away and hierarchy becomes irrelevant.
>
> (Kuhlmann and Philp, 2009)[1]

This chapter describes the strategy implementation practices of one of the most interesting financial institutions of the last decade: ING Direct USA (the American subsidiary of ING Direct). This company has attracted a lot of attention in the business press with its unorthodox perspectives on banking, and it is heralded as one of the most innovative firms in the global banking industry. Many organizations have tried to enter the American banking industry with innovative business models, but the incumbents have always been able to defend their markets successfully. ING Direct USA has been the exception to the rule – rising through the ranks of over 14,000 financial institutions to become one of the thirty largest banks by assets and deposits in the US.

In this chapter, I demonstrate that ING Direct USA's success is not only due to its unconventional perspectives on banking, but also to clear strategic choices and a disciplined implementation of the operational excellence model. I have discussed the bank's strategy and implementation with Arkadi Kuhlmann, the founder of ING Direct, and other top managers of the company, and the interviews have revealed that ING Direct USA is a great example of a well-aligned and highly committed organization. In my opinion, this is a key driver of the company's phenomenal growth from 2000 to 2012.

In 2012, ING Direct USA was sold to Capital One for US$ 9 billion, and the company is now called Capital One 360. Therefore, I also describe what happened and what led to the sale of this remarkable company.

ING Direct USA: a rebel in the US banking industry

For the last couple of years, ING Direct has been one of the greatest success stories in the financial services industry. The Dutch ING Group launched a new bank in 1997 in Canada and attracted Arkadi Kuhlmann, an inspiring and charismatic finance professor with a solid business sense, as CEO of the initiative. Together with Hans Verkoren and Dick Harryvan, two top executives from the ING Group, he developed a new concept in the financial services industry. The unit in Canada became so successful that ING Group set up ING Direct ventures in eight other countries.

ING Direct USA was launched in September 2000. As he did in Canada, Arkadi Kuhlmann railed against the banking industry's high fees and a financial culture that encourages people to save too little, consume too much and invest too recklessly.[2] ING Direct USA played Robin Hood to the big banks 'by empowering the average guy to empower himself.'[3] The company was there to help Americans save more and to revolutionize the American retail banking industry by making saving cool and smart. Arkadi describes it as follows:

> Our purpose is to be a servant of the average person. Rather than getting people to spend more – which is what most banks do – our approach is to get Americans to save more – to return to the values of thrift, self-reliance, and building a nest egg. ING Direct was born in an age of broken promises. The last thing America needed was another bank, but that did not mean America did not need us. ING Direct's mission is to make it easy to save by offering the same great values to all Americans.

The company concentrated on customers from 'Main Street' – customers who had been misled or abandoned by so many other financial institutions.

Arkadi Kuhlmann rejected the characterization of ING Direct as an Internet bank, even though the web was its primary customer channel (ING Direct USA had no branches). The company offered high dividend rates and differentiated from other e-banks via fast, easy, no-hassle service. There were no minimums and no fees. Its slogans were simple and had a clear message – the 'Save Your Money' slogan attracted a lot of interest – and they captured customers' attention with their bright orange colour and by communicating in a humorous, 'anti-establishment' tone (see Figure 10.2).

The company used guerilla-marketing techniques to emphasize its message – quite uncommon in the banking industry. For example, in Baltimore and Washington DC, ING Direct surprised over 8,000 people with a free movie at two participating Regal Cinemas. In a similar way, it offered free gas in Baltimore to 1,000 drivers, at three selected Shell stations, and asked them to put that money into an Orange Savings Account. And it let commuters ride the Boston 'T' lines for free one morning, while ING representatives danced around in orange Paul Revere costumes.

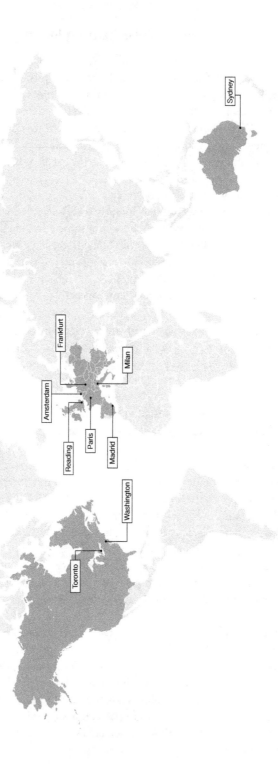

FIGURE 10.1 ING Direct's international presence

Source: Company information

FIGURE 10.2 Outdoor advertising from ING Direct USA

Source: Company information

ING Direct's cafés were another uncommon feature of the marketing strategy. The cafés – located in major cities, such as New York, Washington, Philadelphia and Los Angeles – were not substitutes for branches. Instead, they introduced customers to the ING Direct brand. When ING Direct started its marketing and operations in Canada, early prospects were somewhat suspicious of the new brand, and so they began visiting the company's call centre in Toronto to verify the new bank's physical existence. The ING Direct Canada employees offered those prospects a cup of coffee in the call centre's coffee corner, and that's how the café idea emerged.

Paying high dividends and spending tons on marketing seem like a recipe for red ink. Not for ING Direct USA: the high-volume, low-margin company was a master at efficiently serving low-maintenance customers. ING Direct USA had standardized, state-of-the-art IT systems. The product offering was limited, with limited options for each product. According to Dick Harryvan, CEO of ING Direct Group from 2006 to 2010, this was a deliberate choice:

> In the beginning, we only offered a savings account. If you have one million dollars to spend, the savings market is the best one to target. It's a broad

market, savings is an easy product, and acquisition costs are low. The online savings account has been the ideal product for entering new markets, such as Canada, France, Spain, Italy, and the United States . . . We have been very profitable because we have no branches, and because we have a focused, specific product. Our cost base is one sixth that of a bricks-and-mortar bank. That's why we're able to offer higher rates and charge no fees. While savings is a very profitable product, it's also a good product and attractive to our customers. We have a very good image with young people as well as with older people. In fact, more than 50 per cent of our customers are older than 50. That was a big surprise to us.[4]

ING Direct USA has been very successful with this strategy. In 10 years, the company attracted over 7 million customers and €58 billion in deposits (see Table 10.1 and Figure 10.3). Equally impressive is the level of customer satisfaction that ING Direct USA has been able to achieve. The company doesn't just have customers, it has active 'promoters' for its brand. In 2007, the NPS was 74, which is enormously high.[5] As you will note from Table 10.1, ING Direct USA's profits were very bad in 2008 and 2009; we will explain later in this chapter what exactly happened and to what extent these bad financial results cast a shadow on ING Direct USA's business model.

ING Direct USA: a well-aligned, operationally excellent organization

ING Direct USA had a convincing value proposition – great deals, being responsive, accessible, simple and easy, and passionate – and a convincing cause – leading Americans back to saving. However, not only did Arkadi Kuhlmann create

TABLE 10.1 Financial overview of ING Direct USA (€ million, except when stated otherwise)

€ million	2002	2004	2006	2007	2008	2009	2010	2011 (1H)
Net interest income	147.0	379.9	486.9	519.1	1,061.7	908.3	1,160.0	1,129.1
Profit before tax	43.8	183.6	266.8	268.2	-1,264.7	-539.4	273.4	-145.9
Net income	44.8	115.3	169.7	177.1	-802.3	-344.5	197.6	-105.5
No. of customers (thousands)	789	2,226	4,629	6,524	7,546	7,633	7,686	7,724
Deposits	8,859	22,322	42,896	45,263	55,127	55,279	58,873	56,809
Loans	2,860	7,653	12,311	17,936	25,109	25,943	29,952	28,415

Source: Author's calculations obtained from Bankscope (Bureau Van Dijk)[6]

a differentiated bank with a rebellious image, he also built a well-oiled machine designed to deal with high-volume, low-margin commodity products.

This is illustrated in Figure 10.4, which shows ING Direct USA's Operational Excellence Pentagon. ING Direct USA is the most aligned operationally excellent company in our database of ninety-eight operationally excellent firms. The company received extremely high scores on all fifteen core dimensions of operational excellence. This result is truly remarkable.[7] Let's investigate it in greater detail.

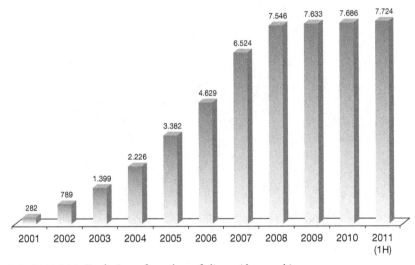

FIGURE 10.3(A) Evolution of number of clients (thousands)

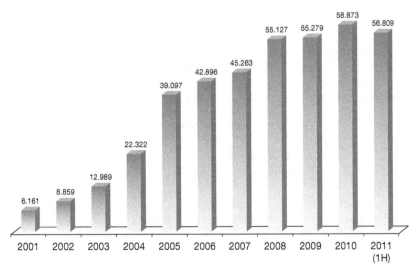

FIGURE 10.3(B) Evolution of deposits (€ million)

Source: Data obtained from Bankscope (Bureau Van Dijk)[7]

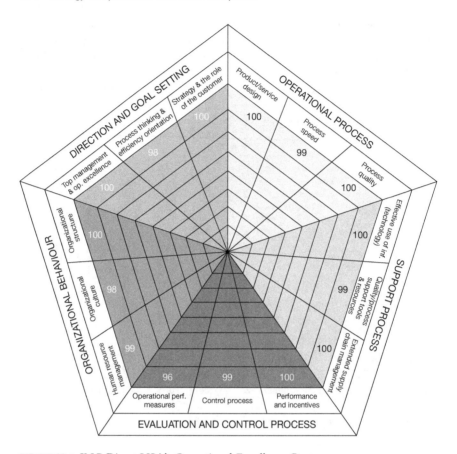

FIGURE 10.4 ING Direct USA's Operational Excellence Pentagon

Direction and goal setting: a long-term focus on process excellence and efficiency supported by top management

Top management and operational excellence

If a company wants to outperform its competitors on cost, speed, quality, dependability and/or flexibility, profits can only come if you get everything right. ING Direct has always seen itself more as a retailer than as a bank, and, from the retailing world, it understood the importance of quality delivery, standardized products and uniform pricing:

> If we ran huge volumes with no mistakes and minimal customer contact, then when we did interact with a customer it had to be right and it had to be good. The bank offices also needed to look smart and efficient. To attract staff, our operations needed to be straightforward and laid out in a simple way, much like aisles in a grocery store or the flow of a manufacturing setup.[9]

Members of top management in an operational excellence firm need to have a thorough understanding of the company's operational processes. To achieve process excellence, it is crucial that top management be completely aligned with the company's process orientation, and that they actively and visibly support this. Arkadi Kuhlmann did not talk a lot about processes explicitly, but the process orientation was always implicit in his messages.

ING Direct has always aimed to offer simple products allowing customers to save time and money. ING Direct USA has created value for consumers by coming out with commodity products and making them very simple. This required a thorough understanding of the company's underlying operational processes. Arkadi Kuhlmann once said: 'You can turn mortgages into simple products too. But that necessitates re-engineering the product and the processes behind it. And to some extent, you need to reengineer the customer as well.'[10] Figure 10.5 is a photo that I took in ING Direct's café in New York, in May 2006. Today, so many years later, getting a mortgage in only 7 minutes is still more the exception than the rule in the banking industry.

Strategy and the role of the customer

Many financial institutions are driven by their operations but forget to introduce the customer's perspective. Today (as in the past), compliance and control are the

FIGURE 10.5 ING Direct USA's mortgage application

key priorities of most banks, and the customer is a necessary evil that perturbs operations but, fortunately, brings in the money too. However, that's not how Arkadi saw the customer's role. Arkadi liked to take regular shifts in ING Direct's call centre – helping existing customers with routine transactions, helping new ones to sign in and listening to the voice of the customer. In this way, he collected a lot of information on how to improve the company's products and operations.

Still, Arkadi did not always follow the customer's advice. When a customer insisted on receiving a printed statement of her account, Arkadi refused . . . and closed her account. ING Direct was for everybody, as long as the customer behaved in the way ING Direct wanted. In 2004, the company fired more than 3,500 customers who did not play by the bank's rules. Those customers relied too heavily on the call centres or asked for too many exceptions to the standard operating procedures.

Operational processes: a strategic role for the operations function

Product/service design

ING Direct USA's mission was to redefine financial services through relentless simplification. The products were simple, the process of signing up was simple, and the experience of using the products was simple. ING Direct emphasized simplicity, not because it felt that people were not smart enough to handle complexity, but because, for it, 'simple' meant honesty (nothing to hide) and trust.

Apart from the traditional banks, ING Direct USA's biggest enemy was internal complexity. That's why the company offered only a few products, and why the criteria for introducing a new product were very strict. To introduce a new product, a country unit would first have to develop a business plan that included: forecasts of demand and marketing expenditures; evaluations of the operational, financial and legal risks associated with launching the product; and clear IT and operational requirements necessary to support the product. Brunon Bartkiewicz, General Manager at ING Direct, explains:

> Every new product reduces our simplicity, increases our risk and defocuses our people. A person who is marketing seven products cannot know all the details, all the figures, all the logic that a person focused on one product does. In the end, the whole game is efficiency: efficiency in marketing, in operations, and in systems.[11]

Process speed and quality and efficiency

ING Direct USA has always been a direct bank, which meant that it could operate more efficiently than most other banks. A big part of its lower cost structure stemmed from the things that it did not offer and in which it did not invest. The company

TABLE 10.2 Comparison of traditional US banks' and ING Direct USA's cost and income structure

	US banking industry (bps)	ING Direct USA (bps)
Interest income	300	170
Non-interest income	125	10
Loan-loss provision	(50)	(10)
Operating expenses	(250)	(70)
Underlying profit margin (pre-tax)	125	100

Note: bps = basis points; 1 basis point = 0.01 per cent.

Source: Company information

did not invest in an ATM network or in traditional branches. It encouraged customers to open accounts online or by using an interactive voice response system, which helped save costs.

Its website was designed to be easy to understand, and customers could select from only a few options. ING Direct USA designed its system for maximum self-service: approximately 90 per cent of the account openings were 'touch-less' (without intervention from a live person).[12] The company's acquisition costs were estimated to be lower than $100. According to Jim Kelly, chief marketing officer of ING Direct USA, a traditional bank's acquisition costs could amount to $300–400.[13]

Maintenance costs were kept low as well. To ensure cheap as well as fast and reliable service, the company designed self-service features for its easy-to-maintain products. This enabled one customer service associate to serve nearly 20,000 customers, while answering 75 per cent of telephone calls within 20 seconds. ING Direct USA made a conscious effort to continue to optimize its website and procedures – resulting in a 17 per cent year-on-year decrease in service calls, even as the number of customers grew by 15 per cent per year.[14] Table 10.2 compares ING Direct USA's long-term cost and income structure with the traditional banks.

Support processes: streamlining tasks and operations and the important role of IT

Effective use of information (technology)

ING Direct USA had two core competencies: marketing and IT. Marketing created the brand and attracted the customers; IT provided the infrastructure to deliver the brand promise and to retain the customers. The company invested heavily in automating its business processes. It used a small group of technology vendor companies to be on the leading edge in using technology to process financial services. For example, ING Direct USA licensed a loan origination system that enabled the bank to process a mortgage with no human intervention. This reduced costs and saved time, while improving the customer experience.[15]

Regarding itself more as a technology firm than as a traditional retail bank, ING Direct USA used an agile IT infrastructure to deliver its simple products, while leveraging consistent architecture across interoperable platforms. The bank had about thirty IT teams – some developed applications, and others were responsible for quality assurance and maintenance. The business owners controlled the IT agenda, so that they could respond more rapidly to changing business needs.[16]

Looking back at the ING Direct USA story, Arkadi Kuhlmann commented:

> Technology played a key role in our case. In retrospect, the change may seem more like evolution than revolution, but making the leap to a retail model allowed us to use the new technology *for* our customers. It helped change the way consumers think about money and the way they go about doing their banking.[17]

Quality and process support tools and resources

All this required ING Direct to manage its processes in a very rigorous way. All processes were documented, and there were detailed guidelines and procedures for the organization's core processes. The company was constantly looking to simplify financial products and financial transactions, and it used tools such as Lean Six Sigma to achieve the efficiency of the manufacturing industry.

ING Direct strived to have its various departments in close contact with each other. The process flow was specified for the entire organization, considering processes from multiple departments simultaneously. Streamlining processes was a key element in ING Direct's business architecture, and so the company had a strong business process orientation.

Evaluation and control processes: measuring and tracking process excellence and efficiency

Control process

Another important element of ING Direct's business model was its obsession with measuring. Measuring how customers react to marketing campaigns and online advertising is a natural activity for an online bank, but, at ING Direct USA, performance measurement did not stop at the marketing department. The company's operations centres competed with each other for recognition and monthly bonuses based on their ability to meet sales and service goals. Everybody in ING Direct measured and was measured. Some performance measures were posted daily on an Intranet site, accessible to everyone within the company. The performance measures were continuously analysed and were the input for action plans to improve products and processes.

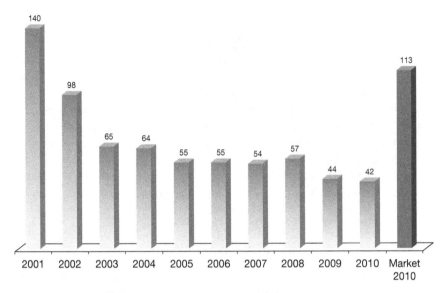

FIGURE 10.6 Evolution of ING Direct's operational cost base to retail balances (excluding marketing) (bps)

Source: Company information

Operational performance measures

All operational performance measures had a direct impact on the company's five high-level targets: (1) total profit, (2) non-marketing expenses/ending assets, (3) net retail funds entrusted (on balance sheet) growth, (4) net mortgage growth and (5) call-centre service level. Efficiency and cost-effectiveness were monitored carefully. Figure 10.6 presents the evolution of the operational costs of ING Direct (all countries) from 2001 to 2010. There we can see that the expense-to-assets ratio (excluding marketing expenses) for ING Direct (all countries) decreased from 140 bps in 2001 to 43 bps in 2010. The average for the market in 2010 was 113 bps. And, in 2009, the company carried US$36 million in assets per employee, versus US$6 million at its peers.[18]

Organizational behaviour processes: creating a business process orientation throughout the entire organization

HR processes

You cannot be a rebel in the banking industry when your organization is made up entirely of traditional bankers. That's why ING Direct USA paid great attention to recruiting the right people, hiring employees with non-banking or untraditional backgrounds. Unlike other operational excellence firms, ING Direct

USA has focused on getting the mavericks and outliers on board. Kuhlmann looked for people who had something to prove – the recipe for being passionate about a rebellious idea. The company hired employees with diverse skill sets to foster greater creativity and innovation, something you would expect more at a product-leader organization.

Nevertheless, ING Direct USA applied the HR practices that I find in many operational excellence firms. The company scores in the ninety-ninth percentile for HR management in our Operational Excellence Pentagon (see Figure 10.4), which means that the employees in the organization understand the concept of flow and standardized work. In addition, the company invested a lot in training to facilitate understanding of the entire process, so that people could be moved easily to other units within the organization. Last, but not least, a lot of emphasis was placed on stimulating effective teamwork.

A particular organization structure and culture

ING Direct USA has been able to create a particular organization culture. This culture was captured in *The Orange Code* (see Figure 10.7), a set of twelve principles that explain what the company is and what it stands for.

According to Arkadi:

> The Orange Code is unique in that it declares a set of principles in the form of a challenge rather than just a list of lofty goals. It's a realistic approach, and it invites ongoing conversation about how the people at ING Direct can live those principles every day.[19]

The company also used its Code as an element of appraisal and evaluation (see Figure 10.8). An employee was a role model if he/she performed very well *and* lived the values.

A key element of that culture was the open communication and teamwork. Management worked hard to ensure that no silos developed, and no one had a job title – which was simply a logical extension of Principle 10 – 'We will be for everyone'. Everybody was in the bonus programme, and the metrics were the same for everyone.

The company also hired Hay Group to set up more formal leadership development initiatives, such as succession planning, executive assessments, organizational development and leadership training programmes.

Strategic commitment at ING Direct USA

All these initiatives led to highly satisfied customers and very committed employees. Employee satisfaction surveys indicated that the employees were proud to work for the company, and that they liked to contribute actively to implementing the company's strategy.

1. We are new here.

2. Our mission is to help people take care of the wealth they make.

3. We will be fair.

4. We will constantly learn.

5. We will change and adapt and dwell only in the present and in the future.

6. We will listen. We will invent. We will simplify.

7. We will never stop asking why. Or why not.

8. We will create wealth for ourselves too. But we will do this by creating value.

9. We will tell the truth.

10. We will be for everyone.

11. We aren't conquerors. We are pioneers. We are not here to destroy. We are here to create.

12. We will never be finished.

FIGURE 10.7 The Orange Code

Source: Company information

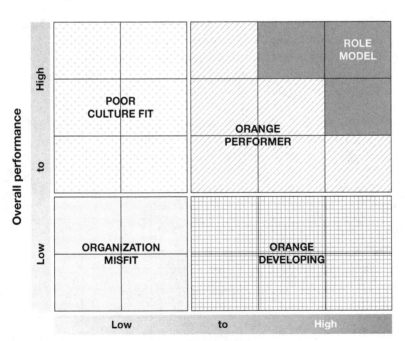

FIGURE 10.8 The Orange Code as an element of organizational fit

Source: Company information

Why was Arkadi Kuhlmann able to create such a motivated and committed workforce? Arkadi would definitely point to the company's mission and the importance of the Orange Code. In his book *The Orange Code*, his co-author Bruce Philp describes it as follows:

> ING Direct got phenomenal performance out of its organization by making its brand an instrument of leadership. As a consequence of that leadership decision, the traditional wall between marketing and operations was torn down. Each served the other, and both served the same greater purpose. The wall between the consumer and the organization got torn down too. ... This all works because everybody is pulling together, and they are pulling together because more effort was put into culture than into process. Manage the culture, and the culture will manage the business. Manage the culture with an idea, and it will grow it.[20]

Culture – this is what drives the performance of an organization. In the case of ING Direct USA, the mission and purpose were essential elements of the company's culture. But I believe there is more than that. One of the main reasons for ING Direct's success in the United States is the level of management maturity that Arkadi and his management team have been able to create. They have built an organization around the operating model of operational excellence, and they have been able to involve many people in this idea. This is illustrated in Figure 10.9, which depicts ING Direct USA's maturity profile.

ING Direct USA is one of the few companies that have reached the level of the committed organization. The company has become a connection of individuals.

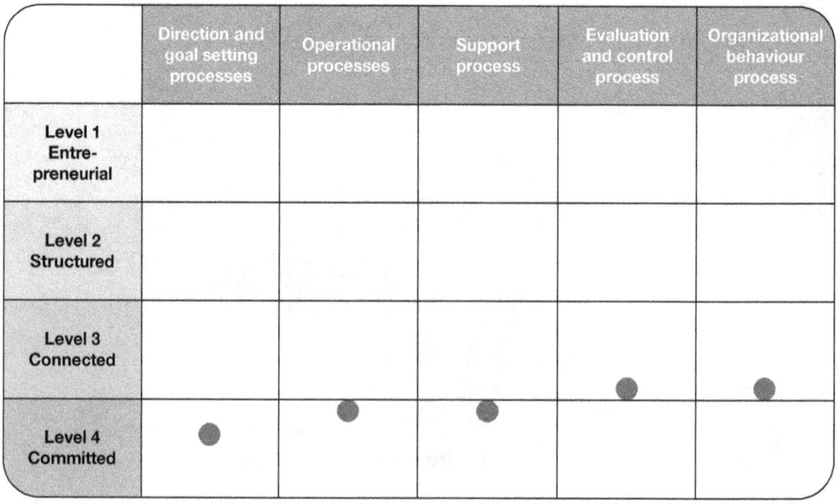

	Direction and goal setting processes	Operational processes	Support process	Evaluation and control process	Organizational behaviour process
Level 1 Entre- preneurial					
Level 2 Structured					
Level 3 Connected				●	●
Level 4 Committed	●	●	●		

FIGURE 10.9 ING Direct USA's maturity profile

The top management team has launched operational excellence activities, while also ensuring that these activities are supported and carried out by all employees.

For example: the mission, vision and values of the company were developed collaboratively after numerous discussions and were fully integrated in the organization culture. In Chapter 4, I wrote that, in committed organizations, the vision and the mission really *live*. This is absolutely true for ING Direct USA. The company had a sense of purpose that was reflected in its culture. The vision and the goals were ambitious and fostered a spirit of continuous improvement and innovation in the organization. The company had strategic plans that were developed and revised by cross-functional teams.

Companies that reach the committed level have their *operational processes* tracked and improved continuously. Process re-engineering is carried out quickly and efficiently, because the employees adapt easily to a changing work environment. Again, ING Direct USA scored well on all these things.

ING Direct USA also had highly mature *support processes*: team communication was an ongoing activity, routine work was facilitated by the extensive use of IT systems and other automation tools, and employees spent a lot of time on system improvements.

As already indicated, performance management was key at ING Direct USA, and this was not restricted to financial figures, but included measures of efficiency and customer satisfaction. In the company's performance-oriented culture, everybody had to manage their individual performance indicators.

Furthermore, everybody felt responsible for carrying out activities to get a job done. Good performers were rewarded, and the others were stimulated by the good performers' best practices. Everybody received support and training to improve.

In summary, ING Direct USA had a structured way of working, regarded the business as one entity and practised value-based management. That makes a truly committed organization, and it involves much more than developing inspiring mission and vision statements.

ING Direct USA's sale to Capital One

I have written this case in the past tense, because today ING Direct USA is no longer part of the Dutch ING Group; it is now part of Capital One, a diversified American banking group. The company is now called Capital One 360. Arkadi Kuhlmann did not make the move to Capital One – he left the company in 2012, ready for a new (ad)venture.

I do not know how well the new company is doing or whether it has been able to preserve its unique culture and management style. Some people ask me: if ING Direct USA was such a great success story, why did ING Group decide to sell? I have discussed this question extensively with my colleague, André Thibeault, who is a finance professor at Vlerick Business School.

From the many discussions I've had with him, I've learned that banking is a very difficult profession. It is not about developing and selling a great product at a good price. ING Direct USA had developed a successful savings product and conquered America with it. However, you need more than a successful savings product to be a successful financial institution. Savings is not a business in itself; it's only half of the story.[21]

Banks make money by originating loans or mortgages or by investing in assets, through which they gain an interest income. That's the asset side of a bank's balance sheet. But banks need money to fund those loans and assets, which is the liabilities side of the balance sheet. Typically, banks start their business model with the asset side: they originate loans or mortgages, determine the yield from those assets, and then see how they can fund them as cheaply as possible. The funding can be customers' deposits or can come from the interbank market (where your colleagues lend you the money you need).

ING Direct USA's business model was unconventional because it focused on the liabilities side. In essence, ING Direct USA's story has always been a savings story. Figure 10.10 shows the evolution of the deposits (the liabilities) and the evolution of (mortgage) loans (part of the assets) of the company.

Figure 10.10 shows the success of ING Direct USA in attracting deposits. The company had also created a mortgage product, but the growth in deposits was much higher than the growth in mortgage loans. This was a source of concern, because US regulations require the company to invest more than 50 per cent of its savings deposits in mortgage lending products. After some years, expanding the product range was one of ING Direct USA's major strategic priorities. It is great to collect funds, but you also need to know how to invest them.

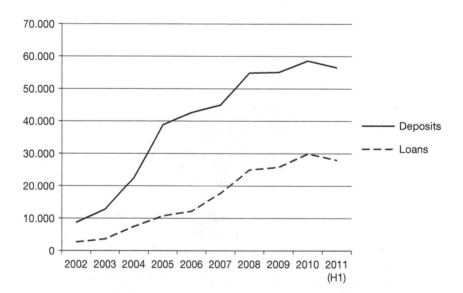

FIGURE 10.10 Evolution of deposits and (mortgage) loans at ING Direct USA (€ million)

In July 2007, the subprime mortgage crisis started hitting the financial services industry. Many people believe that this subprime mortgage crisis put ING Direct USA into financial trouble. However, it is worth noting that, because of its conservative standards in mortgage underwriting, ING Direct USA's mortgage loans exhibited significantly stronger payment performance compared with other banks. The loans were not the problem; the problem was the investments, a significant number of which were in mortgage-related products.

Up to 2007, ING Direct USA had built up a portfolio of more than €30 billion of mortgage obligations (the volume of deposits minus the volume of mortgage loans). In 2005, those investments were considered safe (AAA rating), high-yielding asset categories. But all that changed during the financial crisis, when the market value of ING Direct USA's investment portfolio decreased dramatically. The group had to absorb almost €9 billion in revaluations via equity, and its capital base reduced from €40 billion (2007) to €29 billion (2008). In addition, the capital requirements for those mortgage obligations rose so high that many financial institutions had to seek a lifebuoy from their respective governments. ING Group itself had to enter into an agreement with the Dutch minister of finance. During that period, ING Direct USA's commercial performance was still very positive: customer satisfaction remained high, and the customer base and the deposits continued to grow, albeit marginally.

The help from the Dutch government triggered a reaction from the European Commissioner for Competition, Neelie Kroes, who compelled banks that had received state aid to restructure significantly by selling off substantial assets. The European Commission obliged ING Group to split its banking and insurance operations and to sell ING Direct USA and some of its Dutch banking operations.

On 16 June 2011, ING announced the sale of ING Direct USA to Capital One for US$9 billion. On some blogs, there were discussions about whether Capital One had paid the right price. What was also striking was the reaction of many customers. A journalist for *The New York Times* reported that customers were concerned that, 'ING's brand of low-fee, low-maintenance banking, combined with responsive customer service, would soon be a thing of the past under the new ownership'.[22]

It will be interesting to see how ING Direct USA's integration into Capital One will evolve. Capital One has already changed ING Direct USA's name to Capital One 360. The new owner states that the new company is fuelled by the same commitment to saving its customers' time and money. Time will tell to what extent Capital One has preserved the spirit of the rebel in the banking industry and its well-run operational excellence model.

Key learning points

The case study of ING Direct USA has taught us many things. The first is that operational excellence is essentially about customer centricity (just like customer intimacy and product leadership). Operational excellence enables you to serve your customers better – either by offering them a great price and/or by offering a convenient, hassle-free service.

Operational excellence is difficult – it requires a large number of actions in the various areas of management to get everybody aligned and committed around this orchestrating theme. However, it is not impossible. Arkadi Kuhlmann was able to revolutionize the banking industry with 'an ordinary savings bank'. How might you become the operationally excellent firm in your industry?

Notes

1 Kuhlmann, A., and Philp, B. (2009) *The Orange Code: How ING Direct Succeeded by Being a Rebel With a Cause*, John Wiley & Sons, Hoboken, NJ, p. 125.
2 Taylor, W. C. (2005) 'Rebels With a Cause, and a Business Plan', *The New York Times*, 2 January.
3 Kuhlmann and Philp, *The Orange Code*, p. 7.
4 Heuvel, J. (2005) *Dienstenmarketing* (3rd edn), Noordhoff Uitgevers, Groningen, The Netherlands.
5 The Net Promoter Score (NPS) is a popular measure for customer retention. The NPS is calculated using the answers to one simple question: 'How likely is it that you would recommend Company X to a friend or a colleague?' A company's NPS can be as low as −100 (everybody is a detractor) or as high as +100 (everybody is a promoter). An NPS that is positive, i.e. higher than zero, is felt to be good, and an NPS of +50 is excellent. More information on the NPS can be found in Chapter 12.
6 Thibeault, A., and Verweire, K. (2013) 'ING Direct USA: Asset or Liability for ING Group?', *Vlerick Business School Case Study*.
7 Ibid.
8 The Operational Excellence Pentagon is based on the input of three ING Direct USA managers. We then compared the company's average scores with the scores of the other companies in our database. The scores are percentiles, indicating the percentage of companies that have an equal or lower score for that particular item. High scores imply a high level of alignment.
9 Kuhlmann and Philp, *The Orange Code*, p. 95.
10 Verweire, K., and Van den Berghe, L. A. A. (2007) 'ING Direct: Rebel in the Banking Industry', *Vlerick Business School Case Study*, 307–053–1, p. 6.
11 Robertson, D., and Francis, I. (2003) 'ING Direct: Your Other Bank', *IMD Case Study*, IMD-3-1343, p. 7.
12 Seijts, G., Johnson, P. F., Crossan, M., Compeau, J., and Mark, K. (2010) 'ING Direct USA: Facing the Future', *Richard Ivey School of Business Case Study*, 9B10M090, p. 11.
13 Kirsner, S. (2003) 'Would You Like a Mortgage with Your Mocha?', *FastCompany*, 68 (March), 110.
14 Seijts *et al.*, 'ING Direct USA', p. 12.
15 Bergsman, S. (2006) 'The Orange Mortgage', *Mortgage Banking*, June, 48–53.
16 Seijts *et al.*, 'ING Direct USA', p. 12.
17 Kuhlmann, A. (2011) 'Rock Then Roll Your Business with Arkadi Kuhlmann', available at: http://rockthenrollyourbusiness.tumblr.com/post/11384718757/a-q-a-with-arkadi-kuhlmann-part-v-what-is-your-new (accessed 9 July 2013).
18 Seijts *et al.*, 'ING Direct USA', p. 16.
19 Kuhlmann and Philp, *The Orange Code*, p. 132.
20 Ibid., p. 144.
21 Ibid., p. 132.
22 Carrns, A. (2011) 'Capital One's Response to Outrage Over ING Direct purchase', *The New York Times*, 22 June.

PART IV

Strategy implementation at customer-intimacy firms

11

WHAT DOES IT MEAN TO BE CUSTOMER INTIMATE?

The last part of this book deals with the customer-intimacy operating model. In most industries today, it is difficult to make money by just selling products and services to customers. Stand-alone products and services commoditize rapidly and collapse profit margins. That made Jay Galbraith conclude that the new foundation of profitability is the customer relationship.[1] In response, some organizations have developed value-added strategies, through which they establish long-lasting relationships with their most important customers.

The ability to provide solutions and create and maintain relationships with your most valuable customers can be a durable basis for competitive advantage. In this respect, academicians explore concepts such as customer intimacy, customer centricity, market orientation or market-driving strategies. Unfortunately, the management literature is rather confusing as to what customer intimacy is and how it differs from the other concepts. As a result – despite all the rhetoric – few companies have become truly customer intimate. This also explains why customer intimacy is probably the least understood of the three operating models.

Figure 11.1 shows that a customer-intimacy operating model allows firms either to offer the best service or to become truly connected with their customers. However, both 'best service' and 'best connectivity' leave a lot of room for interpretation. What does a 'best service' value proposition really imply? And how connected should you be with your best customers? These are the topics of this chapter.

Providing more conceptual clarity on customer intimacy

Academicians and consultants use different terms to denote strategies that aim to offer tailored solutions and build lasting relationships with a firm's most valuable customers. Some use the terms *customer focus* or *customer centricity*. Firms are

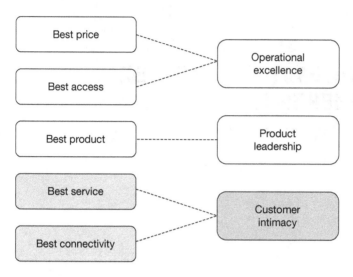

FIGURE 11.1 The value proposition of a customer-intimacy organization

customer-centric when they create and execute highly distinct, competitively dominant and profitable value propositions for different customer segments. Those companies strive to put the customer at the centre of their thinking and they align their entire organizational processes around the customer.

Marketers often use the term *market orientation* to indicate the extent to which a firm implements the marketing concept. The marketing concept, in turn, holds that the key to achieving organizational goals – such as market share and profitability – depends on determining the needs and wants of target markets and then satisfying their desires more effectively and efficiently than the competition does.[2] Along similar lines, George Day defines being *market-driven* as having a superior ability to understand, attract and retain valuable customers. Market-driven firms not only try to satisfy customers, they try to retain valuable customers by building deep loyalty that is rooted in mutual trust and bilateral commitments and communication.[3]

Michael Treacy and Fred Wiersema define *customer intimacy* as segmenting and targeting markets precisely and then tailoring offerings to match the demands of those niches exactly. Customer-intimacy firms combine detailed customer knowledge with operational flexibility, so that they can respond quickly to almost any need, from customizing a product to fulfilling special requests.[4]

What do all of these strategies have in common? In essence, they stretch beyond the core product to provide some added value. For the sake of clarity, the core product can be a consumer good (e.g. shampoo, a mobile phone), an industrial good (e.g. engines, packages) or it can be a service.[5] This implies that a firm provides added value by offering additional services and/or by getting closer to the customer.

I define customer intimacy as the operating model that allows a firm to offer better additional services and/or better connectivity (see Figure 11.2). The overall purpose of customer intimacy is to build longer-lasting and more profitable relationships with your most valuable and loyal customers. Customer retention is the name of the game for customer-intimacy companies. Those companies have realized that sales to existing customers are more profitable than sales to new customers.

Firms moving along the horizontal axis add services and products to their core product and combine it into a single offer. This is often referred to as *solutions* or *bundling*. By moving up along the vertical axis, firms add value through offering longer and deeper relationships to their customers. Whereas the first dimension deals more with *what* the company offers on top of its core product, the second dimension deals with *how* the company interacts with its key customers. In other words, the service dimension tells us something about the nature of the product that is offered to the customer. The connectivity dimension provides insights into how firms interact and build bonds with their most valuable customers. A key feature of customer-intimate firms is that they pay attention to relationship building more than their competitors do.

Customer-intimate organizations ensure that they differentiate from their competitors with their services or with their relationship efforts – relative to the competition, they either provide the 'best service' or the 'best connectivity' in a particular industry. That's where customer-intimacy firms differ from product leaders or operational excellence firms. Companies such as Amazon and Apple provide good service as well, but a service or connectivity orientation is not what pervades those companies. In the case of Amazon, the company has always pursued a process orientation; in the case of Apple, continuous product innovation is the company's overarching theme.

Many people do not see a difference between offering solutions and becoming connected, arguing that offering additional services and solutions requires

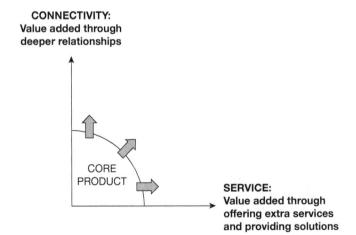

FIGURE 11.2 Creating added value through customer intimacy

customization and connectivity, but this is not always true. A manager of a transportation company told me that some of his customers want many extra services, but they have never engaged in a personal relationship with him. The relationship has remained professional and distant. Other customers like the personal relationship with the manager, but they buy the standard product package. Practice tells me, however, that firms that build a strategy on customer intimacy often go for both better service and better connectivity.

In the rest of this chapter, I will elaborate on what it means to offer the best service or the best connectivity.

Best service: towards providing real solutions

It is fashionable today to declare yourself a 'solutions provider', but, as with many management hypes, there is more to providing solutions than making a simple declaration. The major problem is that few companies understand what solutions really are. As a consequence, companies have no clear idea what it takes and how to organize to become a good solutions provider.

It's not easy to provide a clear definition for the concept 'solution' – most definitions only apply to B2B markets. However, solutions differ from industry to industry, and so, I won't offer a definition, but rather a Service Continuum, along which firms can move to develop more integrated solutions. Firms that want to move to a higher stage need to pass the previous stage. In each stage, companies develop the natural capabilities they need to successfully enter the next higher solutions level.

It is important to note that an organization should not necessarily pursue the highest solutions level, which is the 'business integration model'. For example, in the food retailing industry, the most customer-intimate organizations only provide a wide range of additional services (Level 1), without moving any further along the axis, but some of their suppliers engage in far-reaching partnerships with their most important customers. What matters is where you position yourself relative to your 'best-of-class' competitor or competitive alternative. There are no absolute standards.

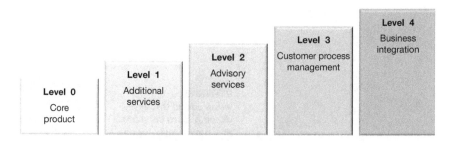

FIGURE 11.3 The Service Continuum: moving up the solutions axis[6]

Level 0: core product

Organizations might enjoy a competitive advantage if they offer a superior core product. In today's world, however, products commoditize, and core product advantages erode quickly. Firms can revitalize their core offer through product innovation or continuous improvement, but, after some time, these advantages are copied, and the firms have to start all over again.

A good core product does not make you customer intimate, but firms that pursue a customer-intimacy strategy should ensure that the quality of their core product is in line with their customers' expectations. Offering solutions and developing relationships with your key customers don't address any quality problems your core product might have.

Level 1: additional services

Offering better products or lower prices is one option for challenging the commodity magnet. Providing additional services is another one. Adding services is a first step towards providing solutions. Here, firms add a variety of complementary products and services to the core product, in order to create additional value for the customer and to differentiate the company's offering from the competition. Figure 11.4 shows that additional services can take many forms.

FIGURE 11.4 A range of additional services

Source: Adapted from Lovelock and Yip (1996)[7]

- Information tells customers how to use a particular product or service better. Some companies educate and train their customers so that they are able to fully utilize all of the core product's features.
- Order-taking flexibility is a second form of additional services and could include placing orders in the language of the customer or through the channel of the customer's choice.
- Hospitality means taking care of the customer; customer-intimate organizations treat customers as guests when they visit the supplier's facilities.
- Safekeeping is about looking after the customer's possessions when (s)he visits a service site. This can range from car parking to packaging and the delivery of new purchases.
- Offering exceptions is another additional service; examples include special requests, handling of complaints and restitutions.
- Payment services offer ease and convenience of payment to the customer. An example would be credit services.
- Customer-intimate firms have clearly defined which additional services to offer, how much of each service they want to offer, and to whom. The answer to these questions is a function of the industry (and that industry's competitive practices) in which the firm competes, the customer's requirements and the firm's service ambition. The most customer-intimate firms offer more additional services and a higher level of performance on those services as well. If customers appreciate the supplementary services that are offered, the firm might charge a price premium for the higher level of service. Most of the time (but not always), the more loyal and better customers receive more favourable treatment.

Case study: Zappos.com: providing a WOW service

Online retailer Zappos.com is known for the great additional services that it offers to its customers. Unlike many other websites that have special rules and lots of fine print, Zappos.com offers free shipping on all domestic orders placed on its website, with no special exceptions or minimum order required. If a customer is not 100 per cent satisfied with his/her purchase, she can return her order to the warehouse for a full refund.

What's more, customers can return their purchase for up to 365 days from the purchase date. (Customers purchasing on 29 February of a Leap Year have 4 years to return their orders.) Wow! Return shipping is absolutely free.

Of course, products must be in the original condition and in the original box and/or packaging. Once a customer's return is received and inspected by the fulfilment centres (usually within 72 hours of receipt), Zappos.com promises to refund the purchase amount within 7 days. Furthermore, the company also offers payment services, and it has a website that provides a lot of information, with operating instructions and useful information on how to deal with the company.

The Zappos philosophy is to do whatever it takes to impress a customer! The company has established a very particular culture and specific HR policies to nurture that service orientation throughout the entire company.

Other companies that are known for their service reputation because of great additional services include SIA, Nordstrom (a leading American fashion specialty retailer), Best Buy (an American retailer of consumer electronics), the Four Seasons and Ritz–Carlton hotel chains and Irma (a Danish supermarket chain).

For all these companies, the coaching and serving role has become a central element in their value proposition, and they invest a lot of resources to fulfil that role in the best way possible. In the earlier stage of the serving and coaching process, these firms offer the extra services to ease the selling process. Although they still focus very much on the transaction itself, the more intimate organizations get rid of the transactional mindset. Coaching and serving then become natural things for them to do. Ultimately, that's where the real competitive advantage of customer-intimate firms resides. After all, products and services can be easily copied – but the flair with which those products and services are offered is more difficult to imitate.

Some product leaders or operational excellence firms also provide great additional services. One example is Miele, the German producer of high-end domestic appliances and commercial equipment. The company has extensive interactive showrooms where you can try out the appliances and where showroom assistants answer all your questions. Miele also offers this service at home through its Miele Home Programme, and the company also offers extensive repair and maintenance programmes if the customer is willing to pay an extra amount of money. However, that does not make Miele a customer-intimate firm: Miele's customer orientation is largely restricted to the sales and service team and does not pervade the entire company. Most product-centric companies must realize that this is as far as their company can go in providing solutions. If those companies want to provide higher-level solutions, then they must make significant adaptations to their entire operating model.

Level 2: advisory services

When firms find that the added value is increasingly coming from their additional services, rather than from their core product, they are ready to move to the next stage on the Service Continuum. Level 2 is the stage at which a company differentiates itself with its advisory services. The focus of the firm shifts from a company's 'own product performance' to a company's 'customer success'. Many definitions of *solutions* refer to this particular stage. Solutions are typically developed as a combination of products, services *and* knowledge that address a customer's pressing business need. It's the *knowledge* component, in particular, that makes the difference.

At this level, companies need to develop a certain level of *expertise* in a particular field, which they then make available to their customers. Suppliers have to step outside their own perspective and start with a desired outcome for their customer. Customers will derive value from solutions through faster deployment, seamless operations, a focus on core activities, fewer up-front costs or reduced support costs.[8]

These advisory services are typically provided for a discrete project, rather than on an ongoing basis.

The initial work involved in building up expertise and creating solutions can be substantial. Organizations need to collect data on product and service performance and customer usage and then combine this with their accumulated knowledge of the customer process. Demonstrating technical expertise is a first step in building the trust that is necessary to developing long-term relationships with key customers. A supplier must also invest significant resources to continuously update and refresh its knowledge base. Although this is costly, it's a crucial investment.

Case study: Baxter Renal Care Division[9]

Baxter's Renal Division (until 2010, one of the three divisions within global healthcare corporation Baxter) is an excellent example of an organization that made the move from product to customer centricity in the late 1990s.

At that time, Baxter's Renal Care Division's revenues came from selling disposable bags of glucose solutions used for kidney dialysis at home. Renal patients with serious kidney problems usually began their treatment at home with peritoneal dialysis (PD) and then moved on to haemodialysis (HD) in the hospital, typically three 4-hour sessions a week. Baxter Renal Care was a market leader in the PD market, but PD was losing out to HD. On a bag-for-bag basis, HD was cheaper, and, at the same time, new PD entrants were competing on price.

Peter Leyland, who was appointed director of the European renal care division in 1997, believed that Baxter Renal Care had to change its focus from selling bags to extending the patient's life (and quality of life). From research, the company discovered that patients chose hospital treatment over home treatment when they did not know how to deal with the illness. Baxter decided to invest heavily in creating and overseeing patient training centres. The aim was to raise patient awareness and speed diagnosis and referral through mobile diagnostic centres and reaching out to practitioners. The company provided patients and practitioners with information on the benefits of different treatments. Baxter provided those services for free – but the costs of the training were more than compensated for by the increased sale of bags and the enhanced survival rates of the patients.

Baxter also provided training on treatment use and lifestyle modification. The company offered patients help when setting up equipment, and it provided them with emergency 24-hour clinical and technical help services by phone and the Internet. All of these training interventions reduced the patients' in-hospital costs dramatically. Baxter also provided support with home care, management of supplies and waste, and drug delivery for home or travel. The company gave its patients a consistent and personalized service.

This example illustrates how Baxter Renal Care Division was able to increase sales and profits by taking a different perspective. It looked at its business with a customer mindset, and it added a lot of advisory services to increase the patients' well-being.

Apart from having technical expertise, customer-intimate organizations also devote a significant amount of time to interacting with the customer. Succeeding in selling diagnostic and advisory services requires the organization to invest time to develop a *customized* response to a customer's needs, but this is where solutions often fail. Although many firms proclaim that they solve customer problems, customers don't always feel that way. They still see the supplier as pushing its products or services. Consultative selling then backfires, mainly because of a lack of trust between buyer and supplier. The supplier might have the expertise, but fails to get intimate.

Customers experience real trust when the solution provider also incorporates product or service components from its competitors. Suppliers should not be afraid to include 'strange bedfellows'. Suppliers, distributors, customers and even competitors may have an important role to play in providing products, services, skills, market knowledge and customer relationships.[10]

Initially, many firms offer the diagnostic and advisory services for free. Some firms, however, hoping to expand new business revenues, see a huge potential in developing the advisory and coaching activity as a separate business activity. The story of how Lou Gerstner launched IBM Business Solutions is well documented in the management literature. The creation of a solutions department can lead to fundamental questions as to what the organization's mission and business definition really are. IBM decided that its core business was no longer producing computers – instead, the company profiled itself as providing ICT consulting services, which brought it into a totally different market to its traditional core market. Be aware that many companies fail to transform their core business into a service business!

Examples of companies that have been successful in providing advisory services are: Tetra Pak, the processing and packaging company, and SKF, the world's largest producer of bearings. With its Performance Solutions programme, GE Healthcare helps leading healthcare systems sustainably improve operational and clinical performance through a combination of advisory services, technology and analytics. Jyske Bank and Svenska Handelsbanken in Scandinavia provide advisory services for better financial management.

Level 3: customer process management

Firms that have built significant expertise in a particular area and that have integrated it in their business offering can go one step further on the Service Continuum. At the third service level, firms go beyond the provision of advisory services: they take complete performance responsibility for particular customer activities, and they remove the customers' problems by assuming the duties that trouble them. Such customer-intimate companies do for the customer what the customer cannot, or will not, do him- or herself. They 'insource' a customer's problems and solve them. Customer process management, however, only works if the customer views this value proposition from a TCO perspective. Customer process management helps reduce a company's overall costs, which include acquisition costs and operating costs.

An important characteristic of customer process management solutions is that suppliers take managed risks and include performance-based contracts. The solutions provider takes on the burden of improving the efficiency and capabilities of the customer's business process and is rewarded based on results. In the worst case, 'no cure' means 'no pay'. Gains are shared – and this can be a very profitable business model for suppliers, provided that they have deep insights into the profit drivers of an industry. Sharing gains can also be a very convincing sales argument, as it shows the supplier's commitment and expertise. However, customers are sometimes sceptical about the performance promises the solution provider makes. Creating trust – once again – is a very important element in convincing customers of the added value of this new value proposition.

Some companies have been very successful with customer process management. Examples include: BASF Coatings with its Integrated Paint Shop, Swedish cement and mineral company FLSchmidt and Johnson Controls' Global WorkPlace Solutions unit. The story of Michelin Fleet Solutions is another illustrative case.

Case study: Michelin Fleet Solutions

In 2000, Michelin, a world leader in the tyre industry, launched Michelin Fleet Solutions, a new venture that started to sell kilometres instead of tyres. The new division's focus was no longer on selling a product (a tyre), but on providing customers with a service: that is, the ability to drive.

Michelin Fleet Solutions offered large European fleets the complete management of their tyre assets during a 3- to 5-year period. By outsourcing tyre management, transportation companies could expect to gain peace of mind, achieve better cost control (fewer breakdowns, lower fuel expenses, better operations management, less administrative burden) and benefit from Michelin's continuous innovation. For Michelin, this was a great way to develop long-lasting relationships with growing transport players and ensure that clients would eventually experience the full value of Michelin tires. Offering solutions was a way to escape the commodity trap by differentiating Michelin's offer from the competition. Michelin charged its clients a monthly fee, which depended on the number of kilometres driven per vehicle. This allowed clients to turn all tyre-related costs into a variable cost directly linked to vehicle use. Michelin's profitability depended on its ability to optimize tyre management activities and to control costs. In the traditional model, a truck breakdown represents an unforeseen cost factor – whereas with Michelin Fleet Solutions, Michelin assumes the industrial risk in exchange for a predictable monthly fee.[11]

The fleet solutions initiative was not launched without problems. Michelin's sales force (which was used to selling tyres) had difficulties showing clients the value of this solution offer. There were also conflicts with the traditional product sales force. And when Michelin started to offer the solution, it discovered that it had underestimated the costs of providing a much more complex selling and delivery process. However, by 2006, Michelin was able to turn its Fleet Solutions business into a profitable venture.

Level 4: business integration

The final stage on the Service Continuum is where the supplier and customer integrate their business processes. Business integration is typically found in B2B markets. In this model, customer and supplier together take responsibility for finding the most productive solutions, changing their processes, their practices and their behaviour in the pursuit of common goals. At the customer process management level, the supplier and customer make a clear demarcation between what is the customer's responsibility and what is the supplier's responsibility. This distinction is less clear at the business integration level.

Business integration implies that the customer and supplier are committed to working closely together to achieve a shared objective and to finding the best solutions for problems that may arise. In this model, suppliers and customers agree that they will create results together. For example, the supplier and the customer can collaborate on design. In this particular case, the customer becomes a fully-fledged member of the supplier's design team. Or the supplier may intervene in the customer's sales process, helping the customer open up new accounts or deal with problem areas. In fact, suppliers and customers can collaborate on any strategic project that is relevant to the customer.

Business integration requires a partnership mindset. The partnership can grow over time and involve the entire synchronization of the two partner operations. This involves the sharing of technology and data and the integration of systems to share supervision of the operations. In this situation, there should be full transparency and trust, as the two partners share sensitive strategic information. Sometimes, supplier and customer jointly redesign their operating models and business processes, as if they were a single company.[12] Supplier and customer often set up a formal alliance or a joint venture to formalize the business integration. Companies that offer these forms of solutions to their customers must possess deal-making capabilities.

ABB, a global leader in power and automation technologies, has used joint ventures to run the operations of its customers. Another famous alliance between a supplier and customer is the partnership between P&G and Walmart.

Case study: business integration between P&G and Walmart

In the late 1980s, Walmart was a major P&G customer, but the relationship was anything but collaborative. Their relationship was actually adversarial, obsessed by day-to-day transactions. It was Sam Walton, founder of Walmart, who pushed for a more efficient collaboration between Walmart and his supplier: 'The way we do things is way too complicated. You should automatically send me Pampers, and I should send you a check once a month. We ought to get rid of all this negotiation and invoicing.'[13]

The two companies found a way to share data across their mutual supply chains. Information sharing allowed for continuous replenishment. This meant that P&G replenished Walmart's inventory based on inventory data from Walmart's distribution centre – which led to substantial cost-savings in logistics.

But the cooperation did not stop at logistics. Representatives of the two companies also looked at collaboration initiatives in billing, payments and category management. All those initiatives meant that the companies had to synchronize their processes and systems, but that is a key factor in making channel partnerships work.[14]

Strategic partnerships lead to mutual obligations, limiting both parties' degrees of freedom. When problems arise, the two partners are obliged to look for solutions, instead of merely switching partners, but that is the price that both supplier and customer are willing to pay to obtain the benefits of the collaboration.

Checklist: 'customer intimacy and best service'

Does your company have a strategy built around customer intimacy? Have you worked out an explicit and clear service strategy? Do you strive to give the best service in your industry? And what does 'best service' mean for your organization?

1   Do you have an attractive product that is sold at an acceptable price? Can customers obtain your product(s) in an efficient and hassle-free way?
2   Does your company provide additional services? Are these additional services a key element in differentiating yourself from your competitors? What additional services do you offer?
3   Do you offer advisory services? Has your company developed a particular expertise that you make available to your best customers? To what extent do competitors offer similar advisory services?
4   Does your company take complete responsibility for selected business processes or activities of your best customers? Does your fee depend on the performance that you have achieved with this 'insourcing'?
5   To what extent have you worked on business integration with some of your key customers? Has your company aligned operations with key customers?

Best connectivity: getting – and staying – connected

The previous section outlined what firms can offer their best customers, in addition to their core product. In this section, I focus on the relationship that a company can pursue with its best customers. This dimension deals more with *how* the company interacts, rather than *what* it offers. The opening statement of this chapter already revealed that building true relationships with your best customers can be the basis of a firm's competitive advantage. A key feature of customer-intimate firms is that they pay more attention to relationship building than their competitors do. But what does relationship building mean? And how far should companies go in relating with their customers?

Generally, when a firm tries to attract a new customer, it often puts significant effort into the customer acquisition process. The firm might take time to figure out what the customer's needs are and how to sell its products or services to potential customers. All too often, however, after the sale is made, a supplier's efforts at interaction with that customer decrease rather quickly. In many cases, the customer becomes a record in the supplier's administration database.

Not so in the case of customer-intimacy firms! Customer-intimacy firms realize that creating a loyal customer base requires continuous interaction with your best customers that extends beyond the customer acquisition phase. This is illustrated in Figure 11.5.

What kinds of interaction do customer-intimacy firms maintain after the customer acquisition phase? Again, there is no single answer to this question. Firms can have different sorts of relationship with their customers, and some firms have chosen to go further than others. For example, some firms have rather impersonal, transactional relationships with their customers, whereas others share information, link or integrate activities, and socialize.

In analogy to the Service Continuum, I have developed a Connectivity Continuum that describes different relationship levels between a firm and its best customers. Figure 11.6 shows that the partnering relationship is the most advanced stage of relationship building. Before a firm has achieved this connectivity level, it needs to have successfully passed the previous stages on the connectivity axis. Again, at each stage, companies develop natural capabilities to successfully enter the next, higher level of connectivity.

It is important to note that the *customer* determines and controls the nature of the interactions with the supplier. For example, if the customer is not open to a personal relationship with his or her supplier, then suppliers should be happy with a convenience relationship, or even a transactional relationship. The firm's job is to provide an environment in which the optimal level of relationship, which may vary from customer to customer, can flourish.

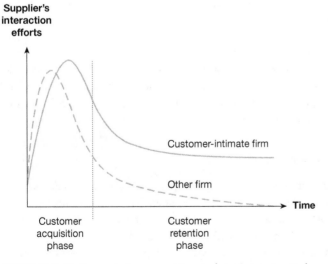

FIGURE 11.5 Customer intimacy: getting and staying connected

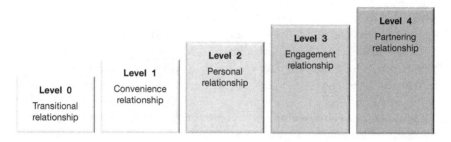

FIGURE 11.6 The Connectivity Continuum: towards true partnerships

Level 0: transactional relationship

The basic level of relationship a firm can have with its customer is a transactional relationship. This relationship, which is most prevalent in everyday or low-cost transactions, reflects a rational orientation on the customer's part. The customer wants to obtain a product or service. For the firm, this implies a relationship that fosters efficiency in transaction and straightforward, no-hassle sales. In such utility relationships, you satisfy your customers when you provide the product or service they want, when they want it and for the price they want to pay. If you do not meet these basic expectations, no relationship or intimacy strategy will ever make up for the flaws in your overall product offer.

This means that you should be careful when probing for deeper relationships, because there is a risk that clients may withdraw as they consider deeper relationships inappropriate or undesired. Of course, this does not mean that suppliers cannot have personal relationship with particular clients, but the decision to engage in deeper relationships is merely an ad hoc decision made by a sales or service representative. It is not part of a broader sales strategy.

If firms would like to strengthen the transactional relationships with their customers, they can increase the number of interaction occasions and make it easier for customers to transact with the supplier. These relationships can also be strengthened by broadening the customer's interaction with other products and services and by engaging in cross-selling activities, or firms can look to make the shopping experience fun and enjoyable.

Level 1: convenience relationship

At the transactional relationship level, suppliers do not see any advantage to knowing the customer better. However, this changes when firms move to the next level on the Connectivity Continuum and start to collect and act upon customer information in a more systematic way. At Level 1, suppliers move away from the very short-term horizon and start to develop relationship capabilities. Firms no longer see customers as strangers but as 'acquaintances'.[15] They reward their loyal customers in many different ways: they give financial rewards, or provide tailor-made products or some other preferential treatment. The customers are open to a relationship, and they expect the supplier to use the information they provide to streamline the entire customer experience cycle – which describes the steps people go through from purchasing a product or service to discarding it (the phases from 'get it' to 'use it' to 'fix it' to 'discard it').

A convenience relationship can only be established if there is a repetitive interaction with the customer. With each interaction, the customer becomes more familiar with the supplier's products or services and modus operandi. Thus, a convenience relationship facilitates transactions primarily by reducing the customer's perceived risk and costs. That's how suppliers can win credibility – that is, the belief that the supplier can and will perform as promised – in the market.

A convenience relationship can involve customization (especially in a B2B environment), but, in general, the relationship has an impersonal character, and the emphasis in the interaction is rational rather than emotional. Consequently, the potential to develop a sustainable competitive advantage through convenience relationship activities is rather limited.[16] However, some firms have developed a sustainable competitive advantage by exploiting the information received from their customers and by learning from the transactions as a whole. For example, both Dell and Amazon have combined customer information management capabilities with a highly developed order and sales system. These companies have created some sense of intimacy with their customers, even if they restrict their interactions to the purely rational level. One of Dell's customers described his relationship with the company as follows: 'From the very beginning, the relationship with Dell has been driven by data, not by dinners.'[17]

Engaging in convenience relationships with your best customers does not make you intimate. I have called the convenience relationship a first step towards more connectivity, because it is a significant step forward compared with the transactional relationship. However, in whatever industry you compete, real customer intimacy starts at Level 2. This is represented graphically in Figure 11.6, where the 'convenience relationship' is still white, not shaded.

Level 2: personal relationship

Firms move to the next connectivity level when they systematically engage in personal relationships with their most loyal customers. Therefore, identifying your *'crown jewels'* is an important task. After all, you need to develop profitable relationships with your customers – which is why most customer-intimacy firms focus their service and relationship efforts on only 20 per cent of their best customers.

Remember: not every customer is a crown jewel! When selecting your 'preferred customers', financial considerations are only part of the picture. Crown jewels are those customers that contribute significantly to your current bottom line or that have the potential to contribute in the future. You also need to look at the relationship orientation of your customers; you can only develop personal relationships with customers who are open to such a personal relationship. Customers are open to personal relationships when they want to interact in a way that involves recognition of their personal choices. That recognition can be a financial reward for their loyalty, such as better rates and conditions, or privileged treatment. Do not underestimate the importance of psychological rewards. Customers enjoy the benefits of talking to a friendly, enjoyable person who takes the time to listen and who is interested in the customer's personal situation.

Typically, firms that aim for personal relationships with their customers invest a lot in their front office people. Great customer experiences are built with *empathic* people – not only do they have technical expertise, they are brimming over with emotional intelligence. In a business-to-consumer (B2C) setting, we see that firms try to put employee policies in place that are focused on retaining core employees. You cannot develop personal relationships with your customers when your sales and service people turn over again and again. In a B2B context, firms that develop personal relationships create key account management structures with their most important customers to embed the relationship in a more structured way.

Personal relationships require two-way communication. This might involve substantial investments from a company. The European bank that I referred to in the introduction of the first chapter of this book, for example, invited all of its customers to its branches for a 1-hour interview. The goal of those meetings was to listen to the customers' financial needs. The bank employees were forbidden to sell a single product – the focus was on *listening*, not selling. Most customers were surprised by this initiative and appreciated it a lot.

Communicating and registering the information in a systematic way – and acting on it – might give a firm a substantial competitive advantage. With each inter-action, a company knows more about the customer, and the relationship has the potential to evolve. What's more, this advantage is increasingly difficult for competitors to copy.

An important difference from the previous level is that the information is not limited to the customer's buying process or product usage, but often includes information on the consumer's identity. Suppliers want to gain insights into individual customers, which will provide the supplier with greater understanding about the right offering. However, the contact database in personal relationships is rather narrow and focused around the product. Also, personal relationships are usually more reactive than proactive – most often, the customer takes the initiative to get in touch.

Case study: personal relationships at Nordstrom

Nordstrom is an American fashion specialty retailer known for its exceptionally broad selection of merchandise and the special ambience in its stores: there is a piano player on the first floor, and you can enjoy a good cup of coffee in the Nordstrom Cafés.

However, the difference is made by the service the salespeople provide. Shoppers are assisted by knowledgeable and friendly salespeople, who are committed to serving their customers throughout the store. The salespeople offer a high degree of personalized attention, as well as services that are uncommon in other retailers, such as calling the customer when suitable shoes or apparel arrive, or providing home delivery.

The salespeople are charged with serving customers, even if doing so means breaching usual procedures. The company uses a CRM tool called the Personal Book, which stores information on customer preferences, purchases and outstanding orders. The Personal Book enables the salespeople to have a more active role in the sales and service process.[18]

Level 3: engagement relationship

Once a firm has the skills to engage in personal relationships, it may decide to pursue a deeper level of relationship with its best customers. In Level 3 – the engagement relationship – the supplier and the customer make a clear commitment to maintain and invest in the relationship. For the supplier, this means that it will engage in a long-term relationship with the customer. The supplier must invest and immerse itself in the life of the customer in order to provide customized solutions. It is also very important that the supplier, not only looks at the business from the customer's perspective, but sometimes even jeopardizes its own profitability in favour of the customer. The customer, on the other hand, is prepared to be open about its strategic challenges and allows the supplier to become its trusted advisor, typically on a broader set of topics than the supplier's product base.

The Tetra Pak case illustrates very well the challenges of moving from a personal relationship to an engagement relationship.

Case study: the challenge of being intimate with a key account[19]

Tetra Pak is a processing and packaging firm known for its customer orientation. Once, an important customer asked for help in stopping its declining sales and the erosion of its margin. The customer had come to Tetra Pak because the company had a lot of market data (Tetra Pak supplied about 80 per cent of the market with packaging solutions). Furthermore, Tetra Pak had already helped the company by advising it to move into a new product market. This time, however, the customer heavily contested the advice of the marketing and sales team. What had happened?

When Tetra Pak analysed its advice, it realized it had been too product-focused: rather than solving the customer's strategic needs – improving the top and bottom lines – Tetra Pak had offered a packaging solution, not really what the customer needed. Furthermore, the customer argued that Tetra Pak had not aligned its goals with the customer's goals. This is precisely what the customer understood when Tetra Pak talked about customer intimacy. The customer wanted an engagement relationship, not just a recognition or personal relationship.

In response to these customer complaints, Tetra Pak successfully embarked on an extensive set of company-wide initiatives to better align with its key customers and to improve customer satisfaction.

This case study reveals a common trap that I find with many so-called customer-intimate firms. They engage in relationships, but fail to take the customer's perspective. Furthermore, such firms do not look beyond their own product solutions – which, again, is a sign of being too narrowly focused. When customers open up to an engagement relationship, the supplier must engage in a certain level of proactivity and be willing to think along with the customer. One manager of a company once noted: 'Signing a contract is not enough. It's like getting married – only once you have signed does the real life begin!' This is typical for engagement relationships.

Level 4: partnering relationship

In engagement relationships, the relationship is driven by the supplier's account manager. The relationship might involve other departments (such as operations or R&D), but the collaboration is orchestrated by the supplier's account manager and the customer's purchasing manager.

At the next level of the Connectivity Continuum, this collaboration is no longer handled by the account and purchasing managers, but by the top management of both the customer and supplier organizations. Firms reach the partnering level when they share goals, management practices and incentives with their best customers. At this stage, both the supplier and the customer acknowledge the importance of each to the other – they are locked in to each other. Ending the relationship is painful and costly (it is like a divorce). A partnering relationship requires commitment to forging a long-term relationship that creates synergies of knowledge and security, and both partners must be willing to adapt and change their operations and management practices. At this level, a customer-intimate firm no longer regards the customer as a customer but as a partner. Obviously, these firms have integrated their businesses, and so partnering inevitably also means pursuing business integration with your customer.

The supplier and the customer have set up various initiatives together, and they manage those initiatives with a collaborative mindset. The collaboration pervades the whole company – a range of functions in both organizations work closely together in dedicated focus teams, and the key to success in such a partner relationship is to make teamwork work. The mentality is one of continuous improvement, and the two partners collaborate intensively to run the business more efficiently and share the gains of their improvement efforts. This is illustrated in Figure 11.7: the customer and the supplier become so integrated that individuals feel more affinity with their team than with their official employer – in fact, the teams run the business.

The difference between a partnering relationship and an engagement relationship lies mainly in the intensity and the scope of the collaboration. Partnering

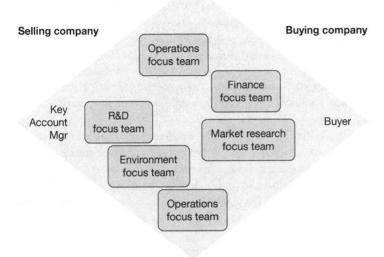

FIGURE 11.7 A partnering relationship between buyer and seller

Source: McDonald (2000)[20]

relationships require that the relationship between a customer and a supplier extend beyond the purchasing manager and the key account manager. It involves many different departments within the two companies. Furthermore, the relationship is a true learning relationship that is strategic for both partners. The case study of Denso and Toyota is a good illustration of such a relationship, built on trust, commitment and cooperation.

Case study: a partnering relationship between Denso and Toyota[21]

One of the most intense partnerships in the world is probably the electrical parts company Denso's relationship with its main customer, Toyota. Denso is one of the few sole suppliers in the TPS (typically, Toyota has at least two suppliers for every component). One of the key characteristics of the Denso–Toyota relationship is the fact that both companies share a common destiny. Denso has invested a lot in skills specific to Toyota's requirements, but the relationship is also based on trust, commitment and cooperation. For Toyota, trust means having high expectations of its suppliers, but treating them fairly and providing them with ongoing training. An interesting fact in the Denso–Toyota relationship is that Denso taught Toyota the principles of quality management (and not the other way around). So, in a partnering relationship, both companies learn from each other. They share responsibilities, they share the risks, and they share the gains.

Checklist: 'customer intimacy and best connectivity'

How important is it for your company to build relationships with your best customers? Are your customer relationships key to your competitive advantage? Does your company have an explicit and clear connectivity strategy? What does 'best connectivity' mean for your organization?

1   Do you meet your customers' fundamental expectations with regard to the delivery of your products? Do you understand how your customers want to relate with you?

2   Are you a credible and reliable supplier to your customers? Do you recognize your best customers, and do you offer them better and faster treatment? Do you make it easier for those customers to obtain and use your goods?

3   Do you take the time to listen to and understand your customers' individual needs and to serve them well? Do you build personal and intimate relationships with your most loyal customers? And what rewards do you offer to your loyal customers?

4   Does your company invest a lot of time and effort in building and maintaining long-term relationships with your most loyal customers? Can you broaden the discussion with your customers beyond your own products and services? When offering solutions, do you sometimes shift your attention from your profitability to the profitability of your customers?

5   Are you partners with your customers, working towards some common objectives and goals? Does the partnership extend beyond your key account manager and the customer's purchasing manager? Have you set up dedicated focus teams to align your operations? Do you share responsibilities, risks and rewards with your customers?

Key learning points

Being customer intimate is about providing great extra services and/or building deep, long-term relationships with your best customers. Few companies specify clearly how they define customer intimacy, leaving room for different interpretations among managers and employees on the content of the value proposition. Winning companies, however, have devised and maintain a clearly stated, focused value proposition. Companies can only achieve excellence in strategy when they are clear about what customer intimacy means in practice and when they consistently communicate this idea to their customers and employees.

This chapter has explored what 'best service' and 'best connectivity' could mean. Both the Service Continuum and the Connectivity Continuum should compel you to think more specifically about your value proposition. It is important that all of the key people in your organization have a common understanding of what 'best service' and/or 'best connectivity' mean, so that you can provide a consistently high level of integration and customization – which will help you stay ahead of your competitors.

Notes

1 Galbraith, J. R. (2005) *Designing the Customer-Centric Organization: A Guide to Strategy, Structure, and Process*, Jossey-Bass, San Francisco, CA, p. 1.

2 Agarwal, S., Erramilli, M. K., and Dev, C. S. (2003) 'Market Orientation and Performance in Service Firms: Role of Innovation', *The Journal of Services Marketing*, 17 (1), 68–82.

3 Day, G. S. (1998) 'What Does It Mean to Be Market-Driven?', *Business Strategy Review*, 9 (1), 1–14.

4 Treacy, M., and Wiersema, F. (1995) *The Discipline of Market Leaders*, Perseus, New York, p. 84.

5 Christopher Lovelock and George Yip distinguish between three types of service business: (1) people-processing services involve tangible actions to customers in person (e.g. airline companies, hotels, restaurants); (2) possession-processing services involve tangible actions to physical objects to improve their value to customers (e.g. warehousing, maintenance, car repair); and (3) information-based services collect, manipulate, interpret and transmit data to create value (e.g. banking, consulting, education). For more information, we refer to Lovelock, C. H., and Yip, G. S. (1996) 'Developing Global Strategies for Service Businesses', *California Management Review*, 38 (2), 64–86.

6 The Service Continuum is inspired by a publication from Corporate Executive Board (2001) *Optimizing Customer Performance: Bringing Discipline to Customer Solutions Strategies*, Corporate Executive Board, Washington, DC.

7 Lovelock and Yip, 'Developing Global Strategies for Service Businesses', 70–1.

8 Kumar, N. (2004) *Marketing as Strategy: Understanding the CEO's Agenda for Driving Growth and Innovation*, Harvard Business Press, Boston, MA.

9 This case study is based on the work of Professor Sandra Vandermerwe: Vandermerwe, S. (2000) 'How Increasing Value to Customers Improves Business Results', *Sloan Management Review*, Fall, 27–37; Vandermerwe, S., and Taishoff, M. (1997) 'Baxter A: A Changing Customer Environment', *Case Study The Management School – Imperial College*, 597–039–1, pp. 1–18; Vandermerwe, S., and Taishoff, M. (1997) 'Baxter B: Total Lifetime Consumer Strategy', *Case Study The Management School – Imperial College*, 597–040–1, pp. 1–10; Vandermerwe, S., and Taishoff, M. (1997) 'Baxter C: Balancing the Score', *Case Study The Management School – Imperial College*, 597–041–1, pp. 1–2.

10 Foote, N. W., Galbraith, J. S., Hope, Q., and Miller, D. (2001) 'Making Solutions the Answer', *The McKinsey Quarterly*, 3, 84–93.

11 Renault, C., Dalsace, F., and Ulaga, W. (2006) 'Michelin Fleet Solutions: From Selling Tyres to Selling Kilometers', *HEC Paris Case Study*, 510–103–1, p. 6.

12 Wiersema, F. (1998) *Customer Intimacy: Pick Your Partners, Shape Your Culture, Win Together*, HarperColllinsBusiness, London.

13 Koch, C. (2002) 'Interview with Ralph Drayer on CPFR, Business Process Automation and P&G's Deal with Walmart', *CIO*, 12 (1 August).

14 Graen, M., and Shaw, M. J. (2003) 'Supply-Chain Partnership Between P&G and Walmart' in Shaw, M. J. (ed.) *E-Business Management: Integration of Web Technologies and Business Models*, Kluwer Academic, Boston, MA, pp. 155–72.

15 Johnson, M. D., and Selnes, F. (2004) 'Customer Portfolio Management: Toward a Dynamic Theory of Exchange Relationships', *Journal of Marketing*, 68 (April), 1–17.

16 Malaviya, P., and Spargo, S. (2004) 'Strengthening Customer Relationships' in Chowdhury, Subir, *Next Generation Business Handbook: New Strategies for Tomorrow's Thought Leaders*, John Wiley & Sons, Hoboken, NJ.

17 Chung, R., Marchand, D. A., and Kettinger, W. J. (2003) 'Dell's Direct Model: Everything to Do with Information', *IMD Case Study*, IMD-3–1149, p. 8.

18 Lal, R., and Han, A. (2005) 'Nordstrom: The Turnaround', *Harvard Business School Case Study*, 9–505–051, pp. 1–35.

19 Shaner, J., and Kashani, K. (2002) 'Tetra Pak (A): The Challenge of Intimacy with a Key Customer', *IMD Case Study*, IMD-5–0604, pp. 1–14; Shaner, J., and Kashani, K.

(2002) 'Tetra Pak (B): Hear Me, Know Me, Grow Me: The Customer Satisfaction Initiative', *IMD Case Study*, IMD-5–0605, pp. 1–9; Shaner, J., and Kashani, K. (2002) 'Tetra Pak (C): Implementing New Initiatives', *IMD Case Study*, IMD-5–0606, pp. 1–5; Shaner, J., and Kashani, K. (2002) 'Tetra Pak (D): Results Achieved (and the Remaining Issues)', *IMD Case Study*, IMD-5–0606, pp. 1–6.

20 McDonald, M. (2000) 'Key Account Management: A Domain Review', *The Marketing Review*, 1, 28.

21 Anderson, E. (2003) 'The Enigma of Toyota's Competitive Advantage: Is Denso the Missing Link in the Academic Literature?', *Pacific Economic Papers – Asia Pacific School of Economics and Government*, 339, 1–38.

12

WHAT DOES IT TAKE TO BE CUSTOMER INTIMATE?

How customer-intimacy organizations implement strategy

Building up a customer-intimate organization means developing a particular set of operational and management competences. Management authors often highlight one aspect of the customer–intimacy challenge. They tell you how to set up and use customer relationship management tools effectively, or they show you how to develop a service-oriented culture. But to become a truly customer-intimate organization requires more than that. Tony Hsieh, the CEO of Zappos.com (the famous online shoe and apparel shop), described the challenge as follows:

> Customer service is not just a department. We have been asked by a lot of people how we have grown so quickly, and the answer is actually really simple . . . We have aligned the entire organization around one mission: to provide the best customer service possible.[1]

The Customer Intimacy Pentagon, which is built around the five levers of the Strategy Implementation Framework that I introduced in Chapter 3, shows the breadth of activities and capabilities that customer-intimacy firms need to master in order to be successful with their strategy. Most companies struggle to get aligned around the mission of 'best customer service possible'. This chapter explains what alignment entails for customer-intimacy firms.

In addition to creating alignment, customer intimacy requires commitment from the entire organization. Not only should front-line employees be empowered to provide great service, customer intimacy also requires commitment from the back-office people and from the staff departments. Only then will the strategy translate into great results.

The Customer Intimacy Pentagon: identifying the fifteen core activities that constitute customer intimacy

Effective strategy implementation means that an organization takes particular actions in support of a particular strategy. This is the essence of strategic alignment. What are the actions that customer-intimacy firms have taken to build a loyal customer base through great additional services and long-lasting relationships? I have identified fifteen core activities that you find in most successful customer-intimacy organizations (see Figure 12.1).

The Customer Intimacy Pentagon: research background

The Customer Intimacy Pentagon is the result of a research project that I and my research associates at Vlerick Business School conducted in the middle of 2010.[2] A first part of the research project involved an extensive literature review on customer intimacy, solutions selling, relationship building, customer centricity and

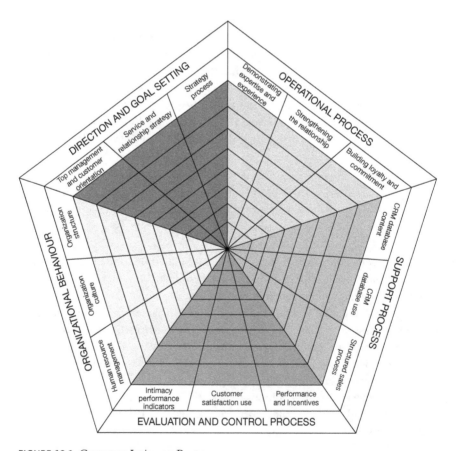

FIGURE 12.1 Customer Intimacy Pentagon

other related topics. Then we explored twenty case studies of well-known customer-intimate firms.[3] The literature review and the case analyses revealed to us the management and operational practices that are found in highly successful customer-intimacy firms.

We then developed a questionnaire and collected customer intimacy and performance data on 207 companies. The managers of these companies had been interviewed by our students or had participated in our executive MBA or executive programmes at our school. We collected responses from at least three managers for each company. The data allowed us to calculate percentiles for each company on the fifteen items of the Customer Intimacy Pentagon. We also asked the managers to benchmark their company's revenue growth and profit margin relative to their main competitors. The performance data allowed us to classify firms as top performers, average performers and bottom performers. In our sample, there were 16 top performers, 176 average performers and 15 bottom performers.

In our research project, we tested whether the top performers were more aligned than the average and bottom performers in the sample. First, we calculated average percentiles for top, average and bottom performers (see Figure 12.2). Second, we examined how many times a company had an item with a percentile higher than seventy-five. The maximum score is fifteen. We calculated average scores for the top, average and bottom performers (see Figure 12.3).

The results indicate that top performers – companies that grow their revenues faster, and have a higher profitability, than their competitors – are more aligned than the average and bottom performers. Figure 12.2 shows that top performers have scores in the fifty-ninth percentile; the percentile for the average performers and the bottom performers is forty-eight and forty-one, respectively. Figure 12.3

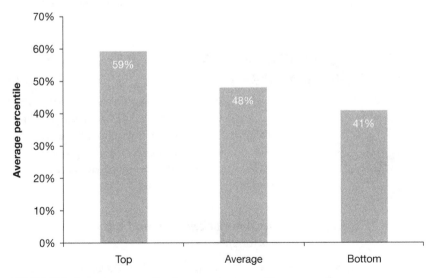

FIGURE 12.2 Average percentiles for top, average and bottom performers

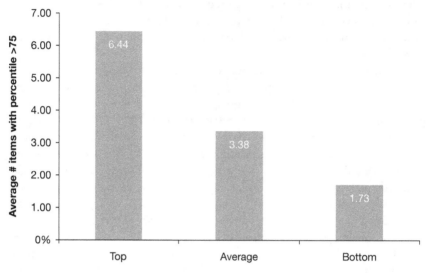

FIGURE 12.3 Number of items with percentile >75 for top, average and bottom performers

indicates that, on average, top performers have 6.44 out of 15 items with a percentile higher than seventy-five. The scores for average and bottom performers are significantly lower. The two figures clearly indicate that there is a correlation between alignment and performance.

What are the core activities that you find in the most successful customer-intimate companies? As with the other operating models, I have identified fifteen core activities that cover all five areas of the Strategy Implementation Framework that I introduced in Chapter 3.

Direction and goal setting: an explicit service and relationship strategy supported by the top

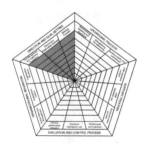

How do customer-intimacy firms use direction- and goal-setting processes to emphasize a service- and relationship-based strategy throughout the company? What is top management's role in this process? And to what extent are customers involved in the strategy process?

Customer orientation and top management

If a customer-intimate organization is like an engine, then leadership is the fuel that starts it and keeps it running. Leaders should formally express their commitment to personalized services: customers must feel special and important. The top management signals its commitment to customer intimacy by deeds and time spent. It is not sufficient to have annual reports and public interviews proclaim a market orientation – employees need to witness behaviours and resource allocations that reflect a commitment to customer intimacy. This can be done in several ways. For example, top managers intervene directly to help solve a customer's problem. Or they spend time visiting key customers and listen carefully to understand their point of view.

In all their communications, they need to show that superior service quality and great customer relations are core elements of the company's culture. This can be reinforced by highlighting customer service successes and failures and emphasizing the importance of customer satisfaction as a key performance indicator for the organization.

The company's beliefs, values, norms and working practices should reflect the ambition to achieve unmatched service behaviour and long-term relationships. This should also be the topic of the company's orchestrating theme – that is, a theme that gives the business an identity in the market and the customer a reason to buy. Such an orchestrating theme ensures company-wide understanding and support for developing customer relations. In light of this, each department can then determine how it can improve customer relations and create measurement standards to track performance. A great case that illustrates a customer-oriented orchestrating theme is the one regarding Jyske Bank in Denmark.

Case study: 'Jyske Differences'[4]

In the late 1990s, Jyske Bank identified the 'Jyske Differences' – the core values that were understood by all employees. The core values were that the bank should: (1) exercise common sense, (2) be open and honest, (3) be different and unpretentious, (4) have genuine interest and equal respect for people, and (5) be efficient and persevering.

Managers looked to the Jyske values and differences for the bank's competitive positioning, and they felt that the 'genuine interest' component of the bank's values dictated a shift from traditional, product-focused selling to a customer-solution approach.

Although the bank's core financial products remained essentially like those of other Danish banks, the way they were delivered changed. This required significant changes in the branches, both tangible and intangible. For example, the branches were redesigned to look like a stylish hotel. Bankers' desks were round tables, to signal equality. Intangible changes included a change in the loan approval process (branches could now underwrite larger loans) and more empowered and better trained employees. Tools were developed to support solution-based service delivery.

Service and relationship strategy

Customer intimacy requires that firms offer additional services and build deeper relationships with their customers – that's how they will differentiate from their competitors. The key question is whether a customer-intimacy firm should offer those services and build those relationships with all of its customers?

The answer is clearly 'no': the best customers should get the best treatment. Then the question becomes: Who are the best customers? The best customers are those for whom the company can do the most and where the company can translate its offering into loyalty *and* superior profitability. Customer-intimate companies must focus on these *crown jewels*, because the high cost of personalized services must be compensated for by the additional profit stream directly attributed to the differential treatment. That's why the 'best customer' must be described in terms of profitability and loyalty at the same time.[5]

According to Werner Reinartz and V. Kumar, managing customers for loyalty is not the same as managing them for profits. Some customers are profitable but not loyal, and vice versa. So, the two authors have argued to classify customers into four loyalty/profitability categories: true friends, butterflies, barnacles and strangers:

- The most favourable customers are the 'true friends', because they are loyal and highly profitable at the same time. The reason is that there is a great fit between the company's offerings and the customers' needs. The company should concentrate on finding ways to bring to the fore their true friends' feelings of loyalty, because 'true believers' are the most valuable customers of all.
- The 'butterflies' are profitable, short-term customers. Again, there is a good fit between the company's offerings and the customers' needs. The classic mistake made in managing these customers is continuing to invest in them after their activity drops off. In practice, this usually means that the company should simply focus on a satisfactory transaction.
- Then, there are the 'barnacles' – loyal customers with low profit potential. If the customer has a 'small wallet', the company must impose strict cost controls. However, if the customer represents a small share of the wallet and could potentially spend more, the company can focus on up- and cross-selling.
- Finally, 'strangers' are customers who have no loyalty and bring no profits to the company. You must identify 'strangers' early and discourage them from doing business with you.

Customer-intimacy firms focus their investments on their true friends, their crown jewels. These are the 20 per cent of the customers who generate 80 per cent of the revenues and who are open to a long-term relationship. This does not mean that a company should get rid of the butterflies and the barnacles, but communication and relationship activities should be addressed primarily to your 'true friends' – it's with these customers that you build a learning relationship. To learn directly from key customers, customer-intimate companies can invite them to the company's premises to take part in personal dialogues or to participate in a customer council. In a B2B context, visiting the customer on site can be very useful:

Butterflies	True friends
• Good fit between company's offerings and customer's needs • Highest profit potential	• Good fit between company's offerings and customer's needs • Highest profit potential
High profitability *Actions:* • Aim to achieve transactional satisfaction, not attitudinal loyalty • Milk the accounts only as long as they are active • Key challenge is to cease investing soon enough	*Actions:* • Communicate consistently • Build both attitudinal and behavioural loyalty • Delight these customers to nurture, defend, and retain them
Strangers	**Barnacles**
• Little fit between company's offerings and customer's needs • Lowest profit potential	• Limited fit between company's offerings and customer's needs • Low profit potential
Low profitability *Actions:* • Make no investment in these relationships • Make profit on every transaction	*Actions:* • Measure both the size and share of wallet • If share of wallet is low, focus on up- and cross-selling • If size of wallet is small, impose strict cost controls

Short-term customers   **Long-term customers**

FIGURE 12.4 Choosing a loyalty strategy

Source: Reinartz and Kumar (2002)[6]

for example, production line or other back-office employees can go on site to see and learn for themselves about the customer's concerns, needs and expectations. These employees are usually fully dedicated to a particular customer to enable them to gain highly specialized knowledge of the customer. The goal is to harness that customer-specific knowledge and combine it with already-developed best practices and expertise to create exceptional results.

Identifying your true friends requires that you measure profitability per customer. It's important to understand and estimate the customer's future value as well. Some companies measure the 'customer lifetime value' to find out how much they can invest in the relationships with their true friends. I will discuss this point later, when I talk about customer-intimacy companies' evaluation and control processes. Retailers such as Staples and Best Buy, and companies such as Tetra Pak and SKF, are quite clear about whom to serve well and where to invest in relationship building.

The strategy process

Customer intimacy requires 'market-sensing' capabilities: that is, the ability to continuously collect information from the market about your competitors and your customers. Customer-intimacy firms use that input to shape their action plans.

Customer-intimacy firms understand the value of customer feedback – and they know that collecting customer data is not an end-point; it's a starting point. Embedding customer feedback into operational processes is essential. Only by listening to what customers are saying and analysing the accumulated data can decisions on the product or service delivery process be properly informed. Customer-intimacy firms have an organized, systematic process for collecting data and translating the input into operational improvements.

However, it's not as simple as that – customer-intimate companies need to have clear lines of communication among those who meet customers, those who analyse feedback and those who interpret the findings. A successful customer feedback programme begins at the frontline, rather than at the corporate centre. This implies that frontline employees – the ones who interact with, and serve, the customer – play a pivotal role in collecting the input and disseminating it throughout the company. They act as gatekeepers of information flows between the company and its customers.

Customer-intimacy firms not only try to get input from their customers, they also actively screen the external environment to detect changes in customer preferences, as well as in competitors' offerings. The ultimate goal is to be market-driven – to understand, attract and retain more valuable customers than any of your competitors do.

Checklist: 'customer intimacy and your direction- and goal-setting processes'

To what extent are your direction- and goal-setting processes aligned with the customer-intimacy operating model? The following questions will help you check whether you have the appropriate direction- and goal-setting processes in place to communicate and translate a strategy built around super-service and deep relationships:

1 Is your top management committed to explaining to your employees what customer centricity means, and do they lead by example? Does a relationship orientation pervade your organization's values, mindsets and norms?

2 Does your company have a clear service and relationship strategy, known by everybody in the organization? Do you serve your best customers better? Do you identify your 'crown jewels', your best and most loyal customers?

3 Does your company screen the market and capture information from your customers in a systematic way? What is the role of your frontline employees in this process?

Operational processes: building credibility, trust, loyalty and commitment

What are the critical operational processes of firms that claim to be market driven and customer-centric? The key operational processes of customer-intimate companies can be seen as a circle that starts with building trustworthiness by demonstrating expertise and experience and by delivering what you have promised. Only when customers are satisfied with their supplier will they open up to tighten the connections. Tightening connections and strengthening the relationship are accomplished by a two-way dialogue between customer and supplier. The third step is to extend the offering with actions that further strengthen customer loyalty, such as customer complaint management, customer reward programmes and customer feedback management. All these efforts should provide the supplier with more information to provide even better products and services, which further increase the company's trustworthiness (see Figure 12.5). Ideally, this is a virtuous circle, where supplier and customer build better and tighter bonds that are increasingly difficult to copy.

Demonstrating expertise and experience

The best-in-class companies that pursue customer intimacy have built a knowledge base to deliver ever-better results for their customers. The entire company is

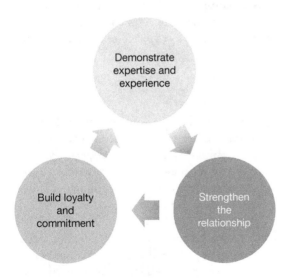

FIGURE 12.5 The key operational processes of customer-intimacy firms

mobilized to create customer-relevant knowledge, disseminate it across departments and use it effectively for the benefit of the customers. Customer-intimacy firms know that the solutions they propose work – and they collect benchmark data, or data from best practices, to convince the customers of their expertise. This is especially important when firms start to offer distinctive advisory services. Demonstrating credibility through expertise and experience is the starting point in building trust with your customers.

Dealing with customer needs and requirements is sometimes so specialized that customer-intimate companies start to work together with other companies that have the appropriate technical and business knowledge. In other words, the strength of a customer-intimate company does not reside solely in what it already knows, but in how it can combine its internal expertise with the expertise of other companies to deliver results that customers want. Customer-intimate firms are not afraid to include 'strange bedfellows' in their solutions.[7] Customers will be surprised to hear that you recommend a solution that includes components of your competitor's product portfolio! This is especially the case in B2B contexts, where customer requirements can be complex. For example, IBM was one of the first companies to recognize that solutions can include components from its direct competitors.

When studying professional service firms, David Maister, Charles Green and Robert Galford developed a model of trust that dissects the crucial elements in building trust with your customers. According to these authors, to win trust you must be credible, reliable and intimate, and you must give up your self-orientation. Credibility can be defined as content expertise plus presence. Reliability is about consistency in your actions. Do you deliver and perform as promised? Intimacy is the ability to make a connection to the interior, emotional state of the client. Greater intimacy means that fewer subjects are barred from discussion. Self-orientation is an attitude that keeps us focused on ourselves rather than on our client.[8] Including strange bedfellows in your solutions is a means to reducing self-orientation and increasing trust.

Strengthening the relationship

Demonstrating expertise and experience helps to open your customer's door. It's a first step in building trust – but it's not sufficient. Customer intimacy requires interactivity. The customer-intimate company recognizes that a *relationship adds value* for its customers only when it is based on personalized interactions. Every relationship is recognized as being unique, based on two-way communication that might change over time. After every transaction and interaction, the customer-intimate company accumulates and remembers information about its customer's needs, preferences and requirements, so that the company can use this information to predict the next actions that will bring more value to the customer. It is necessary to keep communication with the customer open and direct at all times, not just when the company expects something from the customer. This continuous communication keeps the relationship 'warm' and demonstrates to the customer that the company has not 'forgotten' him/her.

Customer-intimacy companies do not focus on general needs but cater to their customers' individual requirements. Customer-intimate companies devote tremendous amounts of energy to listening to their customers. They relentlessly develop in-depth knowledge about the specific preferences and needs of individual customers, because this information contains many valuable indications of value-adding opportunities. Highly personalized interactions are the optimum mechanism for understanding in detail what the customer values and what the sales and service staff can do to deliver better results.

This is where customer-intimacy firms are different from firms such as Dell or Amazon, which are masters of the mass-customization game. According to Joseph Hall and Eric Johnson, the creation of personalized products and services usually involves a combination of 'scientific' processes and 'artistic' processes. *Artistic processes* cannot be precisely pre-specified, and they involve considerable judgement and experience on the part of the employees. In contrast, *scientific processes* are controlled processes, geared towards producing pre-specified, low-variability output. Firms with a business model of mass customization rely most on scientific processes to create personalization,[9] but these firms are unable to achieve true customization. Contrast this mass-customization model with how Zappos.com deals with its customers – Zappos has been able to build emotional connections with its customers in rather unique ways. For example, service excellence means that Zappos has no time limit on calls with customers. On 20 December 2012, the Zappos customer loyalty team in Las Vegas set a new record for the longest service phone call ever: 9 hours and 37 minutes. The customer loyalty team member commented, 'Sometimes people just need to call and talk. We do not judge, we just want to help.'[10] That's what I call intimate personalization!

Customer-intimate companies invest in a single point of contact for their key customers or key customer segments. To build deeper relationships effectively, customer-intimate companies develop a system of 'key account managers' or 'customer segment managers' who are responsible for the company's total relationship with each key customer or with a particular customer segment. This requires significant coordination among the various departments within the firm. The key account manager is the company's representative to the customer (outward facing) and acts as the customer's advocate to the company, ensuring that all of the company's resources are brought to bear on the client's problems (inward facing). The most effective key account managers ensure that their customers' needs are met, and they will do everything possible to mobilize the company to achieve this goal.[11]

Building loyalty and commitment

Customer retention is a top priority for all customer-intimacy firms. It is achieved when firms are able to secure loyalty and commitment from their key customers. Customer-intimacy firms understand that increasing mutual commitment is important, because this ensures that both parties – the customer and the supplier – are willing to maintain and develop a valued relationship. A valued relationship can be built only when there are mutual benefits for both parties. Apart from that, loyalty and commitment can be enhanced in many other ways. What are the most important mechanisms for increasing loyalty and commitment, and thus customer retention as well?

The first element – which is often overlooked – is to address customer complaints immediately and appropriately. Rather than seeing customer complaints as blame for bad performance, customer-intimacy firms see complaints as an opportunity for improvement. Customer-intimate companies ensure that customers' complaints are given a prominent place in the company's information system. The goal is to reveal patterns of organizational practices that directly or indirectly lead to customer complaints and need to be addressed immediately. Every complaint offers opportunities for both ongoing learning and immediate improvement.

Complaint response systems, therefore, should aim to turn a negative experience into a positive one. How can this be done? Well, first, make it easy for customers to complain! Solicit customer input, good or bad. Second, ensure that employees recognize mistakes and empower them to respond to customer complaints without delay. And third, invite senior managers to spend time on incoming service, complaint or information calls. This gives them an anonymous, status-free contact with customers, which helps them understand field-level frustrations and concerns directly, free of the impersonal filtering of reports and memos. It also demonstrates the firm's commitment to deal with complaints.

Case study: how Singapore Airlines deals with complaints

According to company executives, a study by an outside consulting firm revealed that passengers expect more of SIA than they expect of other airlines. Moreover, many customers do not hesitate to complain to SIA about perceived service shortcomings that they would simply ignore on other airlines. SIA senior vice president, Kim Wah Yap, explains: 'Some customers actually tell us that, if we weren't SIA, they wouldn't complain.' The company readily admits that it is responsible for this situation, because for years it has promoted itself as an airline with the highest standards of service.

The company empowers managers at the local level to settle customer unhappiness on the spot. 'We practice what we call "two-level-up" decision-making,' Yap says.

> *'As a manager, you know what your boss can do and what your boss's boss can do. So, we tell our managers to pretend that the bosses aren't around and to go ahead and make the decision for them. This is meant to create customer goodwill by cutting through the bureaucracy.'*

Often, resolving problems with premium class customers doesn't involve any monetary compensation, but is more personal in nature and requires special social skills. 'The high-value customer who has lost some luggage or had coffee spilt on him wants to know: Do you still value my business?' Yap explains. The company usually has a senior executive make an appointment to take the individual to lunch and discuss the matter. 'In Japan, sincerity is more important than any money you can pay them', Yap says. 'Instead, you make an appointment to see them, sit outside their office, and when they are free you walk in, bow, and apologize on behalf of the company.'[12]

Another way to build loyalty is to set up a customer-reward programme that rewards the best customers by giving them a financial discount or preferential treatment, such as shorter lines, faster delivery or easier communication channels. The best customers will appreciate a loyalty programme when the benefits are visible to them and are markedly better than the services offered to regular customers. A company should carefully consider to whom to offer customer loyalty programmes – obviously, you offer those programmes only to your 'true friends'.

Be aware that loyalty can go beyond simple repurchase: loyal customers endorse your products or services. If the loyalty is based on a superior service or relationship, a customer might be willing to pay an extra premium. Some customers even want to collaborate on new product development, or might even invest in you. Therefore, think carefully about your loyalty strategy: is it convincing? Is it relevant to your customers? Does it add value? Do you make them happier with your loyalty programme?

Checklist: 'customer intimacy and your operational processes'

To what extent are your operational processes aligned with the customer-intimacy operating model? The following questions may be useful for checking whether you have the appropriate operational processes to add services and build relationships:

1   Does your company have the expertise and experience to be a credible supplier? Is the knowledge available to all your sales and service staff members? Do you manage that knowledge base well?
2   Does the company maintain a continuous dialogue with its key customers? Are you able to talk about more than your product or service offering? Do you have employees who can engage in intimate conversations with customers?
3   What has your company done to build loyalty and commitment with your key customers? Do you really listen to them? Do you give them a voice that is listened to? Do you have loyalty programmes in place? What do you do with unsatisfied customers?

Support processes: a structured customer acquisition and relationship management

In what support processes do customer-intimate firms invest to increase customer retention? Customer-intimate organizations have implemented a CRM database to collect and store customer information that will be used to provide their employees with relevant data from and about the customer. At the same time, formal sales processes, and rules for how to approach the customer, set standards for everybody in the organization.

CRM database content

In order to have meaningful and intimate conversations with their key customers, customer-intimacy firms collect and capture data about them. Customer-intimacy firms have better, more accurate and more detailed information about their customers than their competitors do. The data gathered contain transactional information (what the customer bought and at what price) and contextual information about customers. At a minimum, a customer-intimate organization should have enough data to assess the likelihood of defection, the current profitability and the lifetime value of each account. Some firms go further and collect data about the history of the relationship, customer interactions at the most important touch points with the customer, the 'share of wallet' – the proportion of his/her overall spending that a customer spends on your products – and potential sales opportunities. Another important source of relevant information is customer complaints. Customer-centric companies invest heavily in CRM technologies to capture, structure and disseminate all the relevant data about and from the customers.

CRM database use

Having the relevant customer data is one thing; using them appropriately is another. How do your employees use your CRM database data? Do they trust the data? Do they share them? Knowledge about the customer is every customer-intimacy company's key asset. Therefore, companies should clearly specify how to feed the database and ensure that employees use it appropriately. Customer-intimate firms define responsibilities for the collection, update and analysis of customer information across the organization. Some companies use messaging systems to update sales people and other employees with new customer and market data. The Ritz-Carlton hotel chain has implemented an efficient process for collecting and updating guest information, and the employees understand that they are responsible for adding any new information to each customer file.

Case study: database management at Ritz-Carlton[13]

Although human interaction and human service systems are at the heart of its customer service, Ritz-Carlton relies on two information systems: one to handle centralized worldwide guest reservations, and a second, local system that keeps records of reservations for each individual hotel and also keeps track of its guests' preferences. The systems are compatible, and when a guest registers at any Ritz-Carlton hotel, the 'guest recognition coordinator' from that hotel can request a guest preference file from the central system and download it to the local one. If new preferences are recorded during the guest's stay, they are added to the local customer file, and the updated file is then sent back to the central database shortly after the guest has checked out.

The complete guest file is available to all staff throughout a guest's stay. What's more, every staff member is expected to use 'guest preference pads' to update guest files. For example, when a staff member engages in conversation with guests, he/she listens for comments such as: 'I don't know why, but I just feel so much better when the beds are made and the bathroom is clean when I come back from breakfast.' Such a remark would be written on a guest preference pad and delivered to the floor supervisor, who would turn it over to the guest recognition coordinator. He or she would then enter the guest's stated preference in the local database later that day.

Structured sales process

Customer-intimate companies have realized that, in order to build relationships with customers, they need to *listen to understand* instead of *listen to sell*. This sales approach is different from traditional product sales, and firms that are considering making the move towards intimacy should understand that this change needs to be managed well. The more structured the sales process, the more customer intimacy becomes a corporate capability, rather than an individual skill.

Customer-intimacy firms define the critical stages in the sales process and assign responsibilities to each part of the process. For example, one retail bank invited its most important customers to the office and had a structured, 1-hour interview with them to listen to their financial needs. The sales people entered all this information into a CRM database for use in their later contacts.

There are many sales process models available that describe how to turn a lead into a deal. What is important for customer-intimacy firms is that they structure, not only the customer acquisition process, but the customer retention process as well. The quality and frequency of contacts are critical in relationship building. So, customer-intimacy firms define guidelines for how many times to contact the top customers and through which channels. Furthermore, they have identified the 'moments of truth' and they know how to deal with customers at these crucial points.

It's also important not to restrict the sales process to the sales department alone. Management needs to understand that both the front and the back offices play a significant role in how to deal with a customer. You would be surprised by how many times, and to whom, your customers talk or mail to people within your organization. Customers not only contact your sales people, they are also in touch with your financial department, with your service staff, maybe even with your production people. Do all of these people know who the top customers are and how to deal with them?

Checklist: 'customer intimacy and your support processes'

Do you have the appropriate support processes in your organization to become intimate with your key customers? Answer the following questions to find out:

1   Does your company have the right data for engaging in intimate relationships with your key customers? Does your customer database include customer-specific information? Are these just transaction data? Or does your database contain more data about and from the customer?
2   Who is responsible for feeding the customer database? Can everybody access those data easily? Are sales and service people informed when new information about key customers is available?
3   Does your company have a structured sales process? Do you measure how many times you contact your key customers? Has your company set guidelines on the frequency and the quality of those customer contacts?

Evaluation and control processes: measures that improve customer loyalty

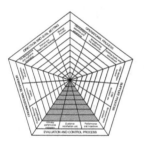

What are the typical evaluation and control processes that customer-intimate firms adopt? What do they measure? And what do they do with the results? Many firms use customer satisfaction programmes to assess their performance with customers. Do customer-intimacy firms also engage in these processes? How do they use incentives to build long-term relationships with valuable clients?

Intimacy performance indicators

Customer intimacy is about moving from a transactional mindset with your key customers to a relational one. This should also be reflected in how you measure your performance. Of course, customer-intimacy firms keep track of the evolution of their financials – revenues, costs, margins – but they include measures of customer retention and loyalty as well. Measuring customer retention is essential to having a tangible indication that a customer relationship is building over time, or not. But how do you measure customer loyalty?

For a long time, firms have been measuring customer satisfaction. Harvard Business School professors Jim Heskett, Earl Sasser and Leonard Schlesinger have demonstrated that customer satisfaction is correlated with customer loyalty, at least in service businesses.[14] However, in recent years, the concept of the NPS has emerged as a more popular measure for customer retention. Fred Reichheld, a consultant at Bain & Company, claims that this measure is the best predictor for company growth. The NPS is calculated using the answers to one simple question:

'How likely is it that you will recommend Company X to a friend or colleague?' The NPS is considered to be a better customer retention measure because for your customers to recommend you requires a higher commitment than just being satisfied. A company's NPS can be as low as -100 (everybody is a detractor) or as high as +100 (everybody is a promoter). An NPS that is positive (i.e. higher than zero) is felt to be good, and an NPS of +50 is excellent. In the academic world, there is a huge debate about whether the NPS is a better measure of loyalty and a better predictor for growth than other customer satisfaction measures. Despite these criticisms, NPS is popular, because it is easy to understand and use.

It is important to note that the NPS is not used by customer-intimacy firms exclusively – operational excellence companies and product leaders use the NPS as well. Customer-intimacy firms do complement customer satisfaction scores and the NPS with other performance measures, such as share of wallet. The assumption is that customer-intimacy firms want to increase their share of wallet with key customers; you cannot develop relationships if the share of wallet is limited over time. Another common performance measure that intimacy firms use is the 'customer lifetime value'. This measure predicts the net profit that can be attributed to the entire future relationship with a customer. It allows firms to estimate how much they should invest in a particular customer. If the customer's lifetime value is low, then the firm should no longer invest heavily in that customer.

Apart from these more generic customer satisfaction/loyalty measures, customer-intimacy firms investigate how well they perform on various service aspects. For example, Starbucks has used a mystery shopper programme – called the 'Customer

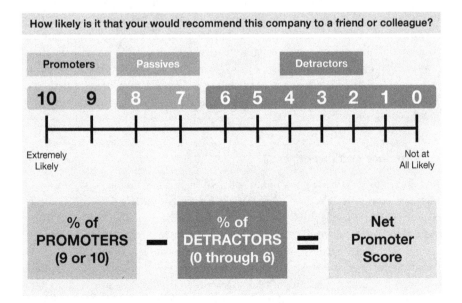

FIGURE 12.6 The Net Promoter Score explained

Snapshot' – that measures each store on four basic service criteria: service quality, cleanliness, product quality and speed of service. In addition to basic service, stores were also rated on legendary service: was the company able to give a customer a memorable experience?[15]

Customer satisfaction use

Measuring customer satisfaction and loyalty is not an end point for customer-intimacy firms – it's a starting point for initiating a whole range of actions in the company. First, intimacy firms discuss the customer satisfaction scores with their best customers. In B2B contexts, the customer satisfaction scores can be used to have a more structured and objective discussion on your performance with some of your top customers. This may signal to these customers that your company takes customer feedback seriously. Tetra Pak launched a customer satisfaction initiative in the late 1990s to listen to the requests and complaints of its largest customers. The poor survey results led to a company-wide change programme to make Tetra Pak more responsive to customers and better aligned with their management issues and priorities.[16]

Customer-intimacy firms use customer satisfaction scores internally as well and disseminate customer satisfaction data to all levels within the organization. They believe that employee awareness of levels of customer satisfaction and loyalty improves responsiveness to customers. For example, a smaller company displayed an evolution of monthly customer satisfaction scores in the printing corner. The employees knew that they would receive a bonus if the average customer satisfaction score was higher than 3.75 out of 5. The managers of this company told me that this was a good way to ensure that everybody was aware that customer satisfaction was a key priority. SIA keeps close track of the compliment/complaint ratio, a tool that it devised for measuring independently generated comments from passengers on good or bad aspects of their experience with the airline. In 2001, the ratio was about thirty-four compliments to one complaint per 10,000 passengers. All letters received went to the heads of the relevant departments for review and possible action.[17]

Performance and incentives

It is common practice to give bonuses based on financial results, but customer-intimacy companies also use customer satisfaction or loyalty scores to allocate bonuses. First, these companies include customer satisfaction scores to assess managerial performance. But they don't stop there: they also involve their sales and service teams in those bonus schemes. For example, Siebel Systems pays commissions to its salespersons, but they do not receive full commissions until a year after a sale, and then only if their customer satisfaction scores are up to par.

One of the key messages of this chapter is that customer intimacy does not stop at the service or sales department. That's why it is important to have bonuses based on customer satisfaction scores for all employees, even those in production units or back-office departments. In the end, back-office people and administrative employees have contact with customers and help to create a customer experience too. Using customer satisfaction and loyalty as reward drivers sends a very strong customer-intimacy signal to your entire organization.

Checklist: 'customer intimacy and your evaluation and control processes'

Do you have the appropriate evaluation and control processes in your organization to become truly intimate with your key customers? The following questions may be useful for assessing how well your evaluation and control processes are aligned with the customer-intimacy operating model:

1   Do your company's key performance indicators include a measure of customer satisfaction or customer retention? Does your company measure the customer lifetime value of your customers?
2   What does your organization do with customer satisfaction scores and input from customer surveys? Do you discuss this input with your core customers? Do you use the information internally to discuss performance and points for improvement?
3   Does your company use the customer satisfaction and retention scores to allocate bonuses to managers, sales and service people and other staff members? How much of the variable part of a person's compensation is based on customer successes?

Organizational behaviour: creating a strong customer service culture

The fifth component of the Strategy Implementation Framework is the organizational behaviour component. Obviously, this is a crucial lever for any organization's strategy implementation. How do customer-intimacy firms use the organizational behaviour lever to build a truly intimate organization? Do these firms have particular HR processes, and how important are the organization's culture and structure in building customer loyalty and retention?

HR management

Developing and maintaining a strong customer service culture is a key task for any company that strives to be truly customer-centric. A service and relationship culture can only be realized by dedicated people who have the responsibility and authority to go the extra mile for the customers. Furthermore, providing excellent service and building deep relationships with key customers require your staff to interact with the customers in an appropriate way. They all must have the same way of thinking about their role and must be motivated to perform: every time and everywhere.

I have already argued that a good customer service value system is a core asset for any customer-intimate organization (see the section on direction and goal setting), but the values need to be translated into the organization's management practices. According to Jacques Horovitz, a professor in service management at IMD and the founder of Château*form'* – a hotel chain that I will present in the next chapter – the key management practices that make a difference in terms of supporting customer-oriented values are usually found in the way people are managed. This topic has received a lot of attention in the service management literature, but some of the recommendations are also relevant for companies operating in more product-oriented industries.

Creating an organization built on service excellence starts with getting the right people on board. The change from transactional selling to selling solutions and relationships often requires a complete transformation of the sales and service organization. In a customer-intimate organization, identifying the right people to hire is not a question of skills, but rather one of attitudes: the disposition of the employee to offer an excellent service to the customer. In customer-oriented organizations, recruiters usually look for people who are open-minded and have excellent communication skills. These characteristics are important to better understand the customer's needs. Employees of customer-intimate organizations are also flexible and people-oriented. Showing a genuine interest in the customer's situation calls for emotional intelligence on the part of the supplier's staff, and a flexible mindset helps one recognize opportunities and link products to needs.

The key to achieving customer satisfaction is consistently to deliver individual attention, resolve problems quickly and show common courtesy, but inspiring a group of employees to adopt these standards is a great challenge. Training plays a crucial role in this process. Customer-intimate organizations give equal importance to technical and non-technical training. Technical training focuses on the skills required to perform the job, whereas the non-technical training concentrates on developing the soft skills and the right attitudes. Technical and non-technical training ensures that service standards are known by everybody in the organization. 'It is only when service standards are woven into the fabric of the organization that service begins to become ingrained in every employee.'[18] Hotel chains such as Ritz-Carlton and Four Seasons and banks such as Svenska Handelsbanken and Jyske Bank have understood this message well.

Apart from the company recruiting the right people and providing training, employees need to be motivated and encouraged to stay in the company. High employee turnover not only imposes a direct cost on the organization, but it might also affect customer relationships negatively. Customer-intimate companies pride themselves on having the best retention rates in their industry, especially in their front-line departments. These companies become preferred employers because of their organizational culture and the way they treat their employees. One of the credos that intimacy firms adhere to is to treat employees like customers.

Organization culture

Customer-intimacy firms all have a pervasive culture that puts the customer at the centre of the firm's thinking. A corporate culture has many facets and levels. Jacques Horovitz has nicely listed the elements that make up a service culture (see Figure 12.7). Such a culture starts with a company's *philosophy* – and a customer-intimacy philosophy starts with the premise that customers are more important than profits. The *customers* drive the organization's behaviour and actions, not the shareholders. Some firms even go a step further and add: 'Employees come first, customers second'. Another element of a customer-intimacy philosophy might be that you first have to give before you receive. Customer intimacy is about 'give and take' – not the other way around!

Next, a service philosophy needs to be translated into the company's values. Values are not idle words – they're the glue that keeps the organization together: they prescribe good behaviour and the appropriate actions for your employees to

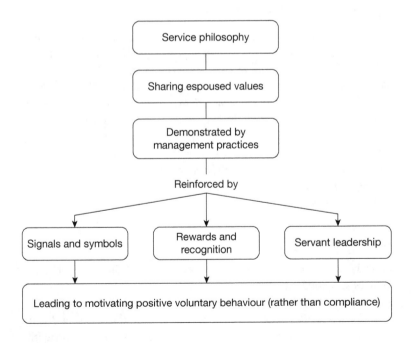

FIGURE 12.7 A customer service culture

Source: Horovitz (2011)[19]

take. Values also need to live, and top management plays a crucial role in this process. I have already discussed this in this chapter's section on direction and goal setting, but it's important to stress that the actions and behaviours of the top management should show a commitment to customers. If top management prefers to spend time with financial analysts rather than visit the distributors and customers, it's sending the wrong signal to the organization.

Once again, the key management practices that make a difference in terms of supporting customer-oriented values are usually found in the way people are managed. The HR practices I've just discussed are important ways to further stimulate a customer-centric culture. The management practices must then be reinforced by signals and symbols and rewards and recognition. Symbols are what a manager shows (his or her car, office, dress); signals are what a manager says and does. Consistent and systematic signals and symbols reinforce customer service. Customer-intimacy companies regularly award prizes to employees who have contributed personally to an increase in the company's customer orientation.

Throughout this chapter, I have referred many times to Ritz-Carlton and Four Seasons. They are good examples of companies that have built a strong customer service culture. Another example is Wegmans Food Markets, a US grocery retail chain that has applied many of these practices and has become renowned for its customer orientation.

Case study: employees first, customers second[20]

Wegmans's shopping experience is driven by the company's value system and its unique culture. The company reiterates these values at every opportunity: 'These values are not just hanging on the wall – employees live them every day.' The values act as a framework for the behaviour of its employees, and all employees are expected to understand and assimilate these values. The company nurtures its culture through storytelling. All employees, including the top managers, are encouraged to share their experiences at Wegmans with others. The company has even introduced a formal storytelling mechanism, called 'Who We Are'. Every meeting at Wegmans – at both the local and national levels – starts with stories about how the company's values are being lived by the employees. The stories are not always about successes – failures are included as well. Storytelling also forms an integral part of the orientation programme for new employees.

Organization structure

Becoming a truly customer-intimate organization is a huge challenge also because it often involves structural change. Designing an appropriate structure is one of the toughest managerial challenges, but, nevertheless, it's a crucial aspect of a firm's successful transformation to customer intimacy. An organization's design defines the roles, responsibilities, authorities and reporting relationships within an organization. The most advanced intimacy organizations revolve around customer segments and customer profit and loss centres.

As firms grow, they typically set up departments that group people with similar functions or roles. The Achilles heel of these functional organizations is coordination. For example, sales people find it difficult to disseminate information to their marketing and production colleagues, and vice versa. Customer intimacy, however, requires a lot of coordination between the various departments. Everybody needs to know who the crown jewels are, and everybody has to know how to deal with the key customers' wishes and needs. The whole organization needs to be directed towards serving and dealing with the key customers. So how do firms organize for that?

Customer-intimacy firms introduce new organizational units and roles – such as customer teams, account managers and relationship managers – to serve the customers better.[21] A customer team is a unit that combines functional experts from marketing, sales, manufacturing, quality and other departments. The customer teams' roles are to anticipate customer needs, ensure that the key customers are served well and relay information to the various departments, such as R&D. You find account teams in both B2C and B2B organizations. For example, companies such as Degussa, Nypro and Citibank have account teams for their most important customers. P&G's account team for Walmart even consists of 250 people, from a wide variety of functions.

Some firms go one step further and have account managers. According to Jay Galbraith, an account manager provides two new factors. First, the account manager becomes a voice for the customer on the management team. Second, (s)he builds and manages the infrastructure that supports customer teams. An account manager plays a coordinating role: this person assumes the role of managing customer information systems and communications across customer teams. (S)he also creates training programmes for the managers and team members, coordinates the planning and is also responsible for customer profitability. Some organizations have even decided to create a separate customer-facing structure by gathering all dedicated customer-specific resources into a single unit, but, in this case, it's very important to build horizontal links with the production and development units. This is the structure that IBM and Johnson Controls have set up.[22]

Another important design feature of customer-intimacy firms is that they allocate a lot of responsibility and authority to the front-office people. Empowering customer contact employees to make their own decisions can enhance customer orientation. Employees have the freedom to look for solutions that appeal to customers, and, rather than working with standardized procedures for dealing with customers, the company chooses to work with looser structures that allow for quick and individualized problem solutions. All this results in flatter organizations, and this has another positive side effect: reducing the number of hierarchy levels within a firm forces top executives to get in touch with customers more often and more closely.

It is worth noting that internal alignment between departments is absolutely necessary. Internal service affects external customer service. A lot of internal communication and cooperation is required in order to meet a customer's needs.

Every department and every employee must be aware that their activities have an impact on providing the best solution to the customer. This is not possible if workers in the back office do not view those in the front office as their own 'internal customers' – a concept that encourages employees to treat their co-workers as though they were customers. The company uses internal customer satisfaction surveys to assess the performance of those back-office departments. The purpose is to raise quality consciousness within an organization, particularly when many employees do not deal directly with the actual (external) customers.

Checklist: 'customer intimacy and your organizational behaviour processes'

Does your organization manage its people and organization in line with the customer-intimacy operating model?

1 Does your organization have the right people to offer solutions and build relationships? How important is 'attitude towards the customer' as a hiring criterion? And to what extent do you train your people in customer and service orientation? Does your company have a reputation for retaining people?
2 Does your organization have a culture of service excellence and of providing superior value to the customer? Does your company award prizes to employees who go the extra mile for a customer?
3 Does your company have an organization structure that is built around the customer? Do you have units with customer profit and loss accountability? Do you have customer teams or account managers that take responsibility for a customer account? Does customer orientation impact the entire organization, including the production and R&D departments?

Commitment and customer intimacy

The Customer Intimacy Pentagon is a great tool for assessing how well your organization is aligned around the operating model of customer intimacy. How many actions and activities have you set up to ensure that customer intimacy is not a promise but a real commitment to your customers? Our research has indicated that more alignment is correlated with better financial results. But that's not enough. Strategy implementation is not only about aligning your organization's activities around a core orchestrating theme – it's also about creating a committed workforce that works towards a common goal. In Chapter 4, I argued that employee commitment and involvement are equally necessary for a successful strategy implementation. Winning companies are able to connect their employees to their strategy and get their employees committed to implementing that strategy.

In that chapter, I described four organizational configurations: the entrepreneurial organization, the structured organization, the connected organization and the committed organization. The four organizations represent four different stages of organizational development and management maturity. The *entrepreneurial firm* is characterized by a continuous search for new opportunities, but lacks the structure and professionalism to continuously offer a great service. When firms take the step to build a more *structured organization*, they build departments with people who perform more or less similar functions or roles. That specialization allows for more professionalization, but it requires more coordination among these functional departments. When firms are not able to link the different functional departments well, they run the risk of creating silos that pursue their own goals. This is what occurs in bureaucratic organizations – they are so internally focused that they have lost sight of the customer.

That's where strategy comes in. In the next stage of an organization's maturity evolution, management starts to look outside and is determined to find a unique position in the market. The top management of the organization defines an orchestrating theme, based on a convincing value proposition, and tries to align the entire organization around that theme. Customer-intimacy firms connect the entire organization around the core theme of excellent service and deep, long-lasting relationships with key customers. This process of alignment often involves a fundamental change in the organization's operating and managerial processes. So, it is important that top management involves the middle managers in that connecting process. This means setting shared goals, changing the organization's working practices, feeding the customer database, reporting on financial and non-financial performance measures and building a performance-oriented culture. When firms have successfully implemented these actions, they have become *connected organizations*. When they are able to involve and commit the entire organization around those activities, they reach the final level of organizational maturity, which I have called the *committed organization*.

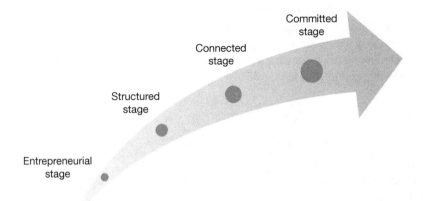

FIGURE 12.8 Effectiveness of the customer-intimacy model at different maturity stages

Many of the activities that I have presented in this chapter assume a company-wide, rather than a functional, perspective. Customer intimacy, just like the other operating models, is an operating model that requires connectedness between the various departments. The fifteen core activities that constitute a customer-intimate organization can only be implemented effectively when an organization has become connected or committed. In this last phase, strategy initiatives are borne not only by middle managers but by all of the employees. This is what true customer intimacy is all about. In the most successful customer-intimate organizations, everybody feels responsible for the customers. When Tetra Pak launched its customer intimacy strategy at the end of the 1990s, it launched a number of corporate programmes. For its Key Account Management Programme, it put every employee – including the receptionist – on a key account team.

Key learning points

In this chapter, I have described in detail what it takes to be customer intimate. You might be a little overwhelmed after reading this chapter: customer intimacy is by no means an easy task. To make customer intimacy work, you need to launch a whole set of activities. Providing solutions requires more than a convincing sales pitch, and it takes more than a dedicated sales team to build long-lasting relationships with your organization. However, when implemented well, customer intimacy gives firms a competitive edge that can be sustained for years.

Managers should think carefully about whom to involve in the customer-intimacy journey. Customer intimacy extends beyond the sales and service departments. It involves the middle managers and employees of the entire organization, and this company-wide mindset requires a level of connectedness that is hard to find in most organizations. Ensuring consistency over different sales or service units and the back-office departments is hard to achieve.

Nevertheless, I believe that customer intimacy can be a successful operating model, even in periods of recession or in commoditizing markets where there is a natural tendency to focus only on price in your sales discussions. The case study that I will present in the next chapter shows that price reductions are not the only solution to the commoditization challenge.

Notes

1 Hsieh, T. (2013) 'Customer Service Is Not Just a Department!', available at: http://about. zappos.com/ (accessed 28 January 2013).
2 See: Verweire, K., Escalier Revollo, J., and Carchon, S. (2010) 'Customer Intimacy: What Does It Mean? What Does It Take?', *Vlerick Business School Research Report*, Vlerick Business School, pp. 1–118.
3 The case studies we examined were: Airborne Express, Best Buy, Wegmans Food Markets, Tetra Pak, Starbucks, Irma, Nordstrom, Svenska Handelsbanken, Baxter Renal Division, Zappos, Michelin, Singapore Airlines, Jyske Bank, Four Seasons, Ritz-Carlton, Superquinn, Rolls-Royce, SKF, Nypro and Johnson Controls Automotive Systems.

4 Hallowell, R. (2004) 'People, Service and Profit at Jyske Bank (abridged version)', *SIMI (Scandinavian International Management Institute) Case Study*, 304–175–1, p. 4.

5 Kashani, K. (2005) 'Countering Commoditization: Value-Added Strategies and Aligning with Customers', in Kashani, K. (ed.), *Beyond Traditional Marketing: Innovations in Marketing Practice*, John Wiley & Sons, Chichester, UK, p. 91.

6 Reinartz, W., and Kumar, V. (2002) 'The Mismanagement of Customer Loyalty', *Harvard Business Review*, July, 93.

7 Foote, N. W., Galbraith, J., Hope, Q., and Miller, D. (2001) 'Making Solutions the Answer', *McKinsey Quarterly*, 3, 84–93.

8 Maister, D. H., Green, C. H., and Galford, R. M. (2000) *The Trusted Advisor*, The Free Press, New York.

9 Hall, J. M., and Johnson, M. E. (2009) 'When Should a Process Be Art, Not Science?', *Harvard Business Review*, March, 58–65.

10 McConnell, A. (2012) 'Zappos' Outrageous Record for the Longest Customer Service Phone Call Ever', available at: www.businessinsider.com/zappos-longest-customer-service-call-2012-12 (accessed 28 January 2013).

11 Georges, L., and Eggert, A. (2003) 'Key Account Managers' Role Within the Value Creation Process of Collaborative Relationships', *Journal of Business-to-Business Marketing*, 10 (4), 1–22.

12 Deshpande, R., and Hogan H. (2003) 'Singapore Airlines: Customer Service Innovation', *Harvard Business School Case Study*, 9–504–025, p. 9.

13 Klein, N., Sasser, W. E., and Jones, T. O. (1999) 'The Ritz-Carlton: Using Information Systems to Better Serve the Customer', *Harvard Business School Case Study*, 9–395–064, p. 6.

14 Heskett, J. L., Sasser, W. E. Jr, and Schlesinger, L. A. (1997) *The Service Profit Chain: How Leading Companies Link Profit and Growth to Loyalty, Satisfaction, and Value*, The Free Press, New York.

15 Moon, Y., and Quelch, J. (2003) 'Starbucks: Delivering Customer Service', *Harvard Business School Case Study*, 9–504–016, p. 6.

16 Kashani, 'Countering Commoditization', pp. 61–105.

17 Deshpande and Hogan, 'Singapore Airlines', p. 8.

18 Day, G. S. (1999) *The Market Driven Organization: Understanding, Attracting, and Keeping Valuable Customers*, The Free Press, New York, p. 8.

19 Horovitz, J. (2011) 'Customer Centricity: The Châteauform' Experience', *Presentation Made for Dexia Lead Program*, 6 May, Brussels.

20 Regani, S., and George, S. (2007) 'Employees First, Customers Second: Wegmans' Work Culture', *ICMR Case Study*, 407–56–1, pp. 1–13.

21 Kates, A., and Galbraith, J. R. (2007) *Designing Your Organization: Using the Star Model to Solve 5 Critical Design Challenges*, Jossey-Bass, San Francisco, CA.

22 Galbraith, J. R. (2005) *Designing the Customer-Centric Organization: A Guide to Strategy, Structure, and Process*, Jossey-Bass, San Francisco, CA.

13

STRATEGY IMPLEMENTATION IN PRACTICE

Châteauform': customer intimacy and beyond[1]

We manage by values, not by rules.

(Horovitz, 2012)[2]

In this last chapter, I present the case of Châteauform' The Home of Seminars – a unique concept of venues and sites dedicated to meetings and seminars in Europe. It is an excellent example of a customer-intimate organization that has been successful for a long period of time in a tough industry. The company was founded in 1996, and, in 2012, its revenues amounted to €92.7 million; the EBITDA was €11.2 million. Table 13.1 provides an overview of the main financials of Châteauform'.

I start this chapter by presenting the Châteauform' concept. Châteauform' has made some strategic choices that have allowed the company to offer a totally different experience to its customers. I then describe the company's operating model and the particular management policies that Jacques Horovitz, the founder of Châteauform', has introduced over time. These management policies explain why

TABLE 13.1 Financial overview of Châteauform'

€ million	2002	2004	2006	2008	2009	2010	2011	2012
Revenues	13.4	22.5	34.7	55.4	54.3	71.0	83.9	92.7
EBIT	2.9	-0.1	2.5	3.9	-1.0	1.3	4.3	4.9
EBIT, %	21.4	-0.4	7.3	7.1	-1.9	1.9	5.2	5.3
Net income	1.4	-0.9	2.5	1.1	-2.2	-0.5	1.6	1.5
No. of sites	6	12	15	24	25	29	31	33
No. of rooms	328	620	768	1,110	1,332	1,530	1,749	1,919

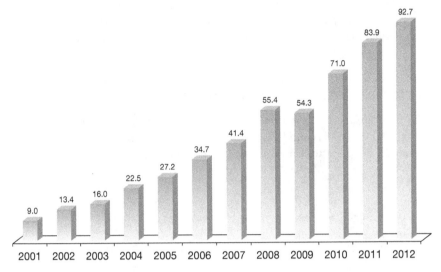

FIGURE 13.1 Evolution of revenues (€ million)

Source: Company information

there is such a high level of strategic alignment and commitment in the company. The last section deals with a topic that most customer-intimacy firms will recognize today: how to manage customers that no longer want to pay a premium price for your extra services or long-term relationships?

The Château*form'* concept

The opportunity

In 1996, Professor Jacques Horovitz, a service marketing specialist at IMD, one of Europe's leading business schools, decided to create the unique concept of Château*form'* The Home of Seminars. Having taught in residential seminars for executive committees and business managers all over the world, he had noticed that appropriate areas for such seminars were hard to find. He saw the opportunity to build a completely new approach to residential seminars, starting from the customer's needs:

> I have been organizing residential seminars for executive committees and management meetings for over 30 years. I have always been struck by how poorly venues cater to such events. Sometimes the meeting rooms are uncomfortable or badly equipped, sometimes the venues themselves are unsuitable – they are frequently too large, and participants feel lost among other groups, wedding parties, business people and holidaymakers. It's often impossible to take an extended break during the working day, because either

there are no activities on offer or there is nowhere to go to unwind, chat and simply get to know other participants. Meals are heavy and lengthy. Participants are once again seated and no consideration is taken of the group's needs.[3]

Châteauform's target segment and core offering

The Château*form'* concept was born out of Horovitz's own country house in Neuville-Bosc, not far from Paris, France. It was to be the first of a series of venues specifically dedicated to corporate meetings, training events and workshops. Clients

FIGURE 13.2 Château*form'* site map

Source: Company website

Château de Neuville-Bosc (France)

La Princesse de Mello (France)

Château de Bellinglise (France)

Le Manoir (France)

Le Mas San Joan (Spain)

Villa Gallarati Scotti (Italy)

Le Chalet de Champéry (Switzerland)

La Grande Abbaye de la Ramée (Belgium)

FIGURE 13.3 Some Château*form'* sites

Source: Company website

were immediately enthusiastic, and soon new sites opened around Paris and, later, further across Europe (see Figure 13.2 for the locations, and Figure 13.3 for some pictures of the sites).

Originally, Château*form'*'s clients were big multinationals from the 500 largest companies in the Paris region, and participants came from all over the world. Over time, the target group expanded beyond those profiles, but Château*form'* has always been dedicated to its target segment: companies that want to organize seminars or workshops for their management teams or employees. This choice of a single customer segment has allowed the company to come up with a differentiated service offering.

Unlike run-of-the-mill seminar venues, participants and teams are offered the possibility to escape from their daily routines and are received at exceptional places – beautiful castles in private parklands or elegant manors or homes on large estates in the countryside. Each venue typically has forty to fifty bedrooms, with a distinct theme and architecture. Works of art cover the walls. Simplicity, not luxury, permeates the décor as well as the property's ambience, and all spaces and surroundings are well maintained. Horovitz comments:

> We are not looking for luxury. We are not aiming at getting 3 or 4 stars. In fact, if you look at the bathroom, the towels have the thickness of those in a 4- or 5-star hotel, but the shower of a 2-star hotel – because when a participant goes to a seminar, he just needs a quick shower and the means to dry up quickly. We definitely focus our service around simplicity, conviviality, and generosity – not luxury.[4]

Meeting facilities include large auditoriums, as well as boardrooms and plenty of seated corners perfectly suited for small group discussions. In addition to being fully equipped with video projector, computer, colour printer, flip charts, digital cameras and other teaching materials, each plenary room also includes the latest audio-visual equipment, such as white boards and interactive boards capable of transmitting information electronically between meeting rooms.

Châteauform' is always on the leading edge of new pedagogic technology. Alongside the advanced audio-visual equipment, it has invented unique concepts such as the round room – a circular room with no tables or chairs, but just steps you can sit or lie on. The round shape symbolizes the idea of cohesive development. Meeting rooms can be configured as the client desires – U-shape, theatre-style, or even in a circle with floor cushions, beanbags and poufs.

Participants are free to enjoy the rural surroundings; each venue provides umpteen choices for leisure, sport and relaxation. Each venue also works with partner companies to provide clients with an array of team activities, such as wine-tastings or painting workshops.

After dinner, guests can relax in the various lounges with open bars, enjoy a game of billiards or pool, or engage in a board game together. Avid singers can entertain their colleagues using Châteauform's karaoke system. Alternatively, each Châteauform' venue offers spa, steam or Japanese bath facilities. One site even offers massage bathtubs with 150 jets. Another offers waterbeds with jets, for a full body massage in 10 minutes. As with technology, whenever Châteauform' discovers a new system for wellness, it will try to implement it.

In summary, the tranquillity of each site, coupled with high-tech meeting rooms, is not only conducive to strategic thinking and productive meetings, but also to a wide range of recreational team-building activities. Together, these elements offer a brand-new combination of work, relaxation and reflection.

Great service and a wonderful experience

The beautiful and functional sites, and the relaxing atmosphere, are complemented by very attentive staff, who are always ready to provide help and assistance. The key message of Château*form'* for its customers is: 'Feel at home far from home'.

A central element of the Château*form'* experience is the presence of a host couple and a chef, called the trio team. The host couple, a husband-and-wife team, manages each property as if it is theirs and looks after the well-being of the participants. They are usually experienced in the service industry and share a strong sense of enthusiasm. Friendly and very entrepreneurial, they live on the premises and are responsible for ensuring that everything works and that their home is warm and well kept. Their attentiveness and hospitality are key pillars of the Château*form'* experience. They are completely in charge, with the ability and flexibility to make all decisions necessary to provide their customers with a great experience.

The chef also contributes to the participants' overall experience during their stay. Meals at Château*form'* are not simply functional – they're a culinary experience. Everything is deliciously fresh and light, and the wines complement the menu perfectly. Morning and afternoon snacks are served in the garden or lounge and vary from sweet dishes, such as French toast with vanilla and candied lemon cake, to savoury, such as herb quiches, homemade terrines and crudités. During each break, fresh fruit juices or iced tea are served alongside the coffee. Lunch is always a buffet, allowing the teams the flexibility to arrive for lunch whenever their morning session ends. Dinner, on the other hand, is seated and provides the opportunity for the chef to introduce the menu he has created.

Flexibility and service are keywords in Château*form'*'s value proposition. Participants are given the opportunity to take over the site as their own for the time of their seminar. The participants can help themselves to whatever they want at any time. Every facility is tailored to their needs, for an all-inclusive fee. For seminar organizers, Château*form'* is a dream come true: it provides all of the ingredients that are missing elsewhere to transform a seminar into a true experience for participants.

Château*form'*'s clients include, not only seminar participants, but also organizing assistants, HR liaisons, key decision-makers from the client corporations as well as consultants, facilitators and professors conducting the meeting sessions. To facilitate the smooth organization of the seminars, a dedicated person (referred to as the nanny) is in charge of assisting the client with all its requirements. The nanny forms the logistic link between Château*form'*'s customer relations services, the client and the site. He or she understands all of the client's requirements and transmits all information to the sites, so that they can prepare their welcome and stay. The customer relations team and the nannies operate from a central location, which is called the Family Home (or the head office), so that the sites can concentrate on serving the customers.

Pricing

There are no hidden surprises for the decision-makers when it comes to the pricing of a seminar package. The average cost per participant for a day is between €210 and €280, slightly under the rate of a four-star hotel, but with no extras. Lodging, meals, open bar, high-tech meeting rooms, recreational and team-building activities – everything is included – even international phone calls made using the bedroom landlines. The concept of 'everyday fair pricing' means that no client can claim to have obtained a special price. Consequently, clients rest assured that they will not pay more, or less, than any other client. Larger transactions, however, do allow for more favourable terms. For example, in the case where a client purchases 1,000 residential packages one year, a 2–3 per cent discount could be granted the following year. In every case, however, clients receive the same conditions. When Châteauform' raises prices, each client receives a personalized letter, introducing the new prices, with a clear explanation of why they have increased.

Delivering the Châteauform' experience

Châteauform's focus on a particular customer segment – companies that want to organize a seminar or meeting – allows it to configure a value chain that is different from that of the traditional hotels. The 'feel-at-home-far-from-home' principle enables the company to save costs while simultaneously increasing value for its customers. For example, as customers can help themselves in the bar, there is no need to hire a barman. The company also has no receptionists, and it arranges payments directly with its customers' HR departments. Furthermore, the company invests very little in advertising: it relies on its customers to spread the word and do the company's marketing. The company then invests the money it saves in things that really matter to its customers: good equipment, good meeting rooms, good food and – above all – great service.

The company has aligned all of its activities around the operating model of customer intimacy. Figure 13.4 shows that Châteauform' has exceptional scores on almost all dimensions of our Customer Intimacy Pentagon. For thirteen of the fifteen core intimacy items, the company has scores that place it in the seventy-fifth percentile or higher.[5] Let's take a closer look at these items.

Direction and goal setting: an explicit service and relationship strategy supported by the top

'The customer is at the heart of all we do'

Châteauform' is truly customer-centric. The customer is the starting point in all that the company does: 'Without the customer, there is no company. Let us never forget this!' This is also the opening statement of Châteauform's booklet, 'Welcome to the Family'.

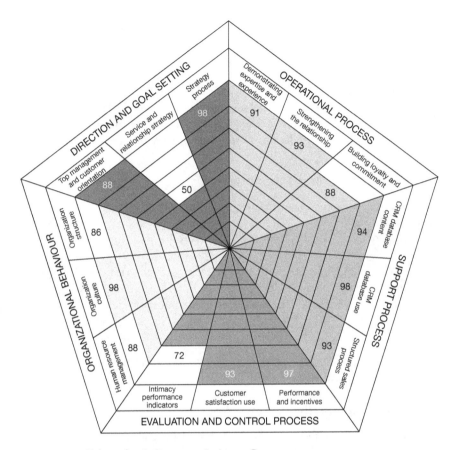

FIGURE 13.4 Château*form*'s Customer Intimacy Pentagon

Customer centricity is also reflected in the company's key concept: 'You're at home here'. The host couple welcomes the customers as if they are coming home. Freedom and flexibility are key elements of Château*form*'s value proposition, and, to make sure participants feel at ease, all of Château*form*'s venues are on a human scale.

Another important element of the Château*form'* promise is that participants can get what they want or need at any time, either by asking or by helping themselves: 'Your rhythm is ours: We adapt to you, not the other way around'.

Customer centricity and customer intimacy are also reflected in the company's values. 'Love for the customer' is the first of the company's seven values, and the company has identified twenty marketing principles to stress that particular value. For example, the company constantly measures customer satisfaction. It also aims to maintain constant contact with its clients and potential clients and adheres to the principle, 'Focus on relationships, not on transactions'. Helping a customer is considered more important than closing a sale.

Strategic goals

At all sites, the permanent focus is on customer satisfaction, not on profits. The sites have budgets, and the Family Home is responsible for the revenues:

> Profit is a consequence, and as such it always shows up too late to make a difference. The key measure of success is customer satisfaction, one customer at a time. Whereas only 30 minutes are spent on the financials during the budgeting process, hours are invested in improving the customer experience.

A better treatment for better customers?

Surprisingly, Châteauform' scores relatively low on the item 'Service and relationship strategy' (see Figure 13.4). Châteauform' is one of the few companies that does not offer more or better services to its loyal customers. Jacques Horovitz explains:

> Everybody is the same. When you treat a particular customer better, you treat another worse. We do not like that. Instead, our philosophy is to know our customers better. The more they come and the better we know them, the more we can deal with their particular wishes.

Operational processes: demonstrating expertise and delivering a great experience

Demonstrating expertise and experience

Because Châteauform' is focused on hosting residential business seminars, it has developed unparalleled expertise and experience in this business. Both the people in the Family Home and the employees on the sites have built up enormous expertise in hosting and running seminars, and this helps to deliver a great customer experience.

The people on the sites – the couples, the chefs and their teams – take care of the customer during the seminar. However, the people in the Family Home play a very important role in delivering a great customer experience as well. They take care of customer relations in general, as well as all other administrative tasks, such as accounting, financial and legal issues, insurance, operations (i.e. the logistics of the client prior to arrival), the price negotiations and invoicing. They also provide assistance with decoration, renovations and construction, as well as HR services such as recruitment, dispute resolution and team training.

When a corporate client contacts Châteauform' requesting a seminar, a person from the customer relations team looks, with the customer, for an appropriate site, responds to the customer's needs and provides advice. The customer relations team proposes the price, and then the nanny takes over. In the week before the seminar, the nanny visits the host couple and provides them with all the necessary information on the new group. Châteauform' collects information about every participant that it has ever served.

Delivering a great experience

During the seminar, everybody at the site does everything possible to make the participants feel comfortable and happy. With its accumulated knowledge about repeat customers, Château*form'* is able to go the extra mile to handle their special wishes. If it is known that a client loves mint tea, then, upon a subsequent visit to any site, (s)he will be served a cup of fresh mint tea. Château*form'* tries to develop true relationships with its customers by maintaining a continuous dialogue. For example, when a customer cannot organize a seminar because every site is booked, Château*form'* informs the client when a new site becomes available, and, after a seminar, the nanny calls the organizer and asks for extensive feedback.

Support processes: further support to deliver a great service

Delights

Château*form'* recognizes that each customer – participants, organizers, decision-makers and facilitators – has different, specific needs. For each segment, the company has defined a collection of best practices – referred to as the 'delights chart' – to ensure an excellent quality of service for everyone. Delights for participants ensure that they feel at home even when far from home. Delights for organizers make doing business at Château*form'* easy. Delights for facilitators provide the assurance of a no-stress, high-tech, high-touch meeting environment. And delights for decision-makers guarantee that there are no surprises after the seminar.

The delights charts explicitly state the reason for every practice, as well as what Château*form'* wants each participant, organizer and/or facilitator to experience – perhaps a bottle of water and a piece of fresh fruit, accompanied by a hand-written welcome note, in the bedroom upon arrival, or a broad selection of freshly baked bread at each of the meals. The way in which this is realized, however, is entirely up to the trio team and staff at each of the sites. For newcomers to the Château*form'* family, training involves, not only observing a site's operations, but also 'chasing new delights' – i.e. finding new delights not yet included in the chart. In practice, the chart is enriched and updated by a committee every other year.

The right customer information

As stated above, the host couple receives all relevant information with regard to the new group in the week before the seminar (for example, the nannies send an Excel file with all information about the seminar participants). This also includes the customer satisfaction scores the customers have submitted at previous Château*form'* seminars. I am a regular teacher in the Château*form'* hotels, and I once asked to have a look at my customer information. The host showed me my scores and all the comments that I had made, and he assured me that he had taken that information into account. For example, when a participant complains about a noisy room, he/she is given a quieter room. Women are given rooms in the main house, and not on the ground floor, and tall people are given rooms to suit their size.

Evaluation and control processes: a performance measurement system that tracks and rewards customer service and loyalty

Continuous customer feedback

During the last day of a seminar, each participant is asked to complete a satisfaction survey, called 'Sweet and Sour', on site (see Figure 13.5). It asks participants to rate their satisfaction regarding all aspects of their experience – from the service and organization to the site itself. In addition, participants are also asked to indicate whether they would return, and to what extent they would or would not recommend Châteauform' to others. As the 'Sweet and Sours' are completed on site, the host couple can use the input right away to fix issues participants alert them to.

The response rate for the 'Sweet and Sour' form is over 90 per cent. All of the feedback is systematically analysed by the customer relations team and compiled into monthly reports. The comments are compiled and form the starting point for investments in the sites each year.

Although 96 per cent of the customers are either completely or very satisfied, Châteauform's goal is to achieve 100 per cent satisfaction. Châteauform' develops a service recovery plan for both the Sweet and Sour evaluations and the feedback obtained from calls to the organizers. Jacques Horovitz comments:

> The recovery should always be generous. There is no standard, there is no limit. In one training session, I even said that you have €1 million per participant for recovery without having to ask. I really mean no limit. If we do something, we have to do it big.

Employee feedback

Châteauform' not only asks the customer for feedback, it also asks its employees on a site for input. The main idea is that an external perspective is a 'Golden eye'. Employees are encouraged to notice points for improvement and to write them down in a 'Golden book', available at every site. This call for feedback is not restricted to the sites: the Family Home too – the company's head office – asks its host couples and other employees for feedback on how well it has served the sites.

Performance and incentives

Salaries contain both variable and fixed elements, the former representing up to 20 per cent of the fixed income. The monthly performance report serves as the

	Completely satisfied	Very satisfied	Satisfied	Barely satisfied	Unsatisfied
Your overall satisfaction:	○	○	○	○	○
Your satisfaction regarding:					
– Our welcome					
Suggestions:	○	○	○	○	○
– The site					
Suggestions:	○	○	○	○	○
– Your room					
Suggestions:	○	○	○	○	○
– The cleanliness					
Suggestions:	○	○	○	○	○
– The meals					
breakfasts	○	○	○	○	○
snacks	○	○	○	○	○
lunches	○	○	○	○	○
dinners	○	○	○	○	○
tea time	○	○	○	○	○
presentation	○	○	○	○	○
service	○	○	○	○	○
Suggestions:					

	Completely satisfied	Very satisfied	Satisfied	Barely satisfied	Unsatisfied
– The leisure activities					
Suggestions:	○	○	○	○	○
– The seminar rooms					
Suggestions:	○	○	○	○	○
General suggestions:					

If you wish to receive news from Châteauform', please leave us your e-mail address: ____

Would you return?

Absolutely	Probably	Maybe	Definitely not
☐	☐	☐	☐

Will you recommend Châteauform'?

Absolutely	Probably	Maybe	Definitely not
☐	☐	☐	☐

Person we could contact on your behalf:
First name: ____ **Name:** ____
Company: ____
Address: ____
Phone: ____ **Fax:** ____ **Email:** ____

Thank you very much for your help.

... do you want to feel at home again for holidays? (see back of the page)

FIGURE 13.5 'Sweet and Sour' evaluation form

Source: Company information

main input for the variable portion. In addition, everyone is paid a bonus if the occupancy rate at the sites is above the budgeted rate (set at 70 per cent). Château*form'* also pays significant attention to non-financial rewards. At the end of the year, all the 'Sweet' notes are collected and compiled in a book that is called 'Bravo for these thank-yous, Thank you for these bravos' – intended for the entire staff. The company believes it is essential to acknowledge everyone's hard work.[6]

Organizational behaviour processes: a company with a strong service culture

I introduced Figure 13.6 in the previous chapter – this figure was developed by Jacques Horovitz and summarizes quite well how he has created a strong service culture within Château*form'*.

Strong values demonstrated by management practices

Creating a strong service culture starts with a company's philosophy. One of Château*form'*'s key philosophies is that 'customers come first'. If the organization performs well on customer intimacy, profit results! Other elements of Château*form'*'s philosophy are that innovation is key, and that customers (rather than employees) should say how good the company is.

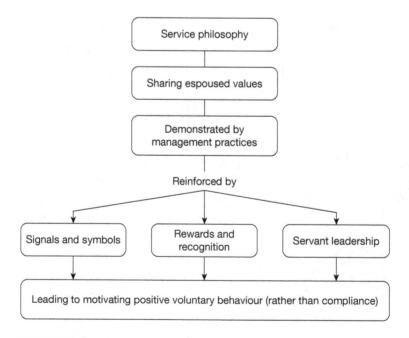

FIGURE 13.6 A customer service culture

Source: Horovitz (2011)[7]

These service philosophies should then be translated into a set of values that are shared with everyone. Jacques Horovitz comments:

> For me, managing by values means, first of all, to have common values. Second, they must be shared or espoused – i.e., people must identify with them. In order for people to believe, they have to be demonstrated by management practices, they have to be reinforced by the leadership, by the rituals and symbols, and by the reward system. So, everything we do in terms of organization or management practices tries to reinforce the values. Consequently, to be able to manage by values rather than by rules, we are ready to experiment in how we manage and control the company.

Captured and described in a booklet entitled 'Welcome to the Family', the shared values form the starting point for the culture at Châteauform' – a culture in which all of the company's activities and behaviours are designed to maximize customer satisfaction. The booklet includes the reasons behind the desired behaviour, as well as suggestions for 'how to . . .'. It enables new employees to immerse themselves in the culture upon arrival, as well as to share the Châteauform' way of living together with other team members. In this way, it provides everyone with the same language and helps give the organization's employees coherence and direction. Everyone is encouraged to constantly check if reality matches with what is claimed – and, if not, to question why.

Once a year, the company organizes a 'kill-the-rules' day. Employees sit together to discuss any rules that have prevented them from living up to the customers' expectations:

> During that day, all of the couples in Châteauform' are asked 'what are the new rules that have popped up?' Rules pop up every year. Everybody seems to believe that, in order to do a good job, you need to issue a new rule: 'Fill in this form, do this, do that'. We list all those rules and immediately kill them. In this way, we reinforce the message that the customer is our central point of attention, not the Family Home. The Family Home supports the sites, not the other way around.

For those who have exemplified and honoured one of the seven values during the year, a shield of merit is presented during Châteauform's annual winter seminar in January – a 2-day get-together devoted to improvement workshops, transformation and change discussions, as well as developing the budgets. This is followed in the summer by a similar 2-day seminar in which best practices are demonstrated, ideas are exchanged and expertise is formalized.

Employees who work for the company for 5, 10, 15 and 20 years are celebrated and receive a special distinction. Employees who work for the company for 5 years are called 'Knights of the Fifth Year' and receive a helmet as a gift (see Figure 13.7). 'Knights of the Tenth Year' receive a full set of armour. And, on the fifteenth anniversary, they receive a fully outfitted riding horse.

FIGURE 13.7 Knight of the Fifth Year

HR practices

Châteauform' pays a lot of attention to hiring the right people. Every new host couple is interviewed by five experienced host couples, and the same procedure applies to selecting a chef. New couples and chefs then attend the 'flying school' for 2–6 months, going from place to place to observe and write an 'astonishment report'. In this way, newcomers not only familiarize themselves with the practices, they also provide an unbiased, fresh look at all Châteauform' sites. Only after they have finished the flying school are they presented with the keys to their homes.

Since 2006, all host couples have also been put under the protection of a godfather or godmother. When they arrive at their new house, the godparent helps them make the transition, over a period of 3 months. The godparent is linked to a particular site – and not to a couple – so that (s)he has a history with the particular property and its staff. The godparent prevents new host couples from repeating mistakes made by others before them. The godparent remains available as a sounding board, or to provide advice, for any problem at the site, be it with an employee or any other HR-related matter.

Decentralized structure

The company emphasizes over and over again that the Family Home supports the sites. Twenty per cent of the Family Home employees' salaries is determined by the customer satisfaction scores. According to Horovitz, this policy was difficult to implement, but it showed Château*form's* commitment to its 'love for the customer': 'Without the sites, we are nothing'. Another interesting management principle is that the customer is the boss, not the host couple or the chef. This is also emphasized by the lack of formal titles.

Strategic commitment at Château*form'*

Jacques Horovitz and his management team have launched many actions that have helped to create a true, customer-intimate organization. At the same time, it is striking to see how Horovitz has been able to get everybody in the organization involved and committed to implementing such a customer-intimacy strategy. This is reflected in Château*form's* maturity profile (see Figure 13.8).

The opening statement of this chapter explains why and how Château*form'* has reached the level of the committed organization (except for its evaluation and control processes): 'We manage by values, not by rules'. Château*form'* has moved beyond the 'entrepreneurial' level: the company has developed enough policies and rules to ensure professionalism and consistency in its service orientation across the different sites. The company has also moved beyond the 'structured' level: the management team at Château*form'* ensures that the employees at the Family Home and the sites work together towards a common goal. Everybody knows who is responsible for what, but Jacques Horovitz makes sure that nobody forgets the big picture – to be the most service-oriented company in the industry. This is typical of a 'connected organization'. The emphasis on values, rather than rules, has helped Château*form'* become a 'committed organization'.

	Direction and goal setting processes	Operational processes	Support process	Evaluation and control process	Organizational behaviour process
Level 1 Entre-preneurial					
Level 2 Structured				●	
Level 3 Connected		●			
Level 4 Committed	●		●		●

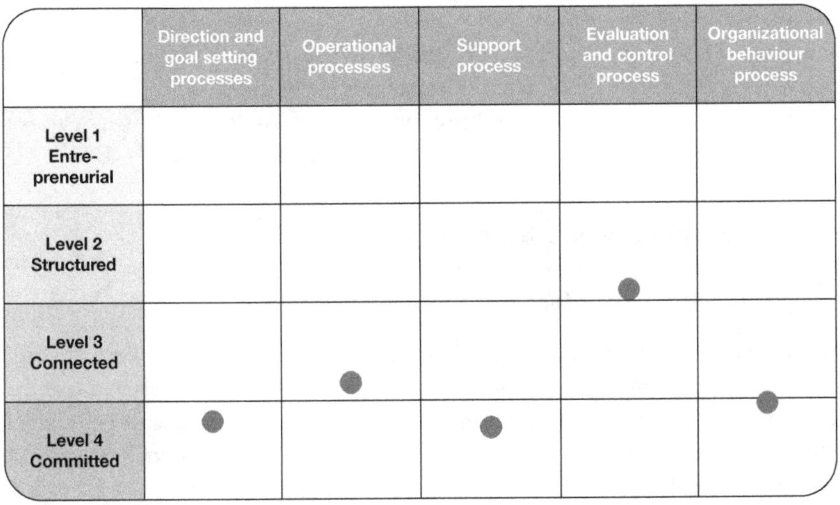

FIGURE 13.8 Château*form's* maturity profile

Châteauform' spends a lot of time developing and discussing the *direction and goals* for the organization. The company's values are not idle words; they are shared and lived by everybody who works there. What is striking is that the discussions on strategy, goals and action plans are not limited to the top management team, but that everybody is invited to contribute and to help shape the strategy and the action plans of the organization.

Châteauform's *operational processes* are well developed and have almost reached the 'committed' stage. The company has defined its core processes, and clear deliverables for each of them, and reviews them regularly. The company has an attitude of continuous process improvement, and it asks its customers and employees for continuous feedback.

Châteauform' helps its employees to deliver a great service in many ways. Capacity planning and competence development are well developed within the company. There is a lot of internal communication on how to improve work practices, and the coordination of the activities and processes is fully integrated into the functioning of the teams. Information flows freely throughout the organization.

Châteauform' has elaborate *evaluation and control processes*. The company measures its performance often, and the performance measures are continuously analysed while action plans are initiated. Everybody is involved in monitoring the results – which is an indication of a 'connected' organization. Nevertheless, Châteauform' has only reached the 'structured' stage for its evaluation and control processes – this is because the company refuses to control through rules and audits. On all the statements of the maturity questionnaire that contained the word 'control', Châteauform's score was rather low. As we've said several times, Jacques Horovitz prefers to manage through values, not rules.

It is no surprise that Châteauform's maturity level is high for its *organizational behaviour processes*. The company pays a lot of attention to the development of its people and to building a participative and supportive – yet performance-oriented – culture. The whole organization is designed in such a way that responsibilities reside with the people who meet the customers every day.

In summary, Châteauform's success not only stems from its high level of alignment but also from the fact that strategy is everyone's job, every day.

Customer intimacy and beyond

The crisis hits Châteauform'

Up to now, I have painted a very rosy picture of the company, but even successful companies face daunting challenges. The year 2009 proved to be very difficult for Châteauform'. It had started well: January sales were 20 per cent, and February a good 8 per cent, above the same months in 2008. However, by March, the global economic crisis had affected Châteauform' – something it had anticipated, but not to such an extent. Demand suddenly dropped by 15 per cent in March, accompanied by an even more worrisome drop in conversion rates. Normally, more than

60 per cent of queries convert to bookings – but this figure halved to less than 30 per cent in just 1 month. From March to June, sales continued to decline sharply, with no clear explanation. This was in stark contrast to the organization's prior performance: even though it competed in a mature market, Châteauform' had known only double-digit growth since its inception in 1996.

Jacques Horovitz decided to call existing clients to ask for their feedback. In those interviews, customers indicated that they still liked the concept, but could no longer afford the rates, or they reserved the experience for the happy few in their company. Customers asked Châteauform' to find a way to reduce prices, so that they could still benefit from the concept, albeit with more limited budgets.

This is a common dilemma for customer-intimacy firms: 'We deliver great services, the customers acknowledge this, but in the end they do not want to pay the price.' How did Châteauform' respond to this situation?

The development of new concepts

When Jacques Horovitz heard the remarks and suggestions of his customers, he turned a challenge into an opportunity. In his previous talks with his customers, budget issues had only been a marginal concern, but, in 2009, that changed: more than 30 per cent of the people he talked to raised the issue of price. At the same time, hotels were slashing their prices. However, Jacques Horovitz was quite clear on this point: Châteauform' would not lower its prices.

The customer relations team would first refer the customers to the cheaper sites, the ones that were further away from a big city. That worked for some customers, but not for all.

So, Jacques Horovitz decided to launch a new concept: 'Châteauform' Campus'. In order to accommodate bigger teams, Horovitz created a campus on the banks of the Seine, in the middle of nature, where participants could meet and work for several consecutive days. The concept of Châteauform' remained: a venue dedicated to seminars and meetings, coupled with high-tech meeting rooms and a nice, friendly atmosphere where participants felt at home. Unlike the traditional sites, however, the Châteauform' Campus had meeting rooms that could host up to 300 participants.

At the same time, Jacques Horovitz launched 'Châteauform' City' to accommodate short-term meetings in the heart of Paris. Again, this new concept was similar to the traditional Châteauform' concept, but what changed here was the amount of interaction between the Châteauform' staff and the customers. Compared with the traditional sites, the staff have less contact with the customers, and so it is more difficult to surprise the customers at every moment of truth. The figures, however, indicate that the concept works: in 2013, Châteauform' City has three sites, all located in Paris, but Jacques Horovitz is considering launching the concept in other big European cities as well.

Châteauform' has already launched Les maisons de Katy et Jacques, where customers can spend their summer or winter holidays with their family, on a number of the existing sites. In this way, Châteauform' has become a corporation with four different concepts. Jacques Horovitz believes that the traditional Château*form'* concept still has high growth potential, but he's curious to see how well the other concepts will fare. He will, of course, rely on his customers to tell him!

Key learning points

This chapter has shown you what customer intimacy means in practice. Achieving high levels of customer intimacy is a difficult task: it requires a company to have a clear strategy and to take a set of well-aligned actions. Customer intimacy also requires commitment from all the managers and staff within the organization. Château*form'* is an example of how to achieve all that. It's also an exceptional case: it's a company that has been very successful – even in difficult periods – by putting its employees and customers at the centre of everything it does. Financial considerations come second.

Château*form'* has set up a whole set of actions – mostly small things – to make its customers feel at home. It is the consistency with which its employees have listened to, and learned from, the customers' comments that has brought the company to where it is today. Jacques Horovitz's main challenge now is to ensure that this culture of asking for continuous feedback and continuous improvement is not lost, even as the company grows.

Notes

1   This chapter is based on the case study, 'Château*form'*': Customer Centricity and Beyond', written by Ghita Greef, Kurt Verweire, Marion Debruyne and Benoît Leleux.
2   This and the following quotations from Jacques Horovitz come from an interview the author had with him in Switzerland, in July 2012.
3   Château*form'* website: www.chateauform.com/en/the-home-of-seminar/the-concept/5 (accessed 19 March 2013).
4   Leleux, B., Nie, W., and Courcoux, A.-S. (2006) 'Château*form'* (A): How to Grow and Maintain Service?', *IMD Case Study*, IMD-3–1660, p. 4.
5   This Customer Intimacy Pentagon was obtained by comparing the scores of three Château*form'* managers on our Customer Intimacy Questionnaire with the scores of 206 other customer-intimacy firms. The scores are percentiles: they indicate the percentage of companies that had an equal or lower score for that particular item. High scores imply a high level of alignment.
6   Leleux *et al.*, 'Château*form'* (A)', p. 11.
7   Horovitz, J. (2011) 'Customer Centricity: The Château*form'* Experience', *Presentation Made for Dexia Lead Program*, 6 May, Brussels.

INDEX

Page numbers in *italic* are tables/figures